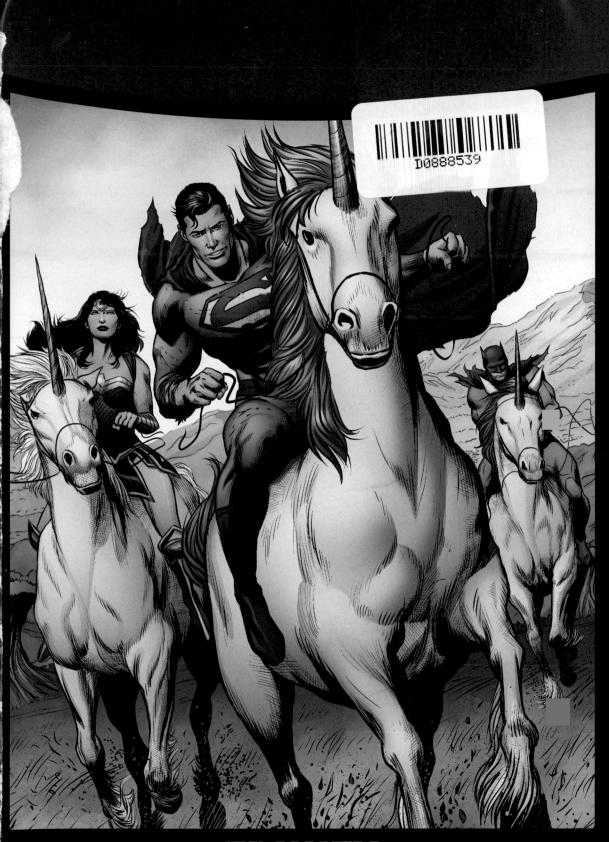

TRINITY

VOL.4 THE SEARCH FOR STEVE TREVOR

TRINITY
VOL.4 THE SEARCH FOR STEVE TREVOR

JAMES ROBINSON
writer

PATCH ZIRCHER * JACK HERBERT * TYLER KIRKHAM
artists

GABE ELTAEB
colorist

JOSH REED * CARLOS M. MANGUAL
letterers

GUILLEM MARCH & TOMEU MOREY
collection cover artists

SUPERMAN created by **JERRY SIEGEL** and **JOE SHUSTER**
By special arrangement with the Jerry Siegel family
BATMAN created by **BOB KANE** with **BILL FINGER**
WONDER WOMAN created by **WILLIAM MOULTON MARSTON**

PAUL KAMINSKI KATIE KUBERT Editors – Original Series • **ANDREA SHEA** Assistant Editor – Original Series
JEB WOODARD Group Editor – Collected Editions • **ALEX GALER** Editor – Collected Edition
STEVE COOK Design Director – Books • **SHANNON STEWART** Publication Design

BOB HARRAS Senior VP – Editor-in-Chief, DC Comics • **PAT McCALLUM** Executive Editor, DC Comics

DAN DiDIO Publisher • **JIM LEE** Publisher & Chief Creative Officer
AMIT DESAI Executive VP – Business & Marketing Strategy, Direct to Consumer & Global Franchise Management
BOBBIE CHASE VP & Executive Editor, Young Reader & Talent Development • **MARK CHIARELLO** Senior VP – Art, Design & Collected Editions
JOHN CUNNINGHAM Senior VP – Sales & Trade Marketing • **BRIAR DARDEN** VP – Business Affairs
ANNE DePIES Senior VP – Business Strategy, Finance & Administration • **DON FALLETTI** VP – Manufacturing Operations
LAWRENCE GANEM VP – Editorial Administration & Talent Relations • **ALISON GILL** Senior VP – Manufacturing & Operations
JASON GREENBERG VP – Business Strategy & Finance • **HANK KANALZ** Senior VP – Editorial Strategy & Administration
JAY KOGAN Senior VP – Legal Affairs • **NICK J. NAPOLITANO** VP – Manufacturing Administration
LISETTE OSTERLOH VP – Digital Marketing & Events • **EDDIE SCANNELL** VP – Consumer Marketing
COURTNEY SIMMONS Senior VP – Publicity & Communications • **JIM (SKI) SOKOLOWSKI** VP – Comic Book Specialty Sales & Trade Marketing
NANCY SPEARS VP – Mass, Book, Digital Sales & Trade Marketing • **MICHELE R. WELLS** VP – Content Strategy

TRINITY VOL. 4: THE SEARCH FOR STEVE TREVOR

DC Comics, 2900 West Alameda Ave., Burbank, CA 91505
Printed by Times Printing, LLC, Random Lake, WI, USA. 11/2/18. First Printing.
ISBN: 978-1-4012-8550-0

Library of Congress Cataloging-in-Publication Data is available.

MIX
Paper from
responsible sources
FSC® C015572

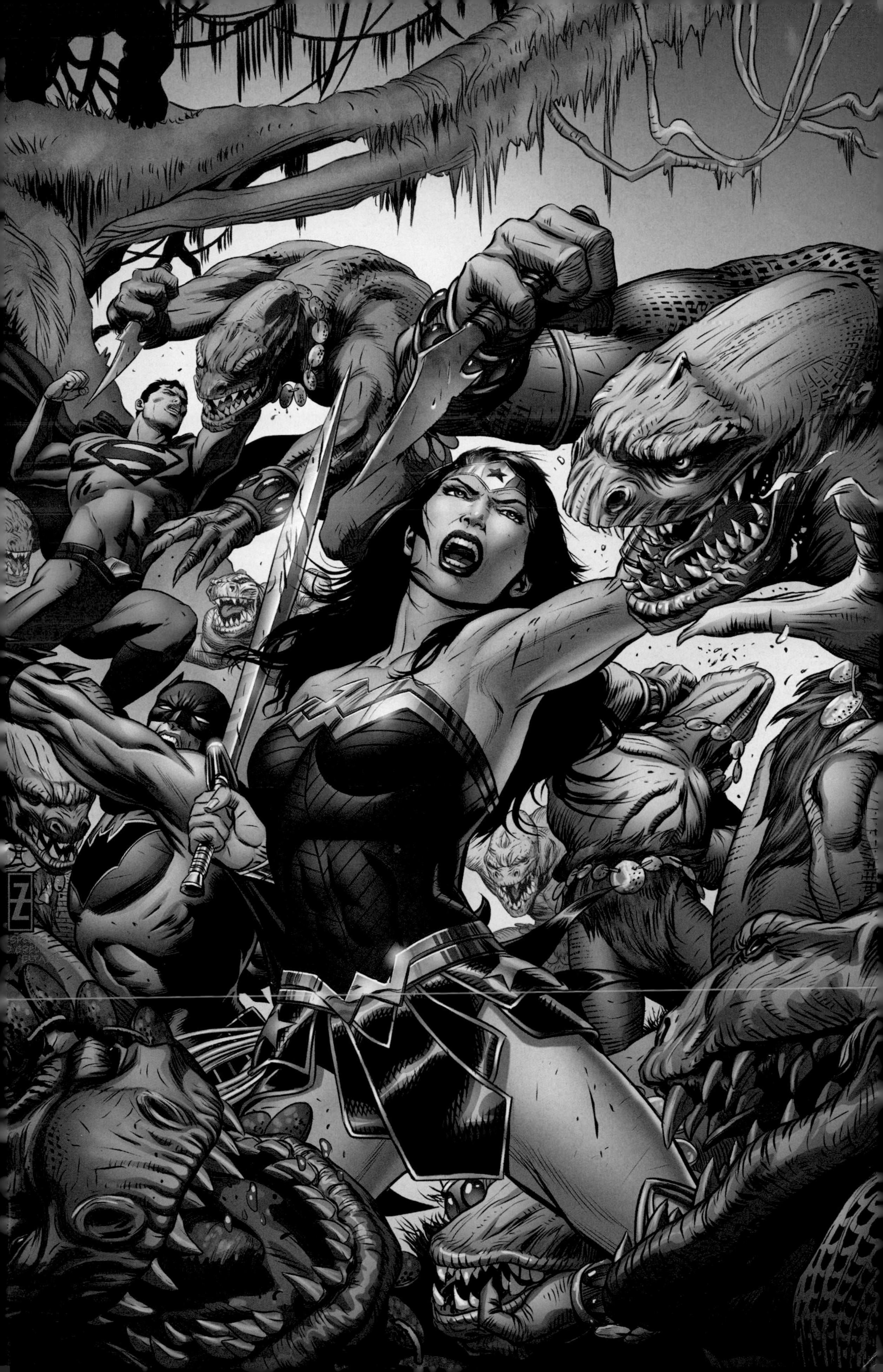

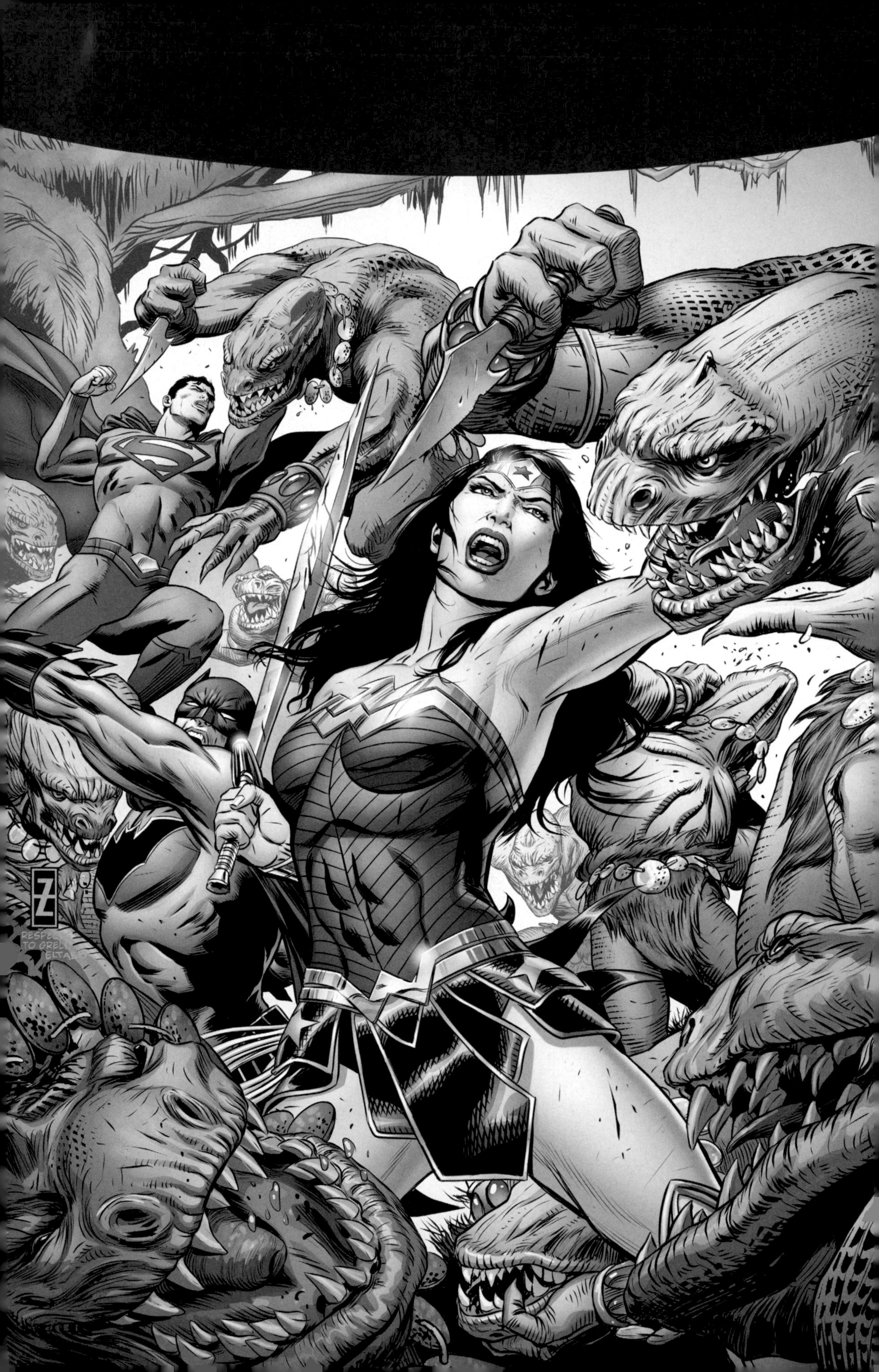

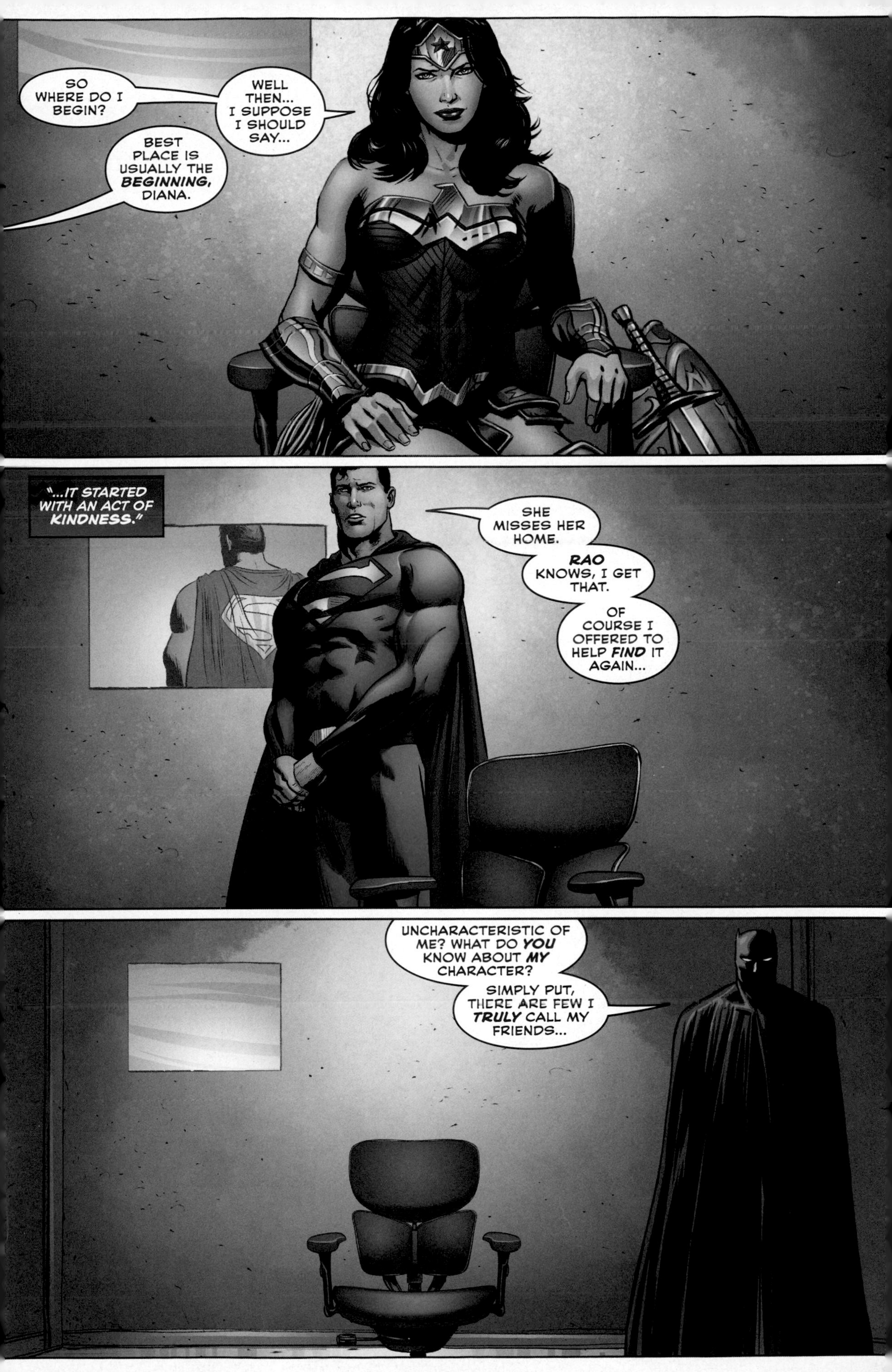
SO WHERE DO I BEGIN?
BEST PLACE IS USUALLY THE BEGINNING, DIANA.
WELL THEN... I SUPPOSE I SHOULD SAY...
"...IT STARTED WITH AN ACT OF KINDNESS."
SHE MISSES HER HOME.
RAO KNOWS, I GET THAT.
OF COURSE I OFFERED TO HELP FIND IT AGAIN...
UNCHARACTERISTIC OF ME? WHAT DO YOU KNOW ABOUT MY CHARACTER?
SIMPLY PUT, THERE ARE FEW I TRULY CALL MY FRIENDS...

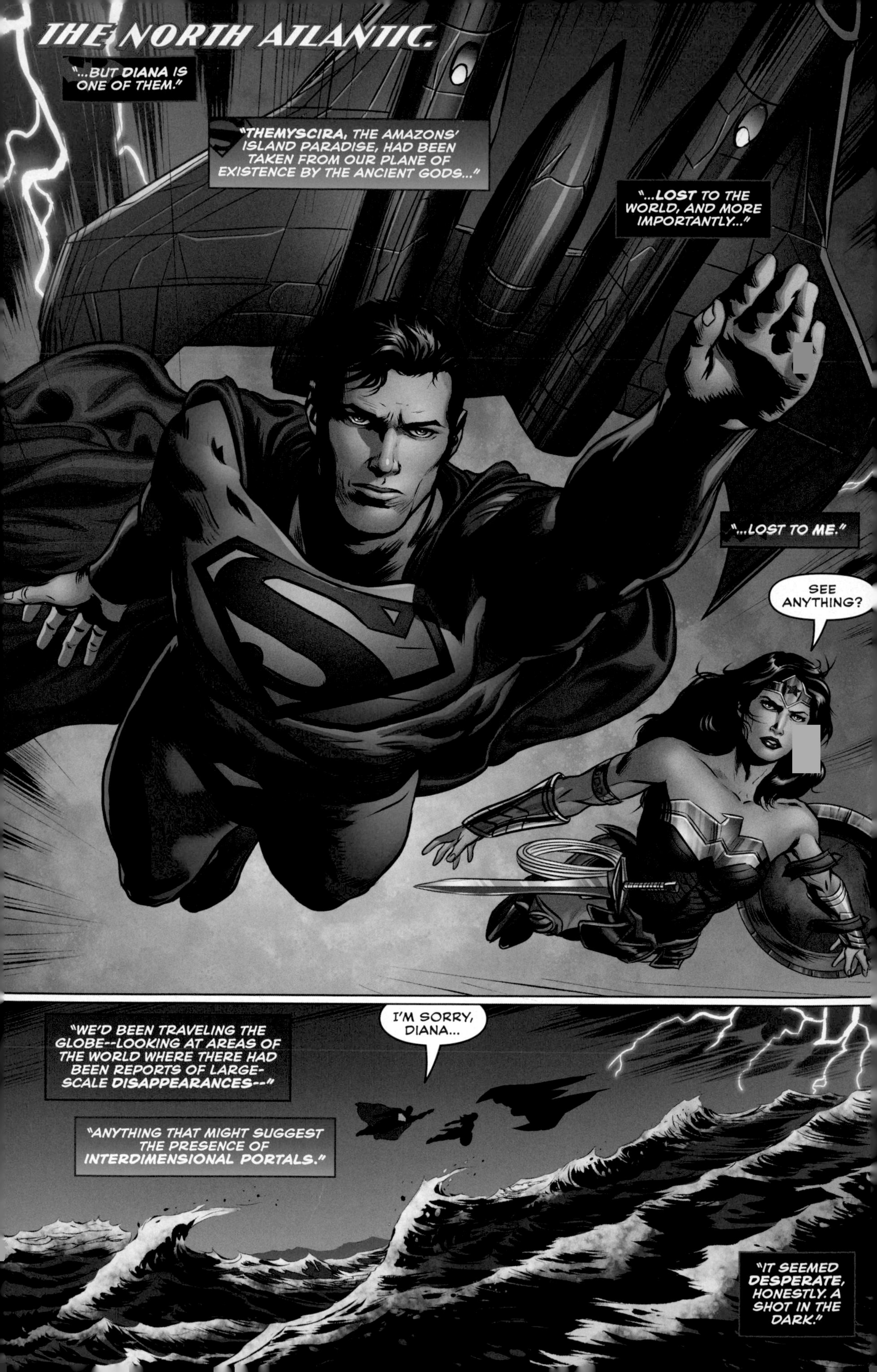
THE NORTH ATLANTIC.
"...BUT DIANA IS ONE OF THEM."
"THEMYSCIRA, THE AMAZONS' ISLAND PARADISE, HAD BEEN TAKEN FROM OUR PLANE OF EXISTENCE BY THE ANCIENT GODS..."
"...LOST TO THE WORLD, AND MORE IMPORTANTLY..."
"...LOST TO ME."
SEE ANYTHING?
"WE'D BEEN TRAVELING THE GLOBE--LOOKING AT AREAS OF THE WORLD WHERE THERE HAD BEEN REPORTS OF LARGE-SCALE DISAPPEARANCES--"
I'M SORRY, DIANA...
"ANYTHING THAT MIGHT SUGGEST THE PRESENCE OF INTERDIMENSIONAL PORTALS."
"IT SEEMED DESPERATE, HONESTLY. A SHOT IN THE DARK."

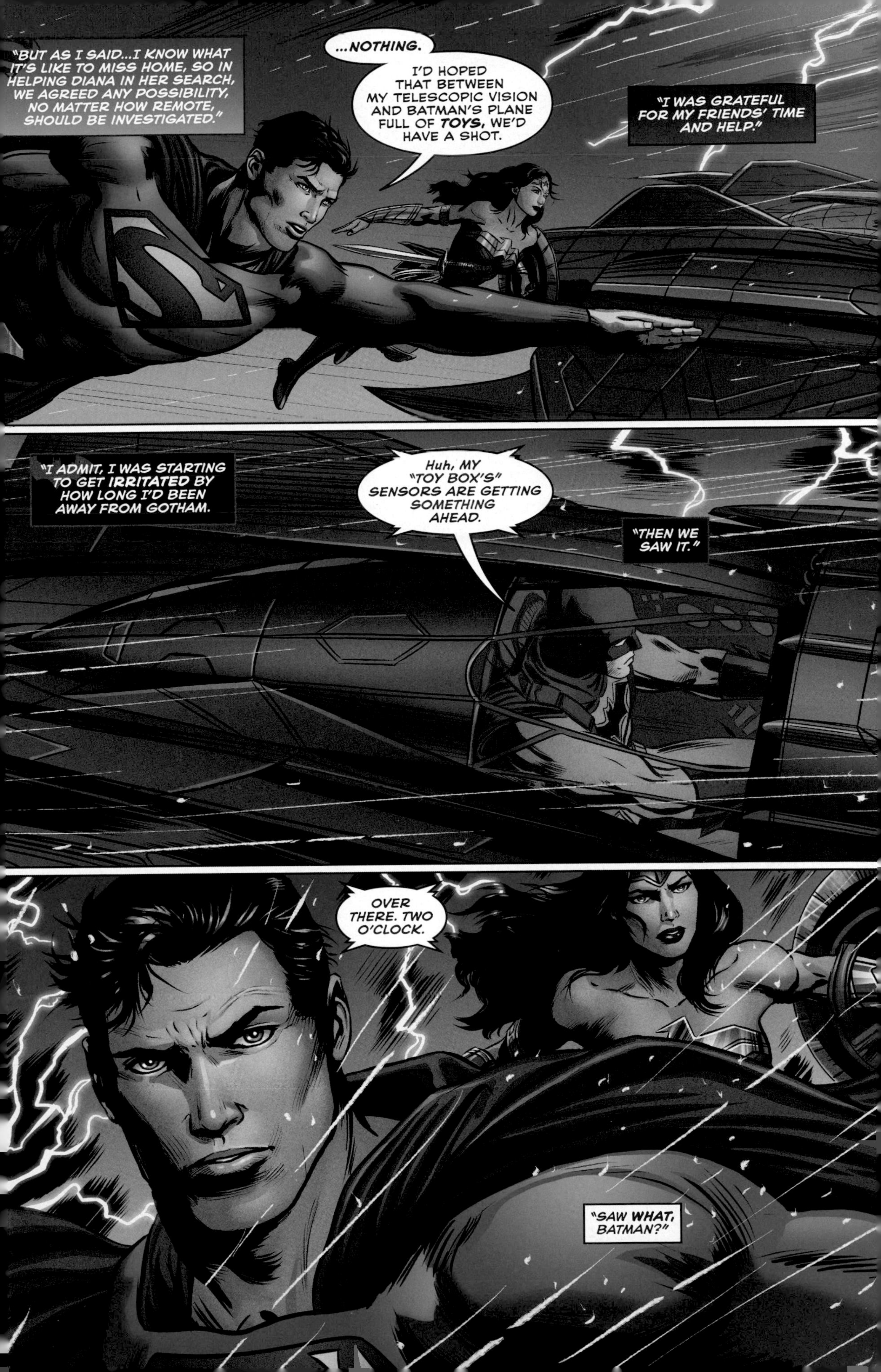
"BUT AS I SAID...I KNOW WHAT IT'S LIKE TO MISS HOME, SO IN HELPING DIANA IN HER SEARCH, WE AGREED ANY POSSIBILITY, NO MATTER HOW REMOTE, SHOULD BE INVESTIGATED."
...NOTHING.
I'D HOPED THAT BETWEEN MY TELESCOPIC VISION AND BATMAN'S PLANE FULL OF TOYS, WE'D HAVE A SHOT.
"I WAS GRATEFUL FOR MY FRIENDS' TIME AND HELP."
"I ADMIT, I WAS STARTING TO GET IRRITATED BY HOW LONG I'D BEEN AWAY FROM GOTHAM.
Huh, MY "TOY BOX'S" SENSORS ARE GETTING SOMETHING AHEAD.
"THEN WE SAW IT."
OVER THERE. TWO O'CLOCK.
"SAW WHAT, BATMAN?"

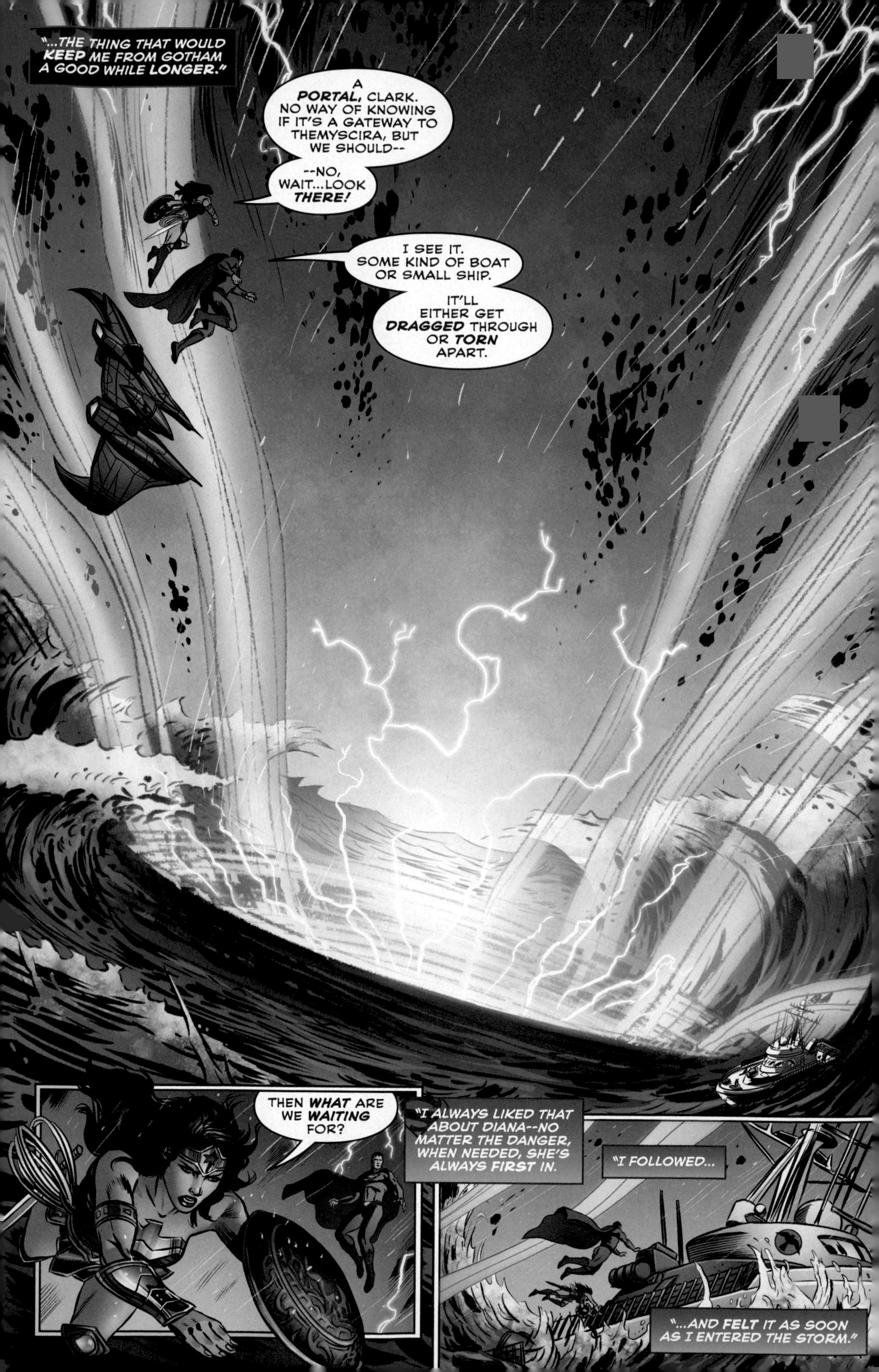
"...THE THING THAT WOULD KEEP ME FROM GOTHAM A GOOD WHILE LONGER."
A PORTAL, CLARK. NO WAY OF KNOWING IF IT'S A GATEWAY TO THEMYSCIRA, BUT WE SHOULD--
--NO, WAIT...LOOK THERE!
I SEE IT. SOME KIND OF BOAT OR SMALL SHIP.
IT'LL EITHER GET DRAGGED THROUGH OR TORN APART.
THEN WHAT ARE WE WAITING FOR?
"I ALWAYS LIKED THAT ABOUT DIANA--NO MATTER THE DANGER, WHEN NEEDED, SHE'S ALWAYS FIRST IN.
"I FOLLOWED...
"...AND FELT IT AS SOON AS I ENTERED THE STORM."

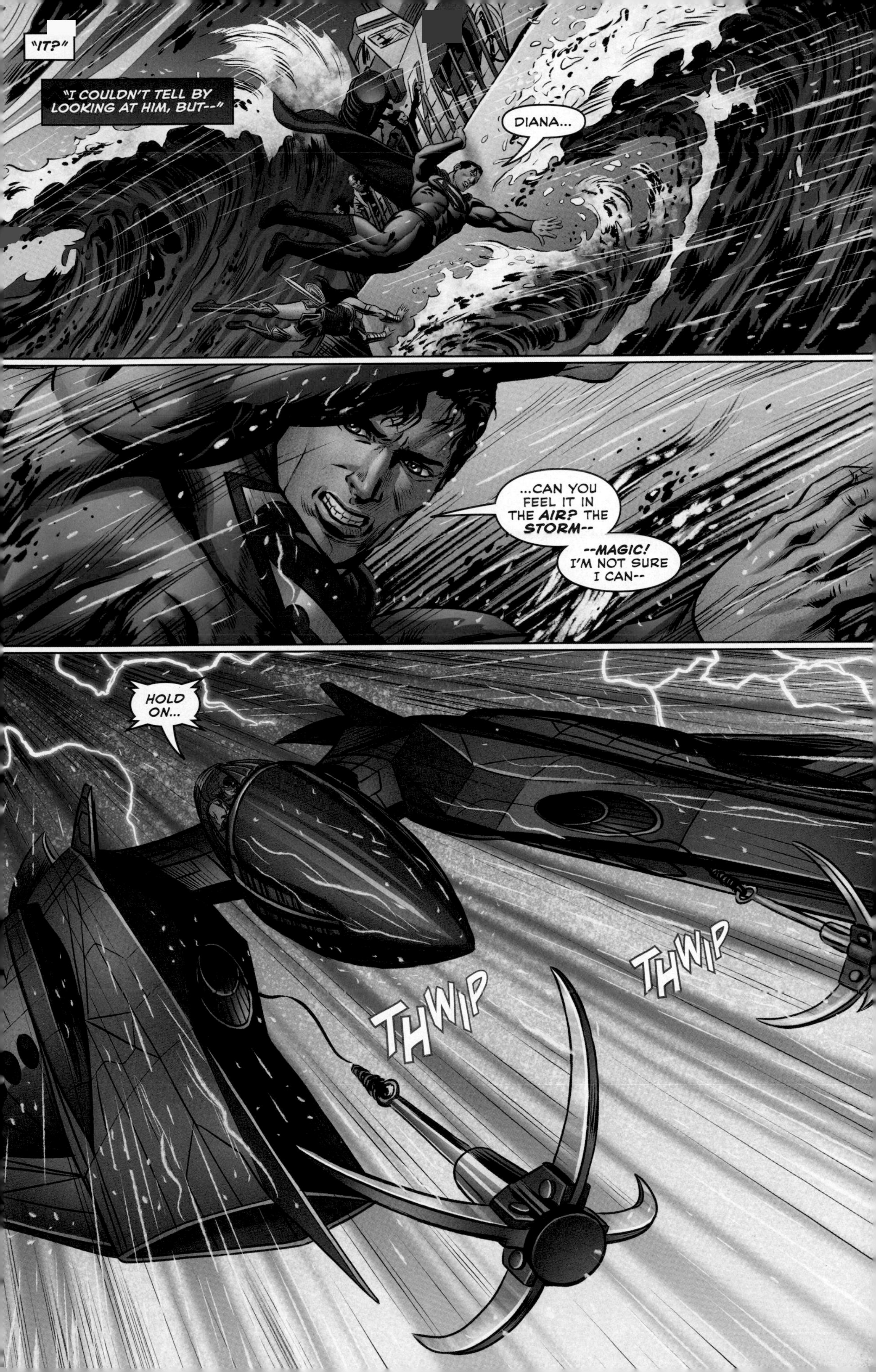
"IT?"
"I COULDN'T TELL BY LOOKING AT HIM, BUT--"
DIANA...
...CAN YOU FEEL IT IN THE AIR? THE STORM--
--MAGIC! I'M NOT SURE I CAN--
HOLD ON...
THWIP
THWIP

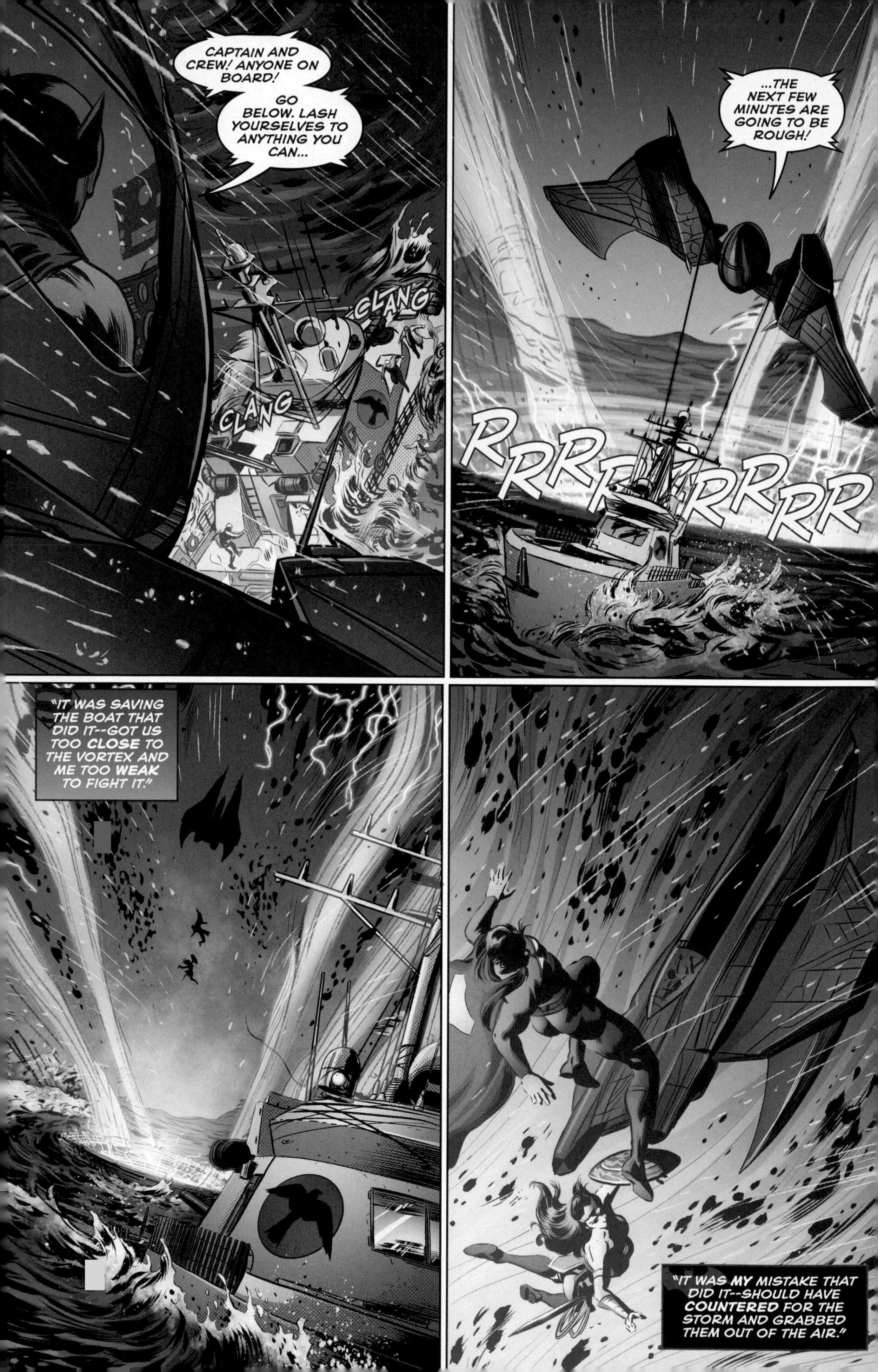
CAPTAIN AND CREW! ANYONE ON BOARD!
GO BELOW. LASH YOURSELVES TO ANYTHING YOU CAN...
CLANG
CLANG
...THE NEXT FEW MINUTES ARE GOING TO BE ROUGH!
RRRRRRRRRR
"IT WAS SAVING THE BOAT THAT DID IT--GOT US TOO CLOSE TO THE VORTEX AND ME TOO WEAK TO FIGHT IT."
"IT WAS MY MISTAKE THAT DID IT--SHOULD HAVE COUNTERED FOR THE STORM AND GRABBED THEM OUT OF THE AIR."

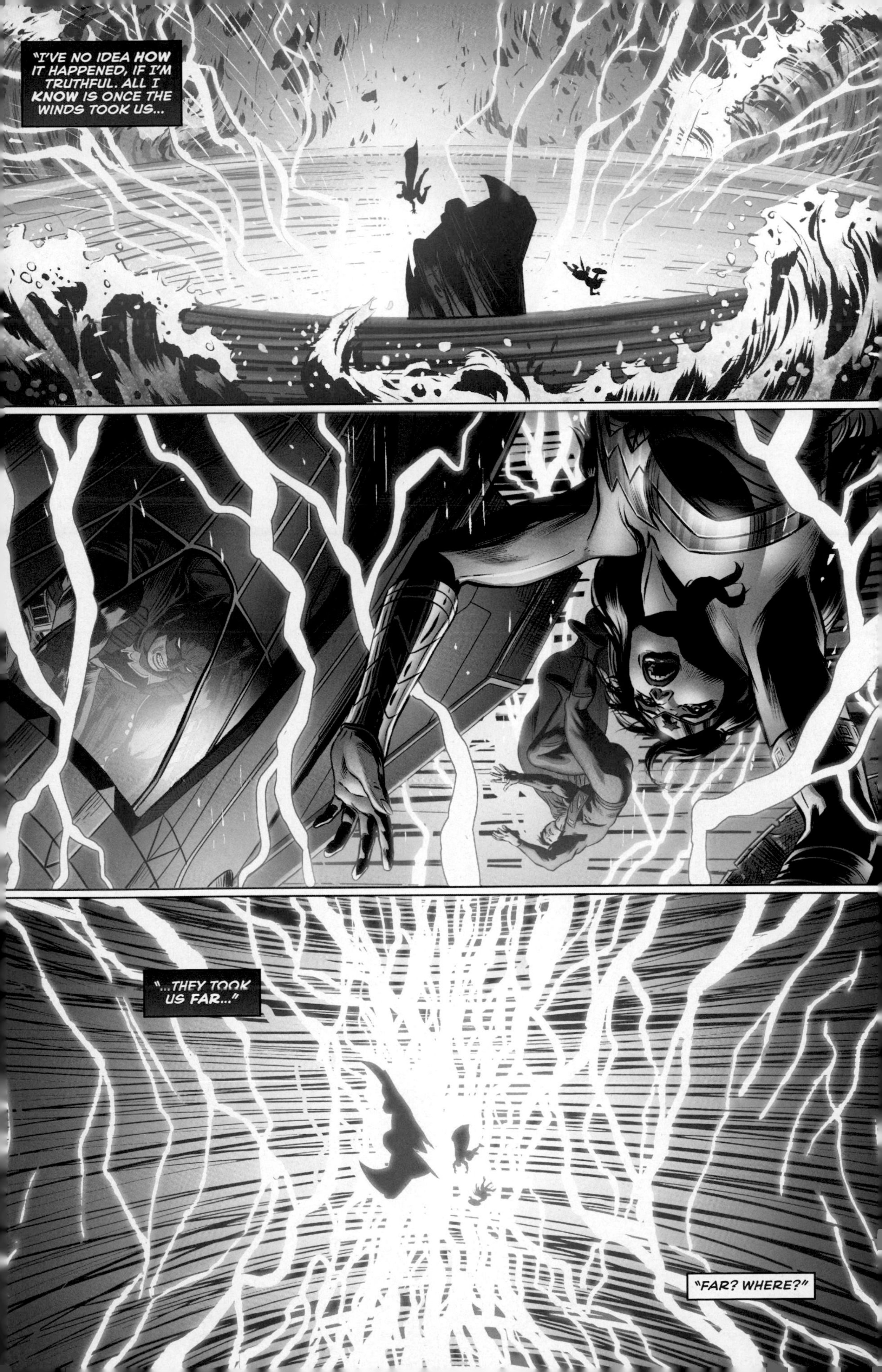
"I'VE NO IDEA HOW IT HAPPENED, IF I'M TRUTHFUL. ALL I KNOW IS ONCE THE WINDS TOOK US...
"...THEY TOOK US FAR..."
"FAR? WHERE?"

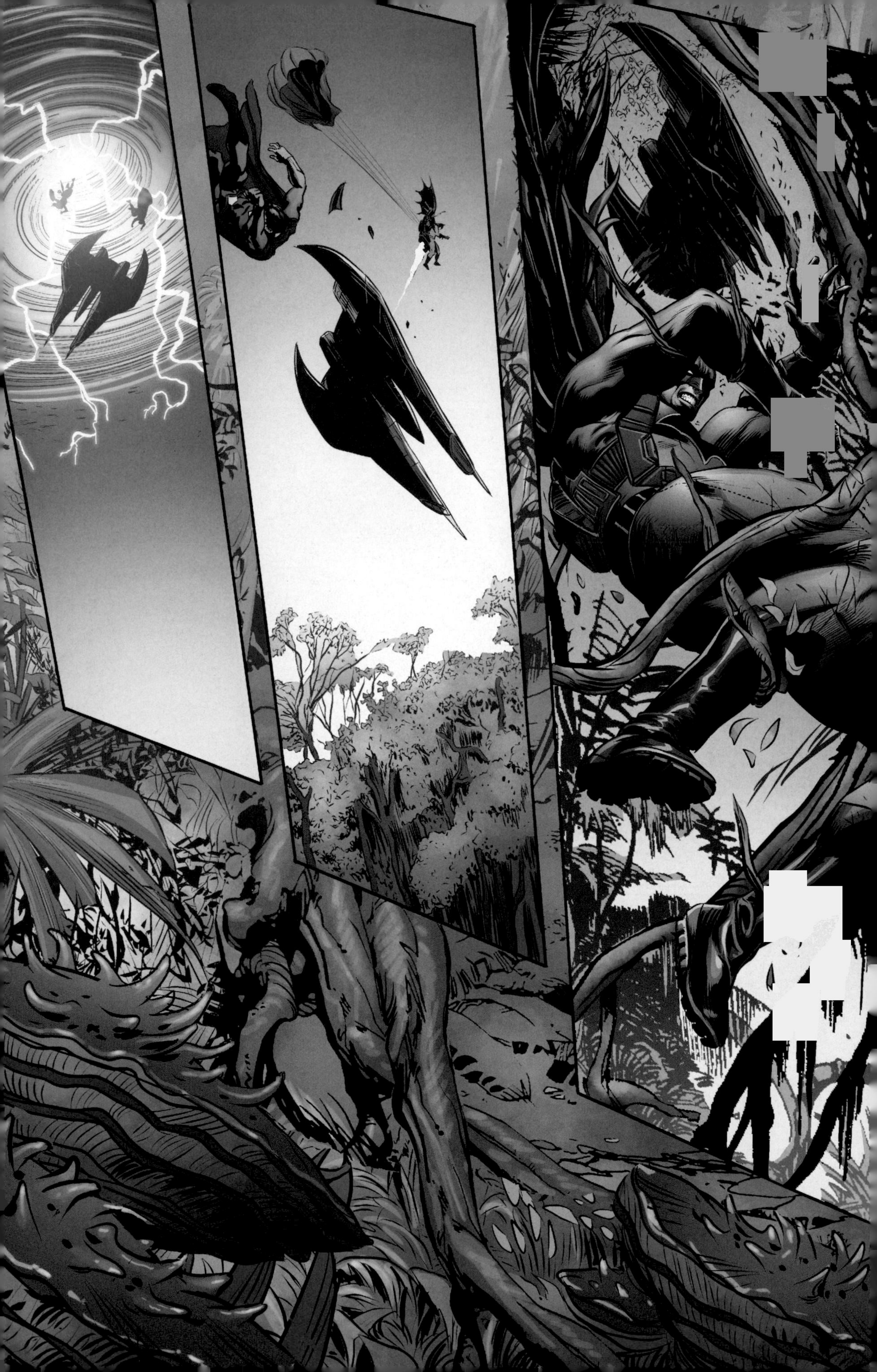

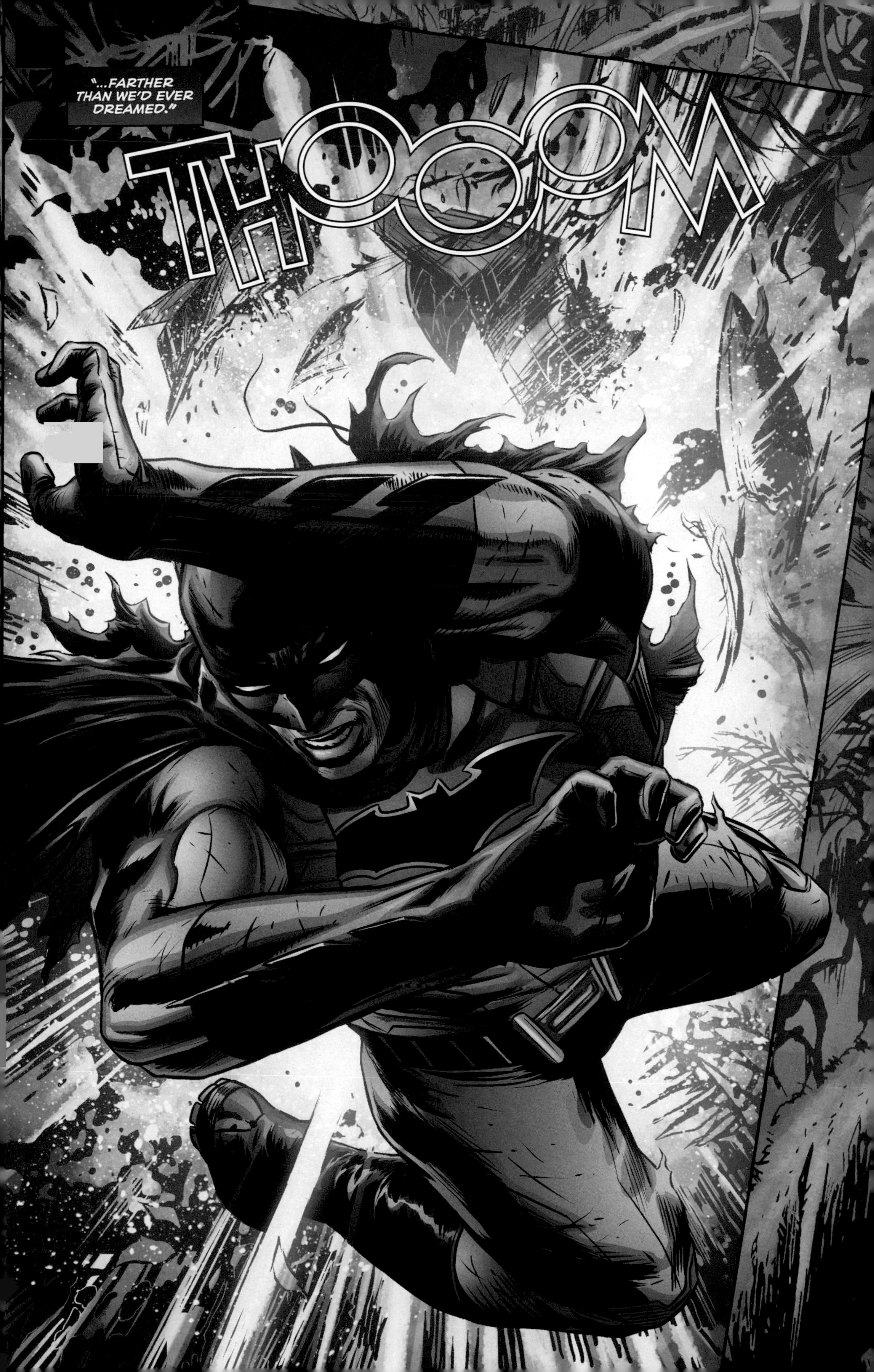
"...FARTHER THAN WE'D EVER DREAMED."
THOOOM

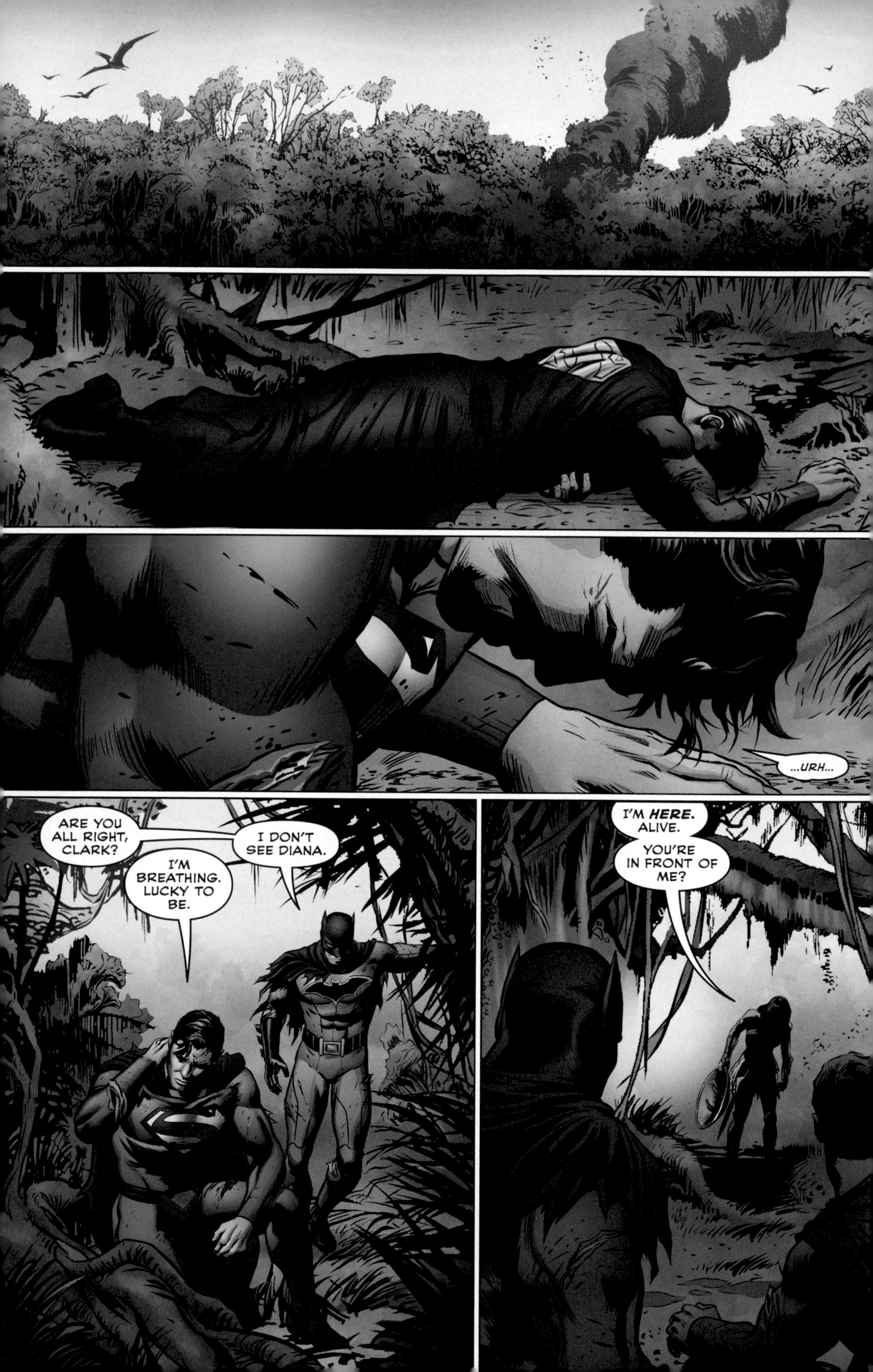
...URH...
ARE YOU ALL RIGHT, CLARK?
I'M BREATHING. LUCKY TO BE.
I DON'T SEE DIANA.
I'M *HERE*. ALIVE.
YOU'RE IN FRONT OF ME?

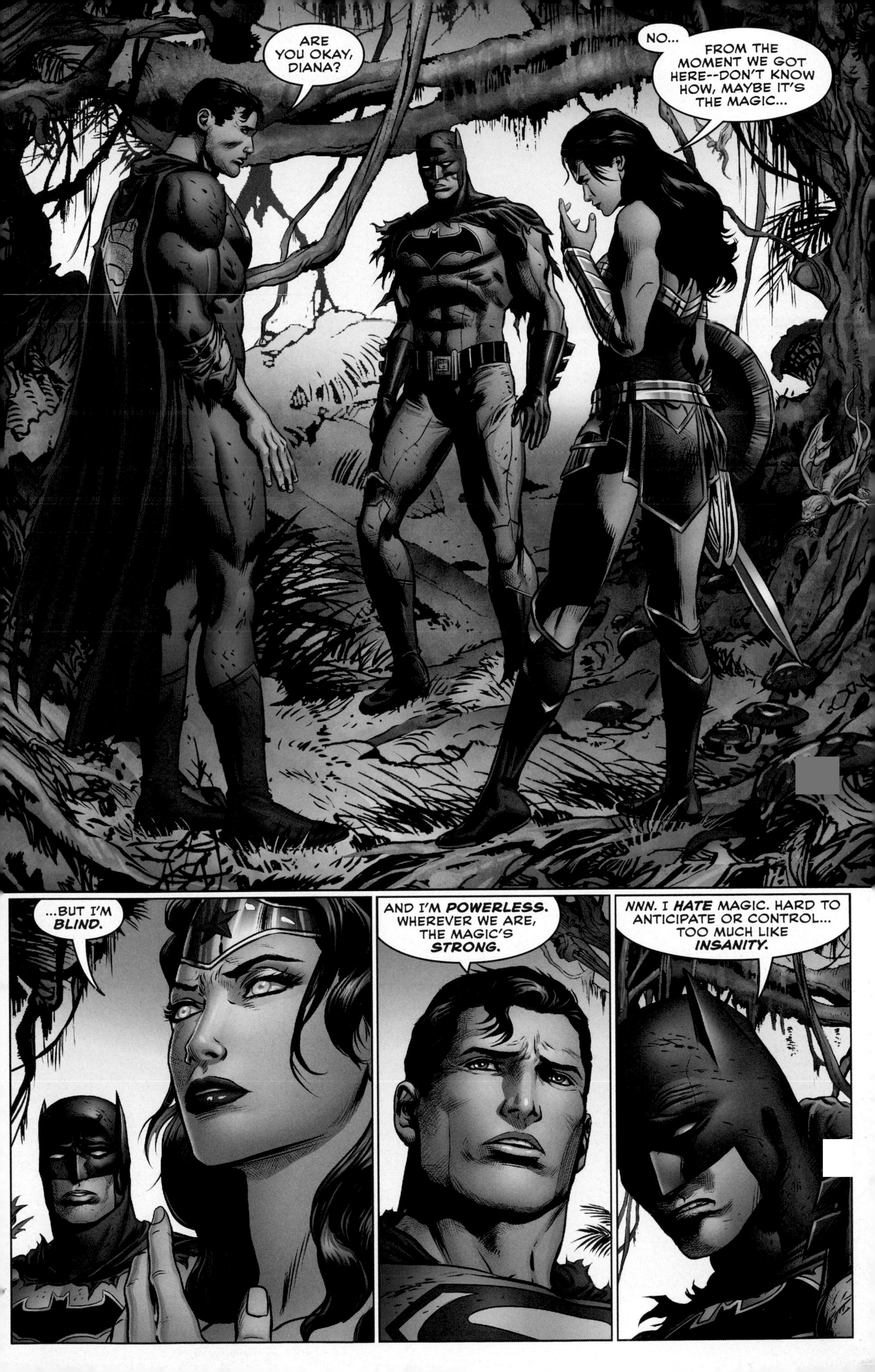
ARE YOU OKAY, DIANA?
NO...
FROM THE MOMENT WE GOT HERE--DON'T KNOW HOW, MAYBE IT'S THE MAGIC...
...BUT I'M BLIND.
AND I'M POWERLESS. WHEREVER WE ARE, THE MAGIC'S STRONG.
NNN. I HATE MAGIC. HARD TO ANTICIPATE OR CONTROL... TOO MUCH LIKE INSANITY.

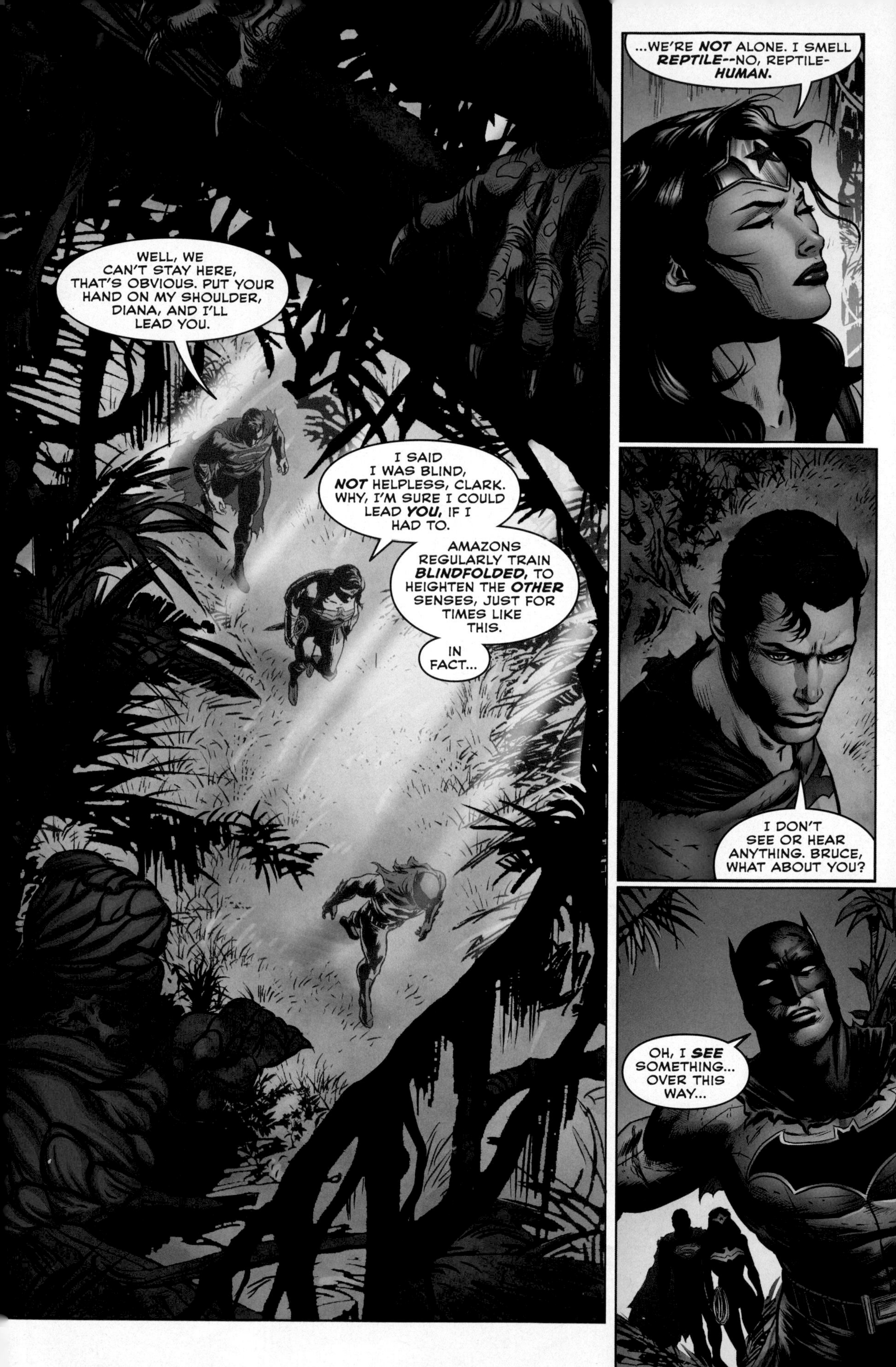

WELL, WE CAN'T STAY HERE, THAT'S OBVIOUS. PUT YOUR HAND ON MY SHOULDER, DIANA, AND I'LL LEAD YOU.
I SAID I WAS BLIND, **NOT** HELPLESS, CLARK. WHY, I'M SURE I COULD LEAD **YOU,** IF I HAD TO.
AMAZONS REGULARLY TRAIN **BLINDFOLDED,** TO HEIGHTEN THE **OTHER** SENSES, JUST FOR TIMES LIKE THIS.
IN FACT...
...WE'RE **NOT** ALONE. I SMELL **REPTILE**--NO, REPTILE-**HUMAN.**
I DON'T SEE OR HEAR ANYTHING. BRUCE, WHAT ABOUT YOU?
OH, I **SEE** SOMETHING... OVER THIS WAY...

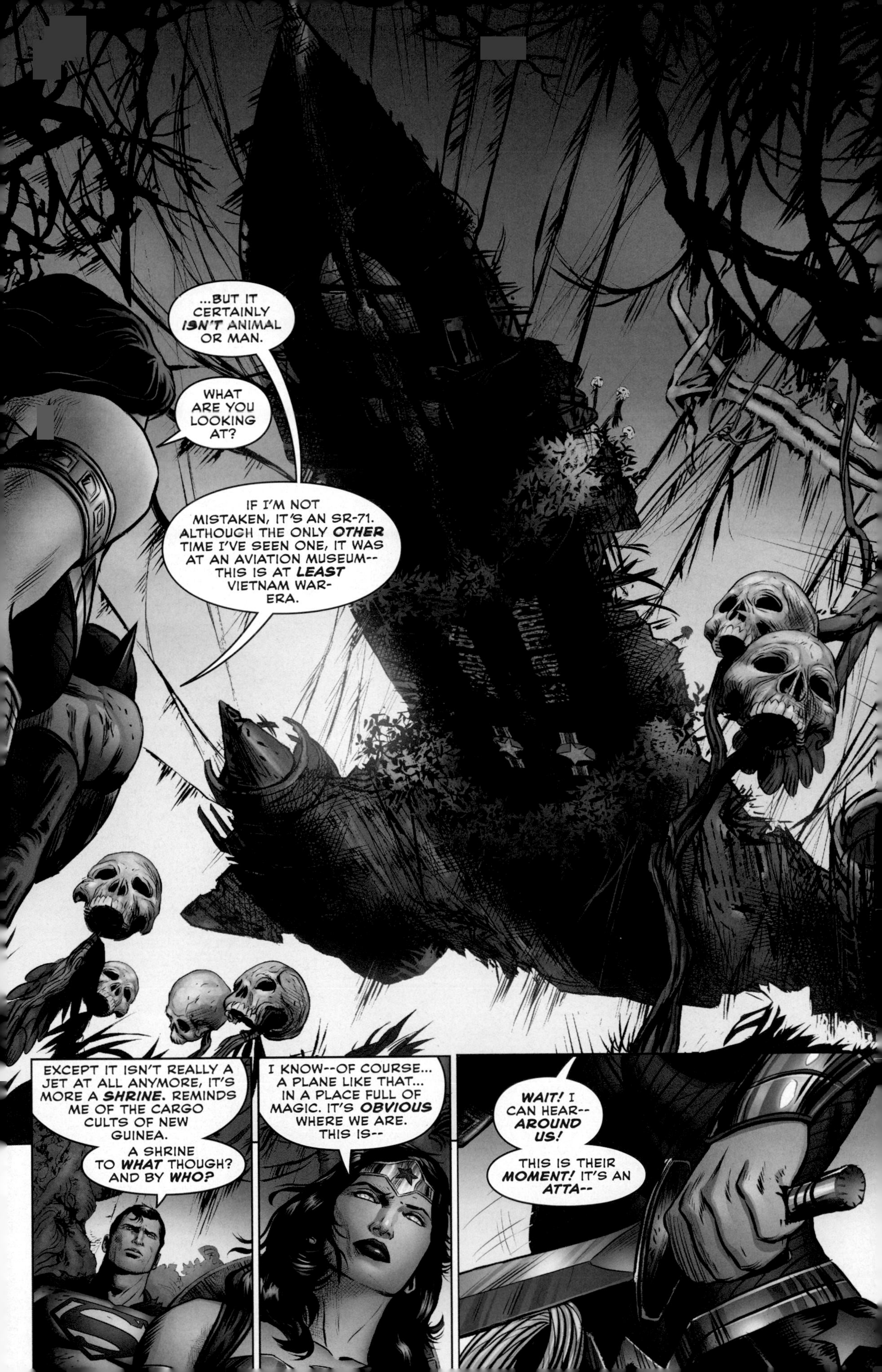
...BUT IT CERTAINLY ISN'T ANIMAL OR MAN.
WHAT ARE YOU LOOKING AT?
IF I'M NOT MISTAKEN, IT'S AN SR-71. ALTHOUGH THE ONLY OTHER TIME I'VE SEEN ONE, IT WAS AT AN AVIATION MUSEUM-- THIS IS AT LEAST VIETNAM WAR-ERA.
EXCEPT IT ISN'T REALLY A JET AT ALL ANYMORE, IT'S MORE A SHRINE. REMINDS ME OF THE CARGO CULTS OF NEW GUINEA.
A SHRINE TO WHAT THOUGH? AND BY WHO?
I KNOW--OF COURSE... A PLANE LIKE THAT... IN A PLACE FULL OF MAGIC. IT'S OBVIOUS WHERE WE ARE. THIS IS--
WAIT! I CAN HEAR-- AROUND US!
THIS IS THEIR MOMENT! IT'S AN ATTA--

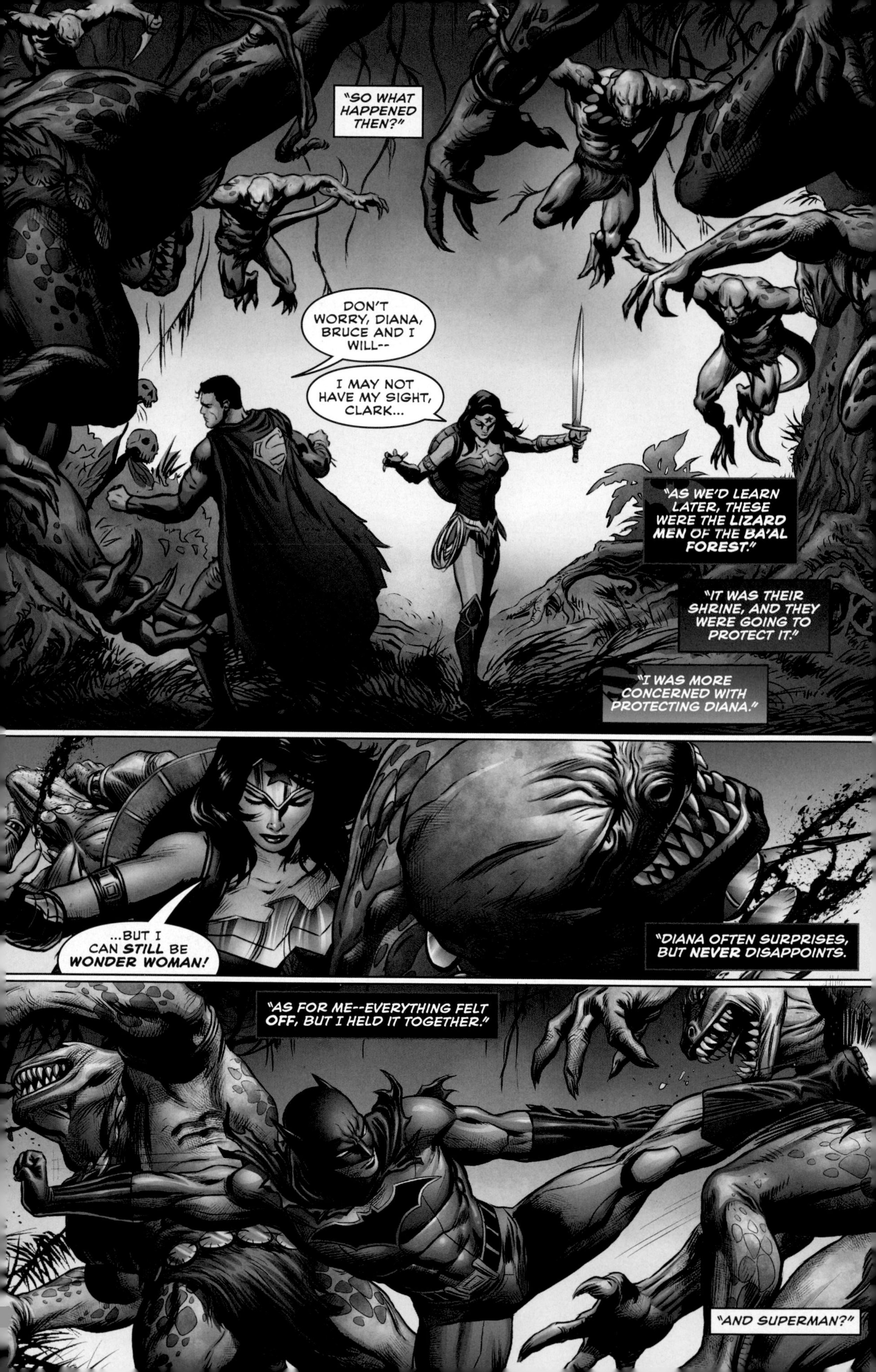
"SO WHAT HAPPENED THEN?"
DON'T WORRY, DIANA, BRUCE AND I WILL--
I MAY NOT HAVE MY SIGHT, CLARK...
"AS WE'D LEARN LATER, THESE WERE THE LIZARD MEN OF THE BA'AL FOREST."
"IT WAS THEIR SHRINE, AND THEY WERE GOING TO PROTECT IT."
"I WAS MORE CONCERNED WITH PROTECTING DIANA."
...BUT I CAN STILL BE WONDER WOMAN!
"DIANA OFTEN SURPRISES, BUT NEVER DISAPPOINTS.
"AS FOR ME--EVERYTHING FELT OFF, BUT I HELD IT TOGETHER."
"AND SUPERMAN?"

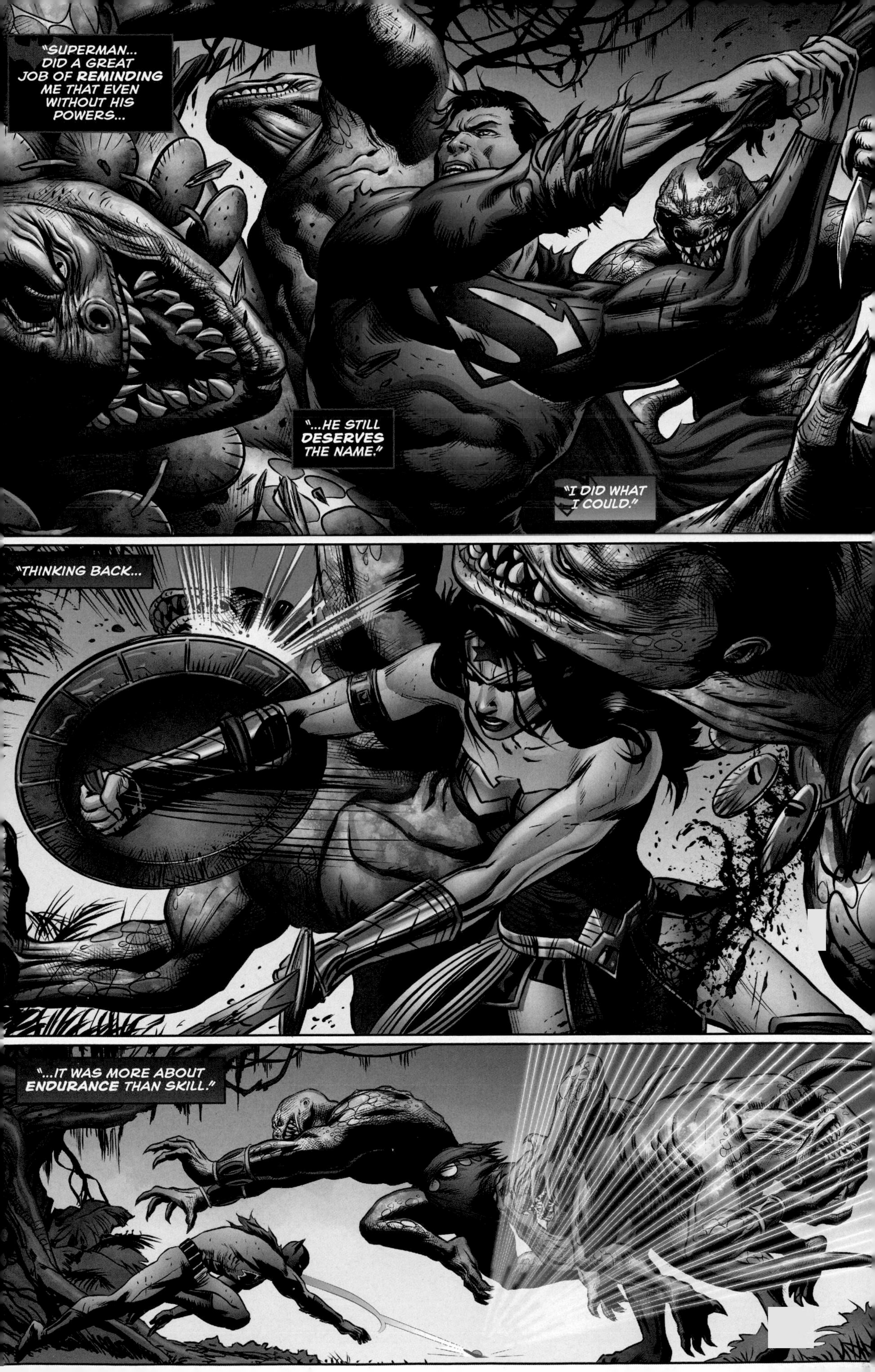
"SUPERMAN... DID A GREAT JOB OF REMINDING ME THAT EVEN WITHOUT HIS POWERS...
"...HE STILL DESERVES THE NAME."
"I DID WHAT I COULD."
"THINKING BACK...
"...IT WAS MORE ABOUT ENDURANCE THAN SKILL."

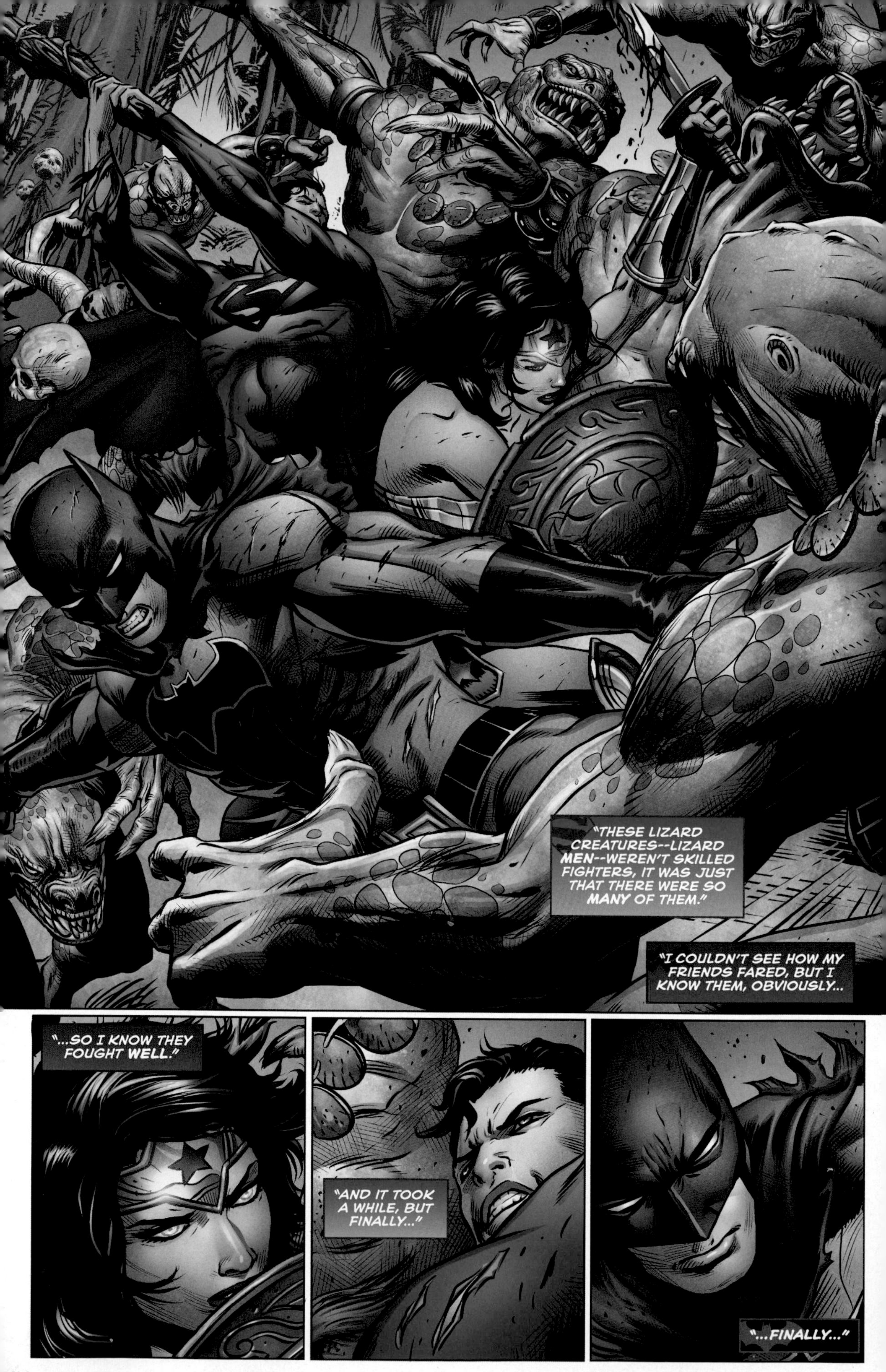
"THESE LIZARD CREATURES--LIZARD MEN--WEREN'T SKILLED FIGHTERS, IT WAS JUST THAT THERE WERE SO MANY OF THEM."
"I COULDN'T SEE HOW MY FRIENDS FARED, BUT I KNOW THEM, OBVIOUSLY...
"...SO I KNOW THEY FOUGHT WELL."
"AND IT TOOK A WHILE, BUT FINALLY..."
"...FINALLY..."

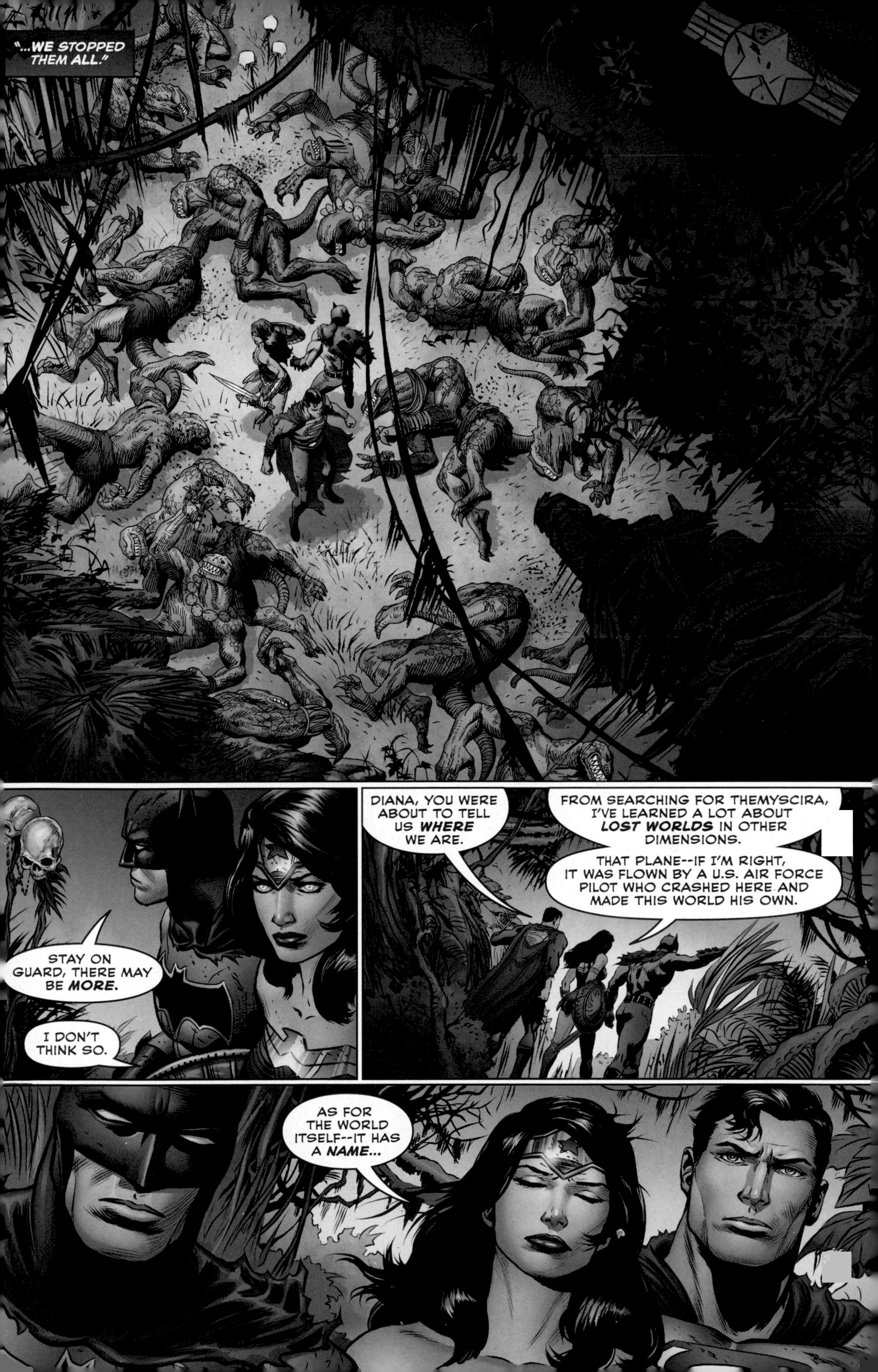
"...WE STOPPED THEM ALL."
STAY ON GUARD, THERE MAY BE MORE.
I DON'T THINK SO.
DIANA, YOU WERE ABOUT TO TELL US WHERE WE ARE.
FROM SEARCHING FOR THEMYSCIRA, I'VE LEARNED A LOT ABOUT LOST WORLDS IN OTHER DIMENSIONS.
THAT PLANE--IF I'M RIGHT, IT WAS FLOWN BY A U.S. AIR FORCE PILOT WHO CRASHED HERE AND MADE THIS WORLD HIS OWN.
AS FOR THE WORLD ITSELF--IT HAS A NAME...

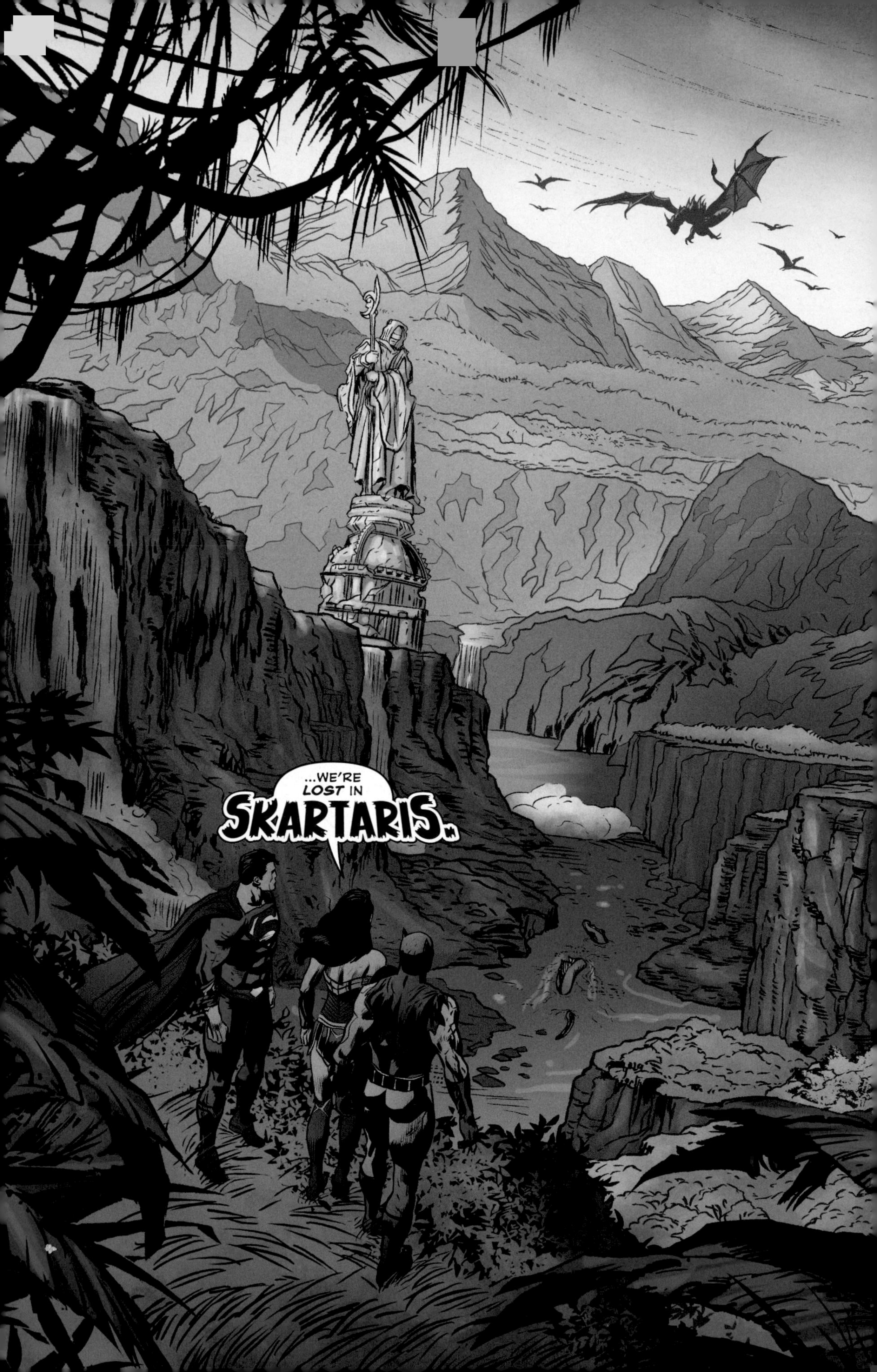
...WE'RE LOST IN SKARTARIS.

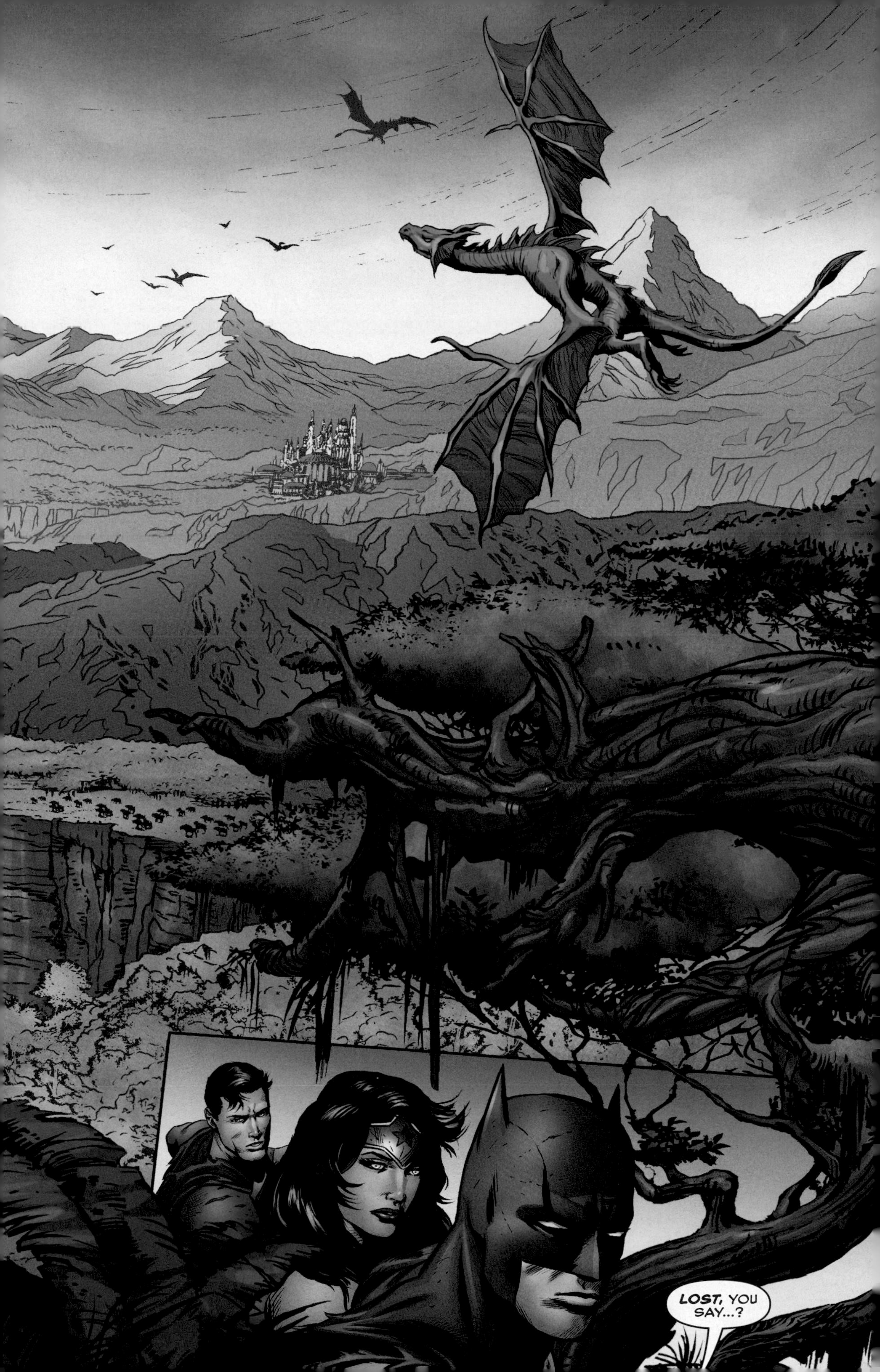
LOST, YOU SAY...?

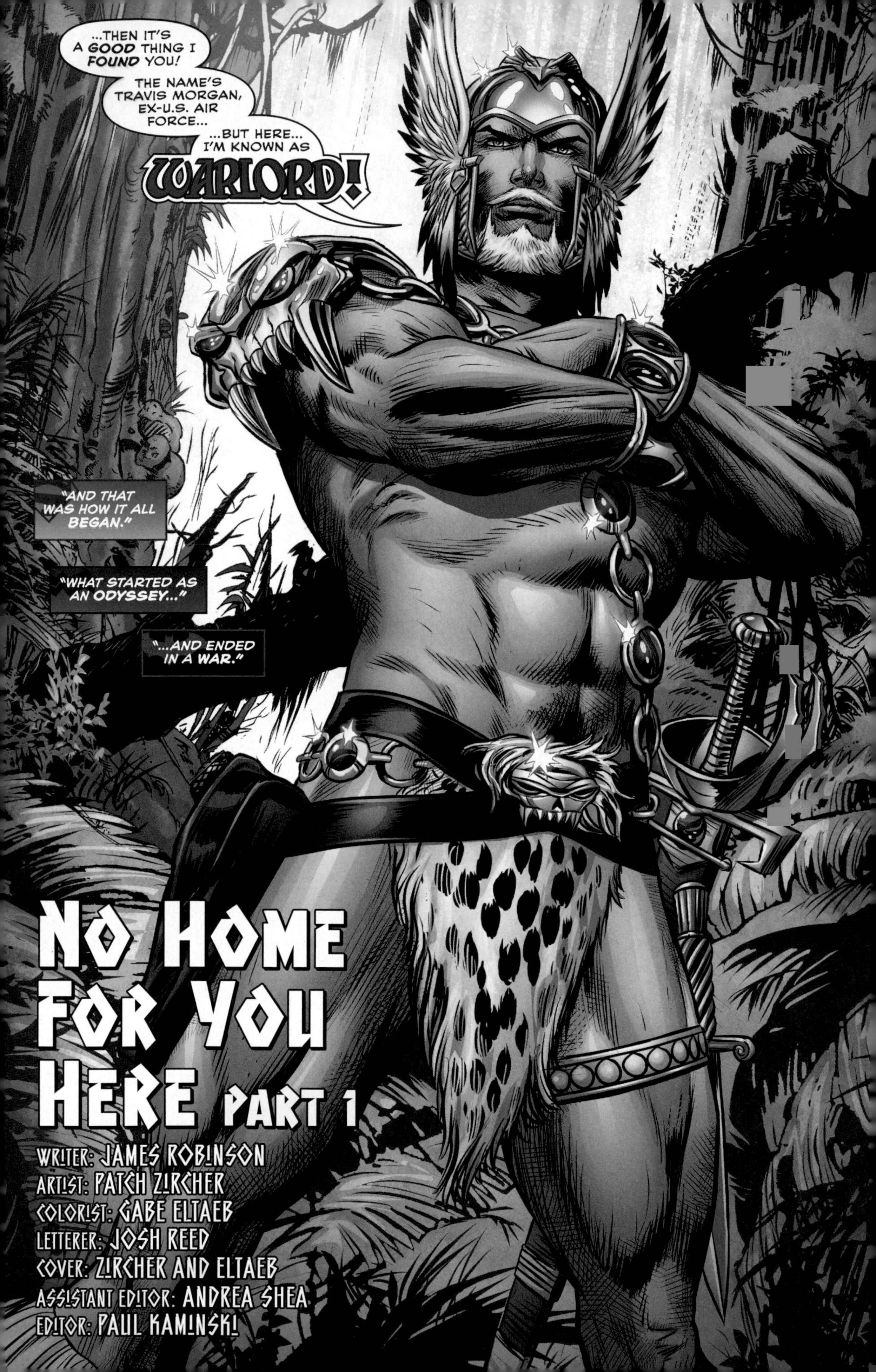

...THEN IT'S A GOOD THING I FOUND YOU!
THE NAME'S TRAVIS MORGAN, EX-U.S. AIR FORCE...
...BUT HERE... I'M KNOWN AS
WARLORD!
"AND THAT WAS HOW IT ALL BEGAN."
"WHAT STARTED AS AN ODYSSEY..."
"...AND ENDED IN A WAR."
NO HOME FOR YOU HERE PART 1
WRITER: JAMES ROBINSON
ARTIST: PATCH ZIRCHER
COLORIST: GABE ELTAEB
LETTERER: JOSH REED
COVER: ZIRCHER AND ELTAEB
ASSISTANT EDITOR: ANDREA SHEA
EDITOR: PAUL KAMINSKI

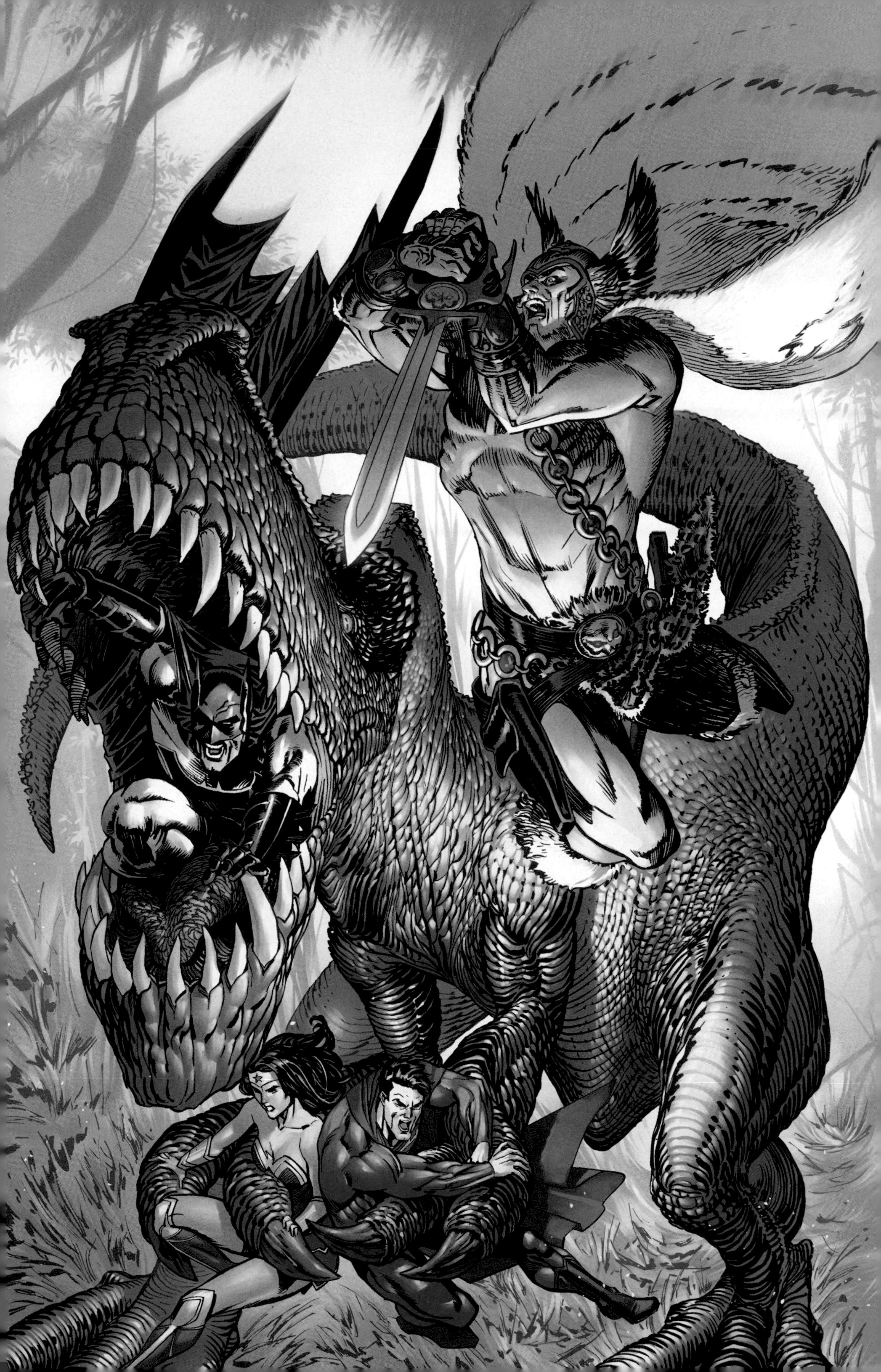

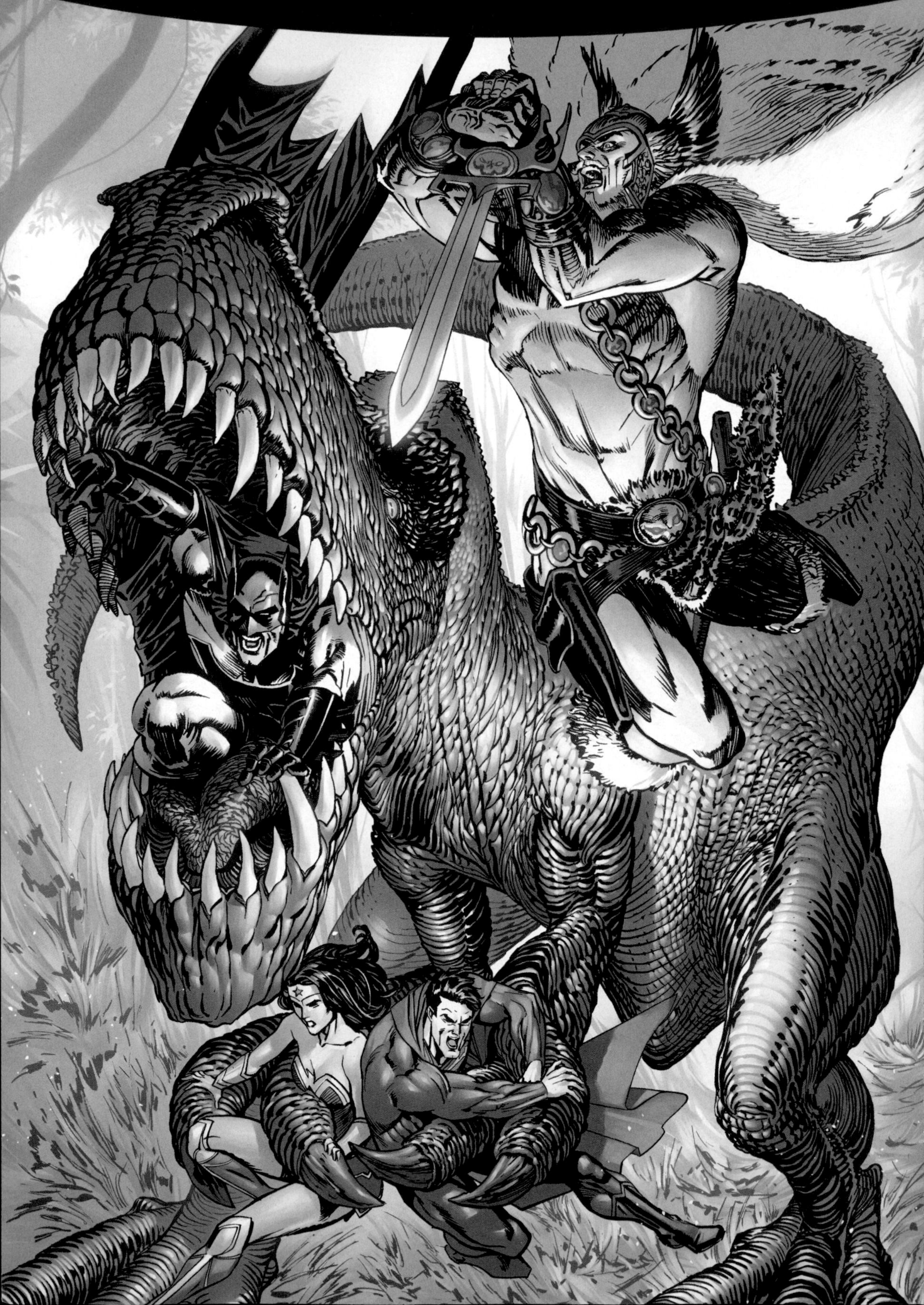

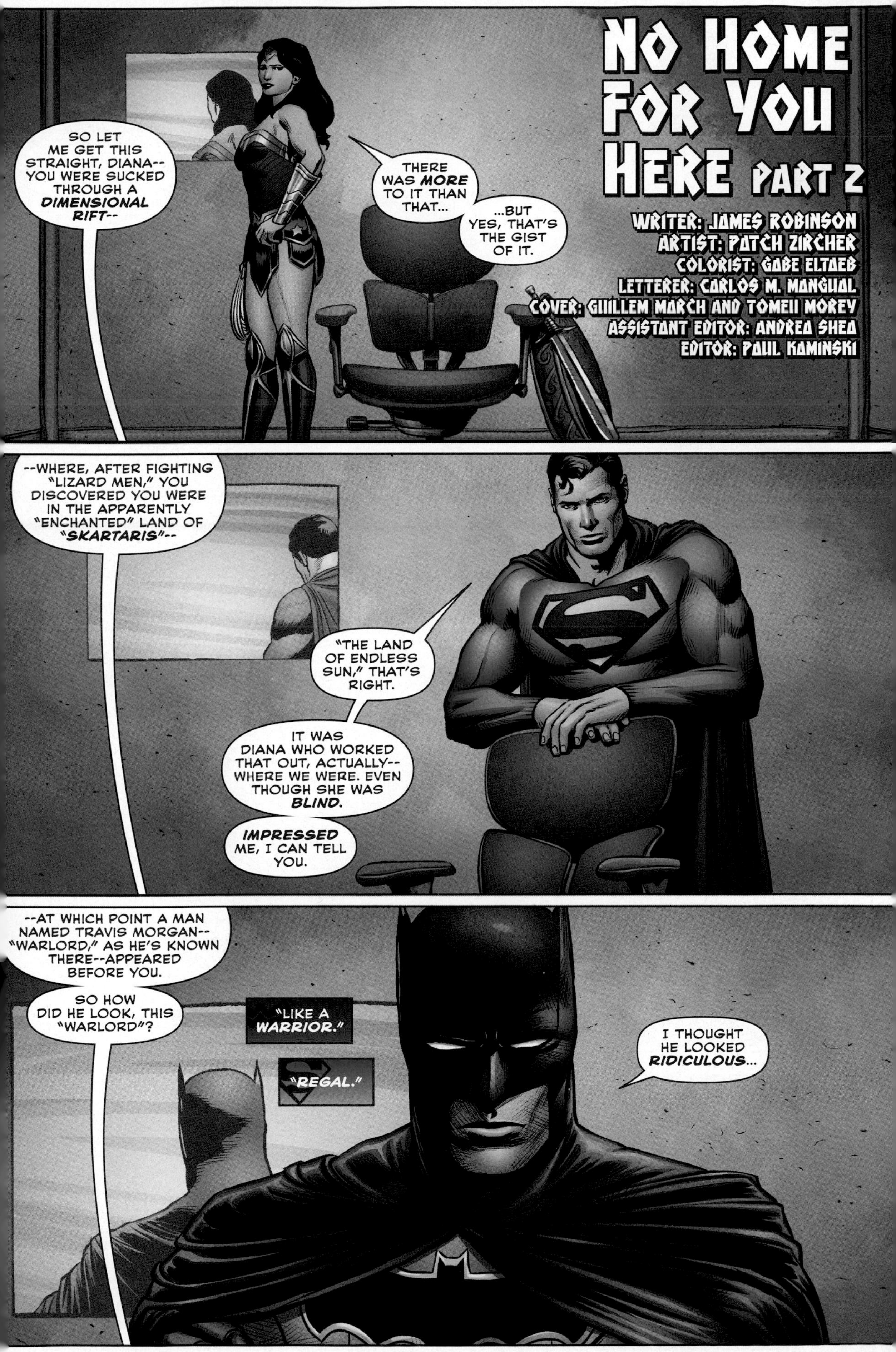
NO HOME FOR YOU HERE PART 2
WRITER: JAMES ROBINSON
ARTIST: PATCH ZIRCHER
COLORIST: GABE ELTAEB
LETTERER: CARLOS M. MANGUAL
COVER: GUILLEM MARCH AND TOMEU MOREY
ASSISTANT EDITOR: ANDREA SHEA
EDITOR: PAUL KAMINSKI
SO LET ME GET THIS STRAIGHT, DIANA-- YOU WERE SUCKED THROUGH A DIMENSIONAL RIFT--
THERE WAS MORE TO IT THAN THAT...
...BUT YES, THAT'S THE GIST OF IT.
--WHERE, AFTER FIGHTING "LIZARD MEN," YOU DISCOVERED YOU WERE IN THE APPARENTLY "ENCHANTED" LAND OF "SKARTARIS"--
"THE LAND OF ENDLESS SUN," THAT'S RIGHT.
IT WAS DIANA WHO WORKED THAT OUT, ACTUALLY-- WHERE WE WERE. EVEN THOUGH SHE WAS BLIND.
IMPRESSED ME, I CAN TELL YOU.
--AT WHICH POINT A MAN NAMED TRAVIS MORGAN-- "WARLORD," AS HE'S KNOWN THERE--APPEARED BEFORE YOU.
SO HOW DID HE LOOK, THIS "WARLORD"?
"LIKE A WARRIOR."
"REGAL."
I THOUGHT HE LOOKED RIDICULOUS...

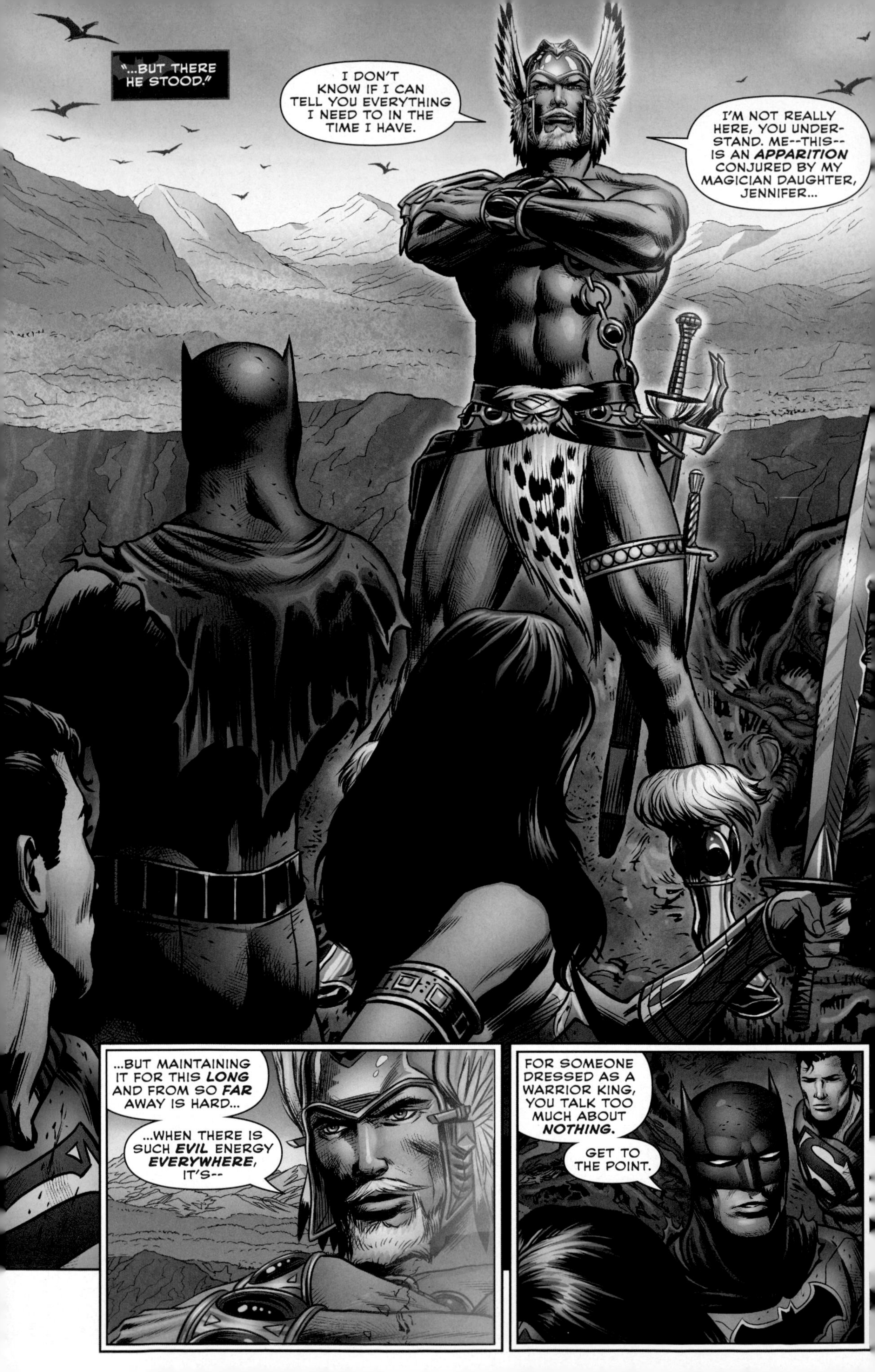
"...BUT THERE HE STOOD."
I DON'T KNOW IF I CAN TELL YOU EVERYTHING I NEED TO IN THE TIME I HAVE.
I'M NOT REALLY HERE, YOU UNDER-STAND. ME--THIS--IS AN APPARITION CONJURED BY MY MAGICIAN DAUGHTER, JENNIFER...
...BUT MAINTAINING IT FOR THIS LONG AND FROM SO FAR AWAY IS HARD...
...WHEN THERE IS SUCH EVIL ENERGY EVERYWHERE, IT'S--
FOR SOMEONE DRESSED AS A WARRIOR KING, YOU TALK TOO MUCH ABOUT NOTHING.
GET TO THE POINT.

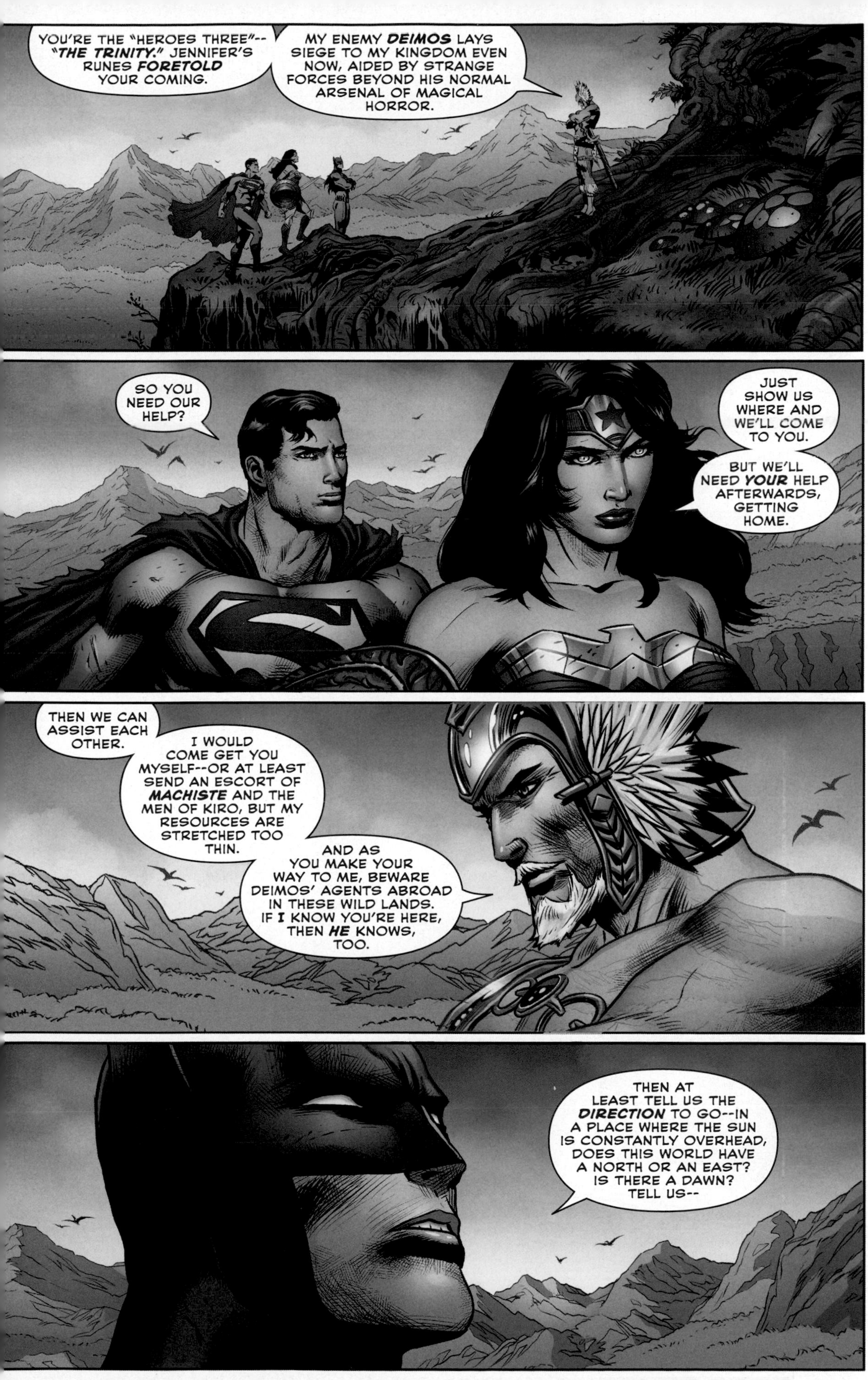
YOU'RE THE "HEROES THREE"-- "THE TRINITY." JENNIFER'S RUNES FORETOLD YOUR COMING.
MY ENEMY DEIMOS LAYS SIEGE TO MY KINGDOM EVEN NOW, AIDED BY STRANGE FORCES BEYOND HIS NORMAL ARSENAL OF MAGICAL HORROR.
SO YOU NEED OUR HELP?
JUST SHOW US WHERE AND WE'LL COME TO YOU.
BUT WE'LL NEED YOUR HELP AFTERWARDS, GETTING HOME.
THEN WE CAN ASSIST EACH OTHER.
I WOULD COME GET YOU MYSELF--OR AT LEAST SEND AN ESCORT OF MACHISTE AND THE MEN OF KIRO, BUT MY RESOURCES ARE STRETCHED TOO THIN.
AND AS YOU MAKE YOUR WAY TO ME, BEWARE DEIMOS' AGENTS ABROAD IN THESE WILD LANDS. IF I KNOW YOU'RE HERE, THEN HE KNOWS, TOO.
THEN AT LEAST TELL US THE DIRECTION TO GO--IN A PLACE WHERE THE SUN IS CONSTANTLY OVERHEAD, DOES THIS WORLD HAVE A NORTH OR AN EAST? IS THERE A DAWN? TELL US--

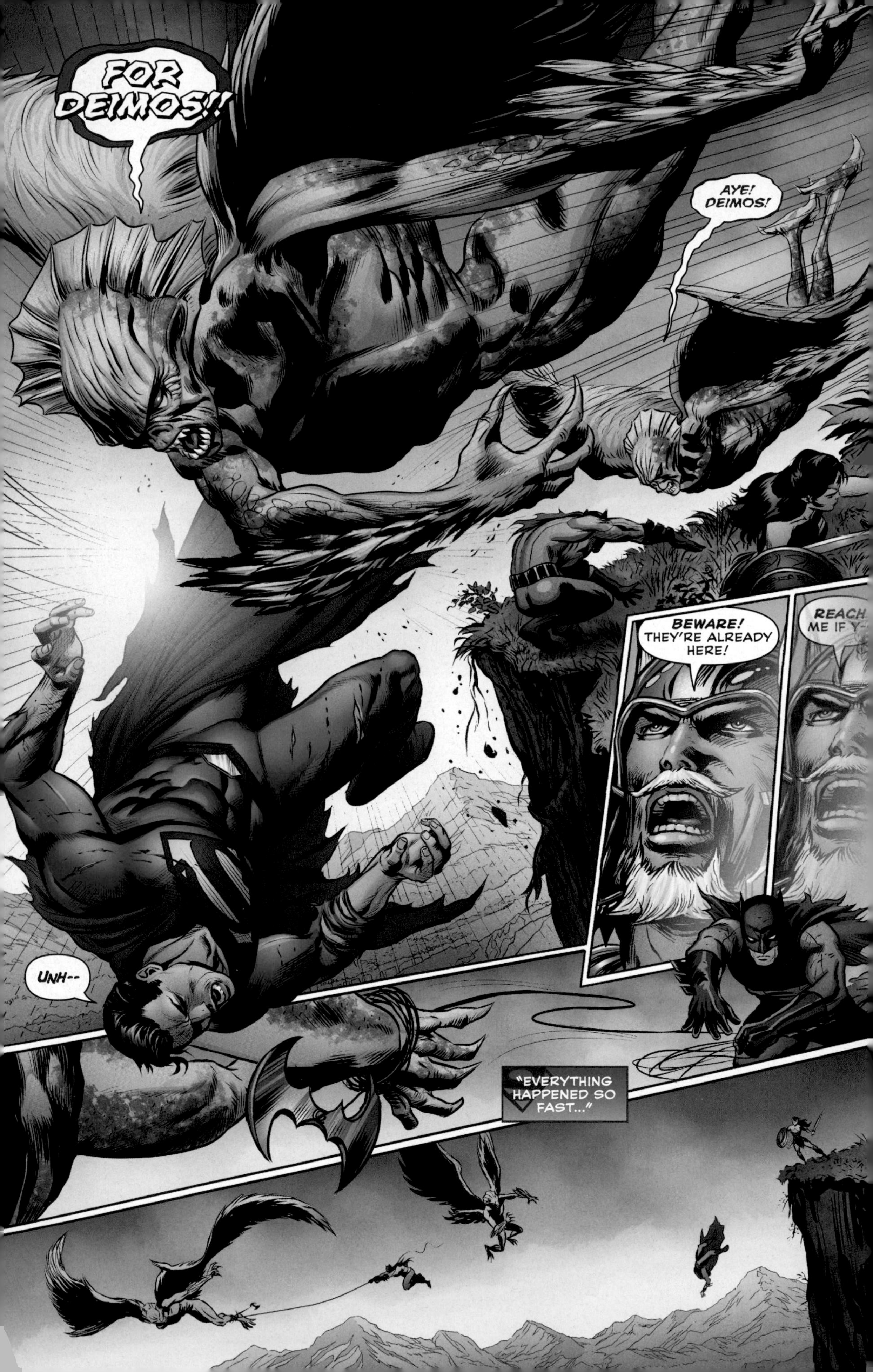
FOR DEIMOS!!
AYE! DEIMOS!
BEWARE! THEY'RE ALREADY HERE!
REACH ME IF Y--
UNH--
"EVERYTHING HAPPENED SO FAST..."

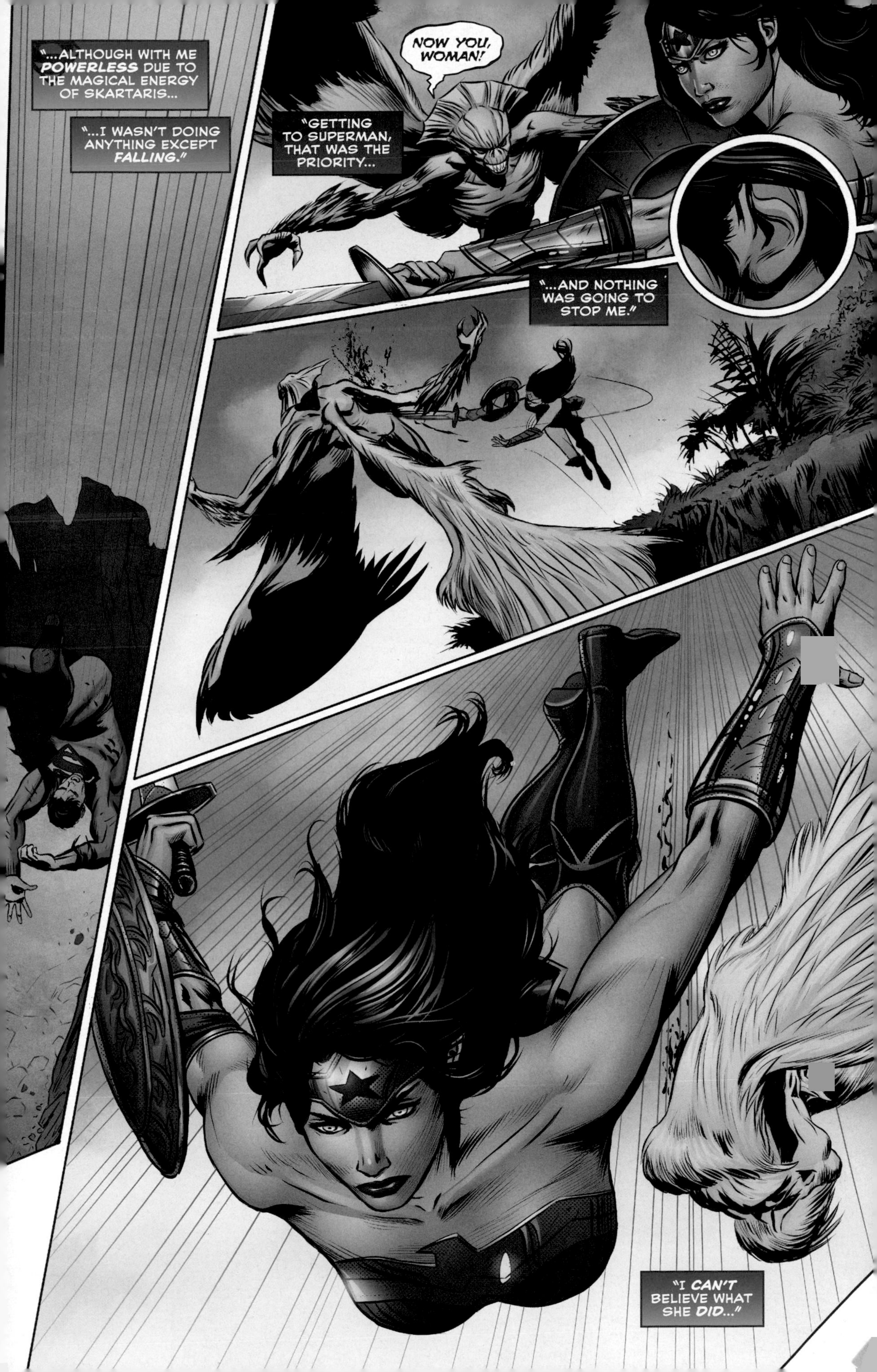
"...ALTHOUGH WITH ME POWERLESS DUE TO THE MAGICAL ENERGY OF SKARTARIS...
"...I WASN'T DOING ANYTHING EXCEPT FALLING."
NOW YOU, WOMAN!
"GETTING TO SUPERMAN, THAT WAS THE PRIORITY...
"...AND NOTHING WAS GOING TO STOP ME."
"I CAN'T BELIEVE WHAT SHE DID..."

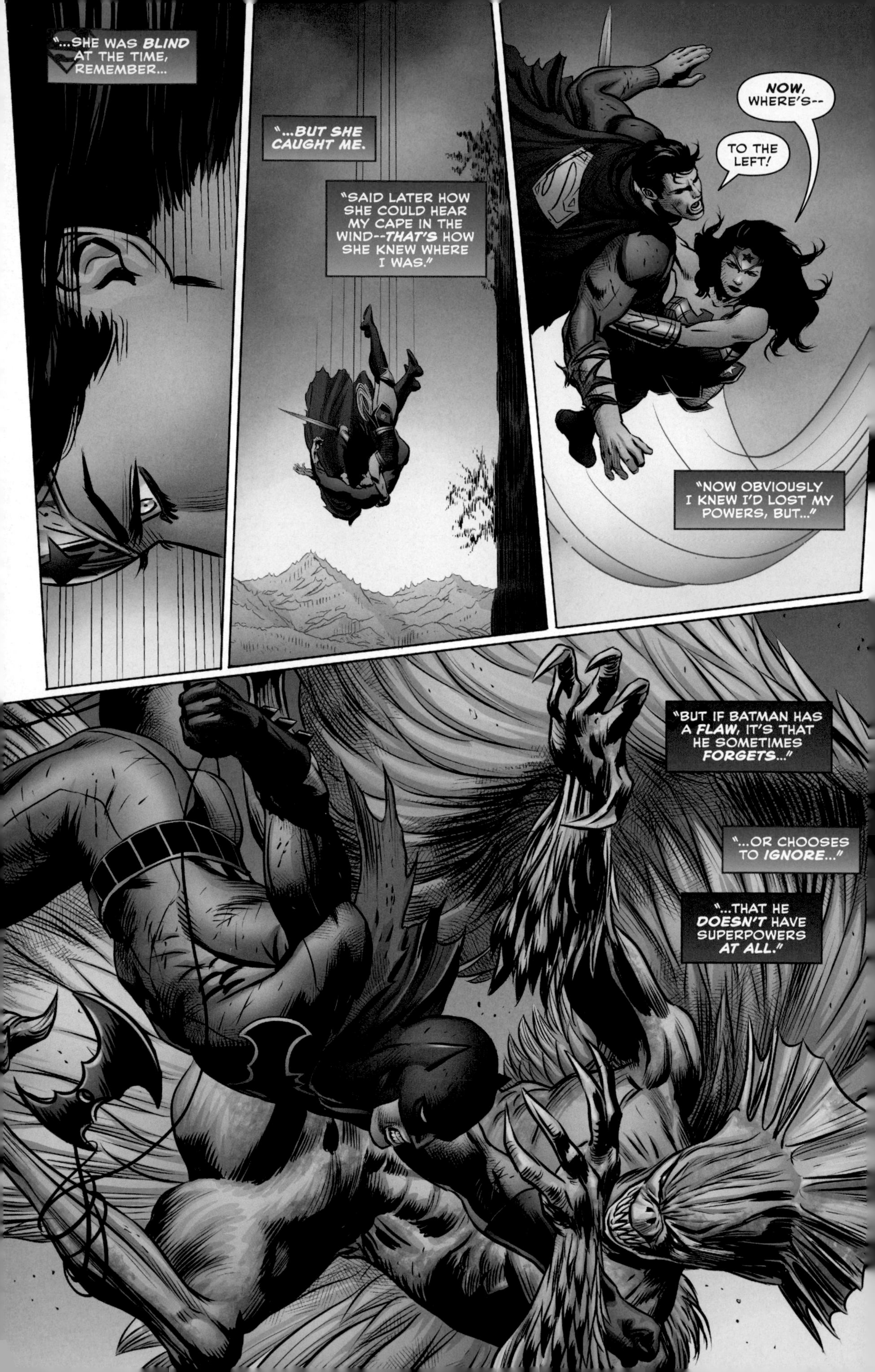
"...SHE WAS BLIND AT THE TIME, REMEMBER...
"...BUT SHE CAUGHT ME.
"SAID LATER HOW SHE COULD HEAR MY CAPE IN THE WIND--THAT'S HOW SHE KNEW WHERE I WAS."
NOW, WHERE'S--
TO THE LEFT!
"NOW OBVIOUSLY I KNEW I'D LOST MY POWERS, BUT..."
"BUT IF BATMAN HAS A FLAW, IT'S THAT HE SOMETIMES FORGETS..."
"...OR CHOOSES TO IGNORE..."
"...THAT HE DOESN'T HAVE SUPERPOWERS AT ALL."

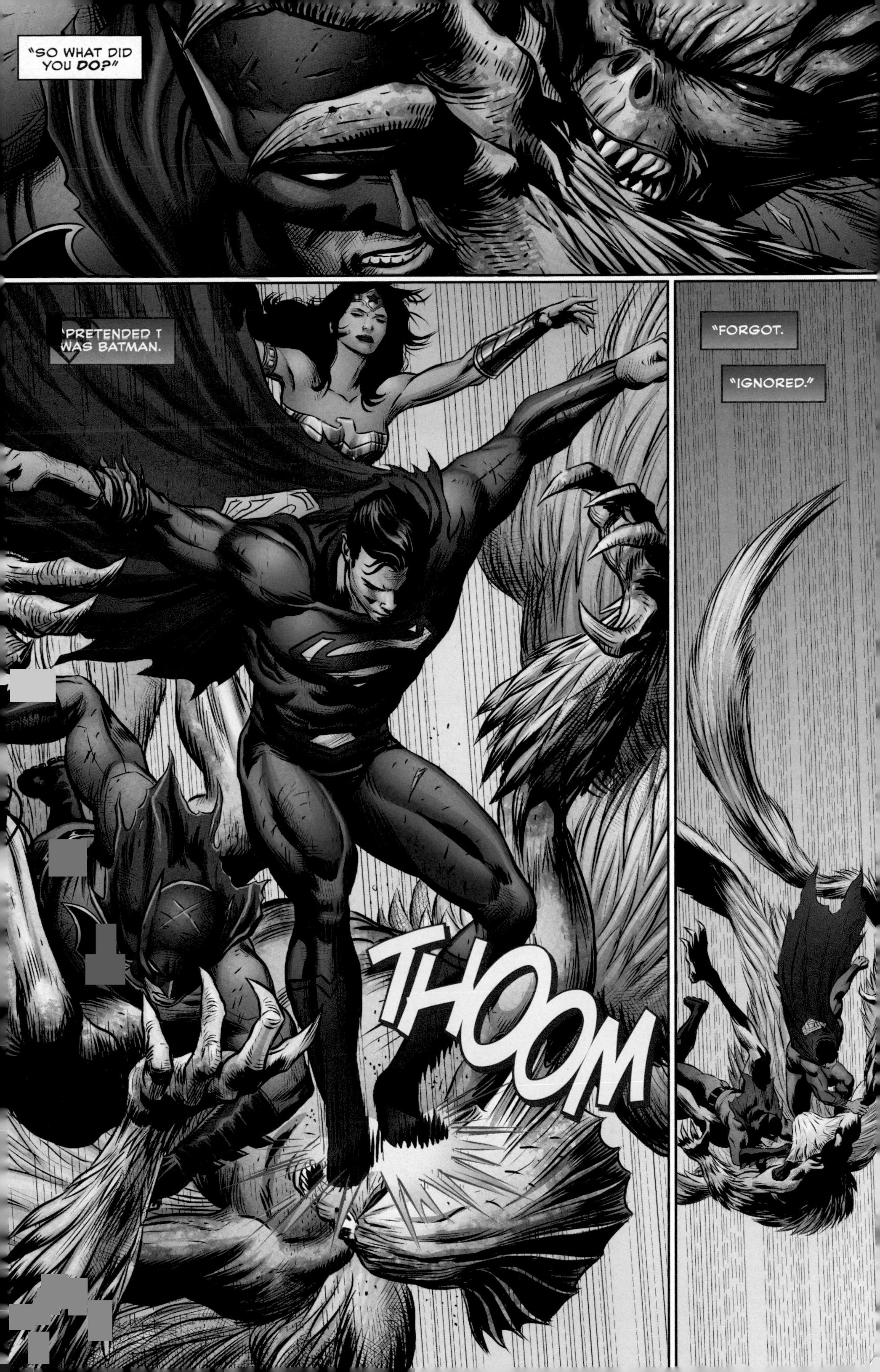
"SO WHAT DID YOU DO?"
"PRETENDED I WAS BATMAN.
THOOM
"FORGOT.
"IGNORED."

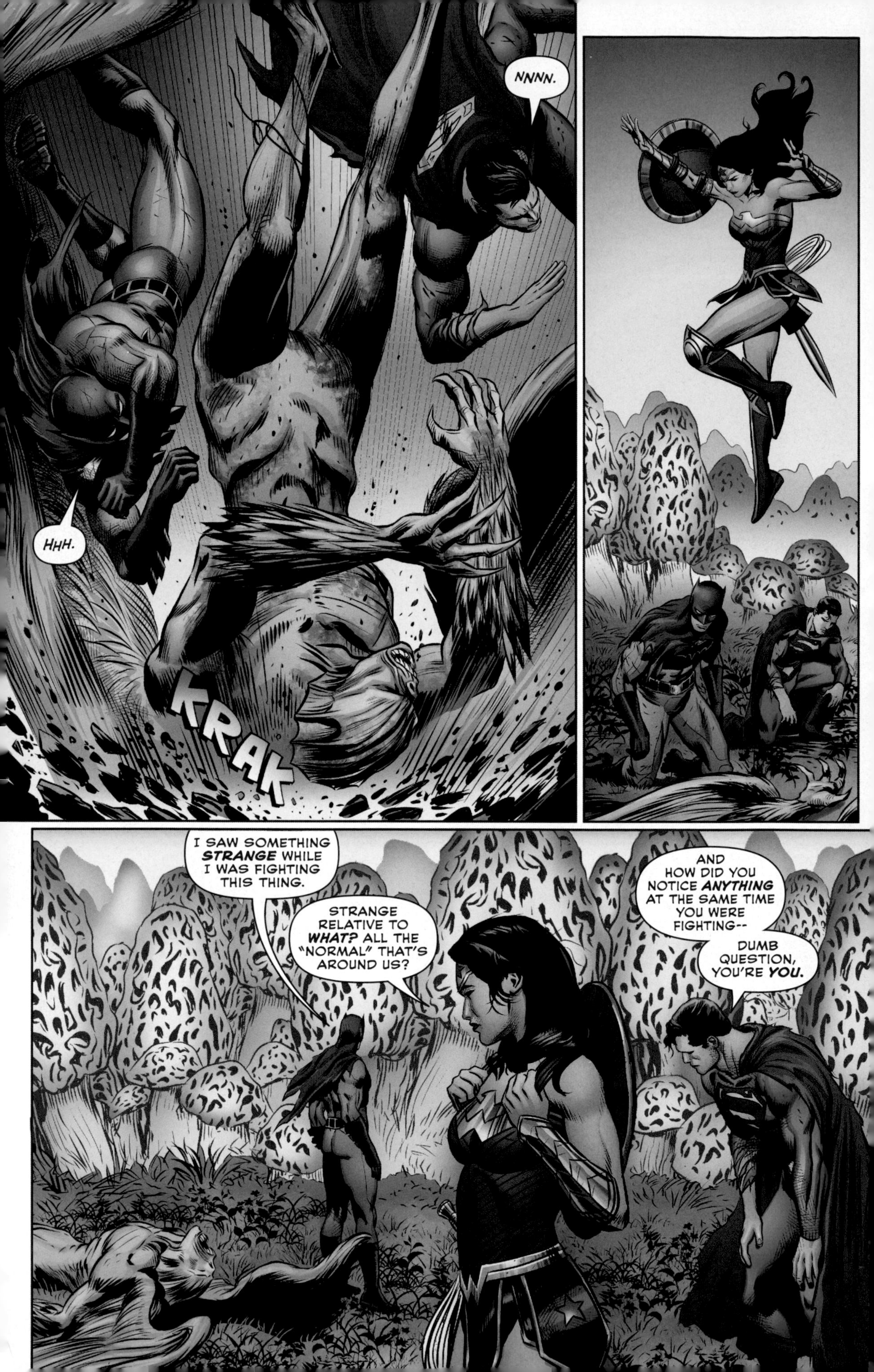
NNNN.
HHH.
KRAK
I SAW SOMETHING STRANGE WHILE I WAS FIGHTING THIS THING.
STRANGE RELATIVE TO WHAT? ALL THE "NORMAL" THAT'S AROUND US?
AND HOW DID YOU NOTICE ANYTHING AT THE SAME TIME YOU WERE FIGHTING--
DUMB QUESTION, YOU'RE YOU.

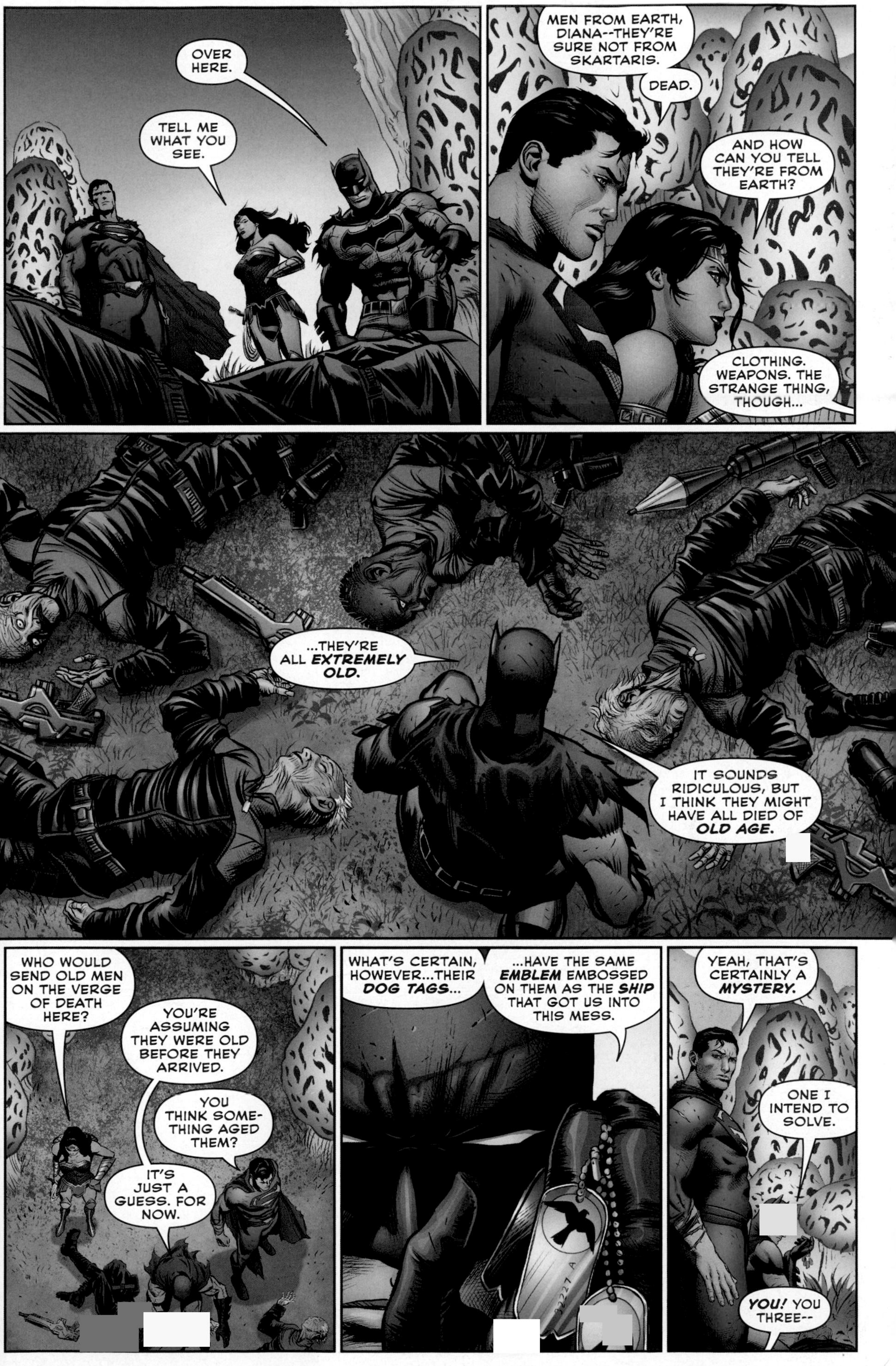
OVER HERE.
TELL ME WHAT YOU SEE.
MEN FROM EARTH, DIANA--THEY'RE SURE NOT FROM SKARTARIS.
DEAD.
AND HOW CAN YOU TELL THEY'RE FROM EARTH?
CLOTHING. WEAPONS. THE STRANGE THING, THOUGH...
...THEY'RE ALL EXTREMELY OLD.
IT SOUNDS RIDICULOUS, BUT I THINK THEY MIGHT HAVE ALL DIED OF OLD AGE.
WHO WOULD SEND OLD MEN ON THE VERGE OF DEATH HERE?
YOU'RE ASSUMING THEY WERE OLD BEFORE THEY ARRIVED.
YOU THINK SOMETHING AGED THEM?
IT'S JUST A GUESS. FOR NOW.
WHAT'S CERTAIN, HOWEVER...THEIR DOG TAGS...
...HAVE THE SAME EMBLEM EMBOSSED ON THEM AS THE SHIP THAT GOT US INTO THIS MESS.
YEAH, THAT'S CERTAINLY A MYSTERY.
ONE I INTEND TO SOLVE.
YOU! YOU THREE--

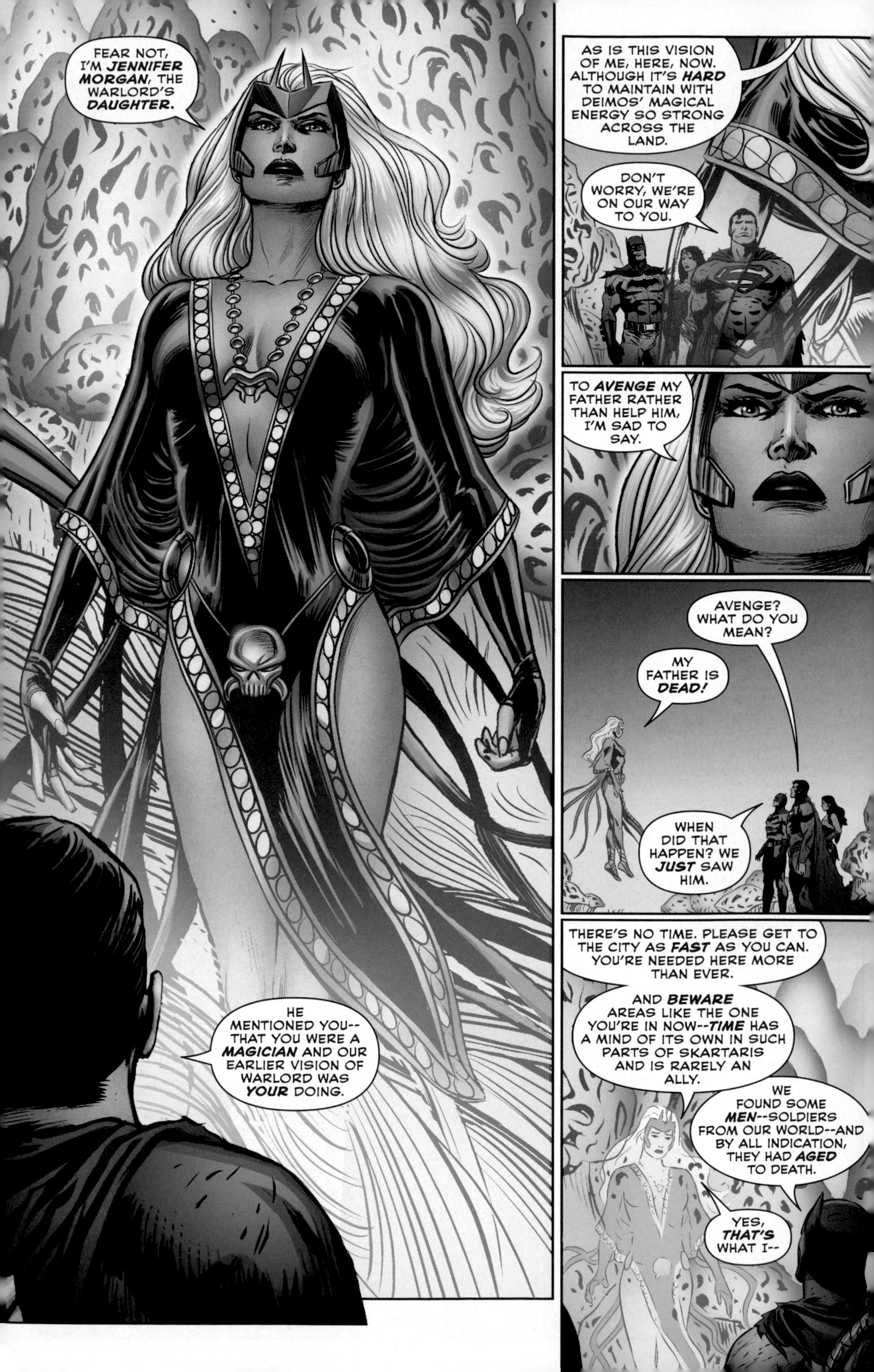

FEAR NOT, I'M JENNIFER MORGAN, THE WARLORD'S DAUGHTER.
HE MENTIONED YOU--THAT YOU WERE A MAGICIAN AND OUR EARLIER VISION OF WARLORD WAS YOUR DOING.
AS IS THIS VISION OF ME, HERE, NOW. ALTHOUGH IT'S HARD TO MAINTAIN WITH DEIMOS' MAGICAL ENERGY SO STRONG ACROSS THE LAND.
DON'T WORRY, WE'RE ON OUR WAY TO YOU.
TO AVENGE MY FATHER RATHER THAN HELP HIM, I'M SAD TO SAY.
AVENGE? WHAT DO YOU MEAN?
MY FATHER IS DEAD!
WHEN DID THAT HAPPEN? WE JUST SAW HIM.
THERE'S NO TIME. PLEASE GET TO THE CITY AS FAST AS YOU CAN. YOU'RE NEEDED HERE MORE THAN EVER.
AND BEWARE AREAS LIKE THE ONE YOU'RE IN NOW--TIME HAS A MIND OF ITS OWN IN SUCH PARTS OF SKARTARIS AND IS RARELY AN ALLY.
WE FOUND SOME MEN--SOLDIERS FROM OUR WORLD--AND BY ALL INDICATION, THEY HAD AGED TO DEATH.
YES, THAT'S WHAT I--

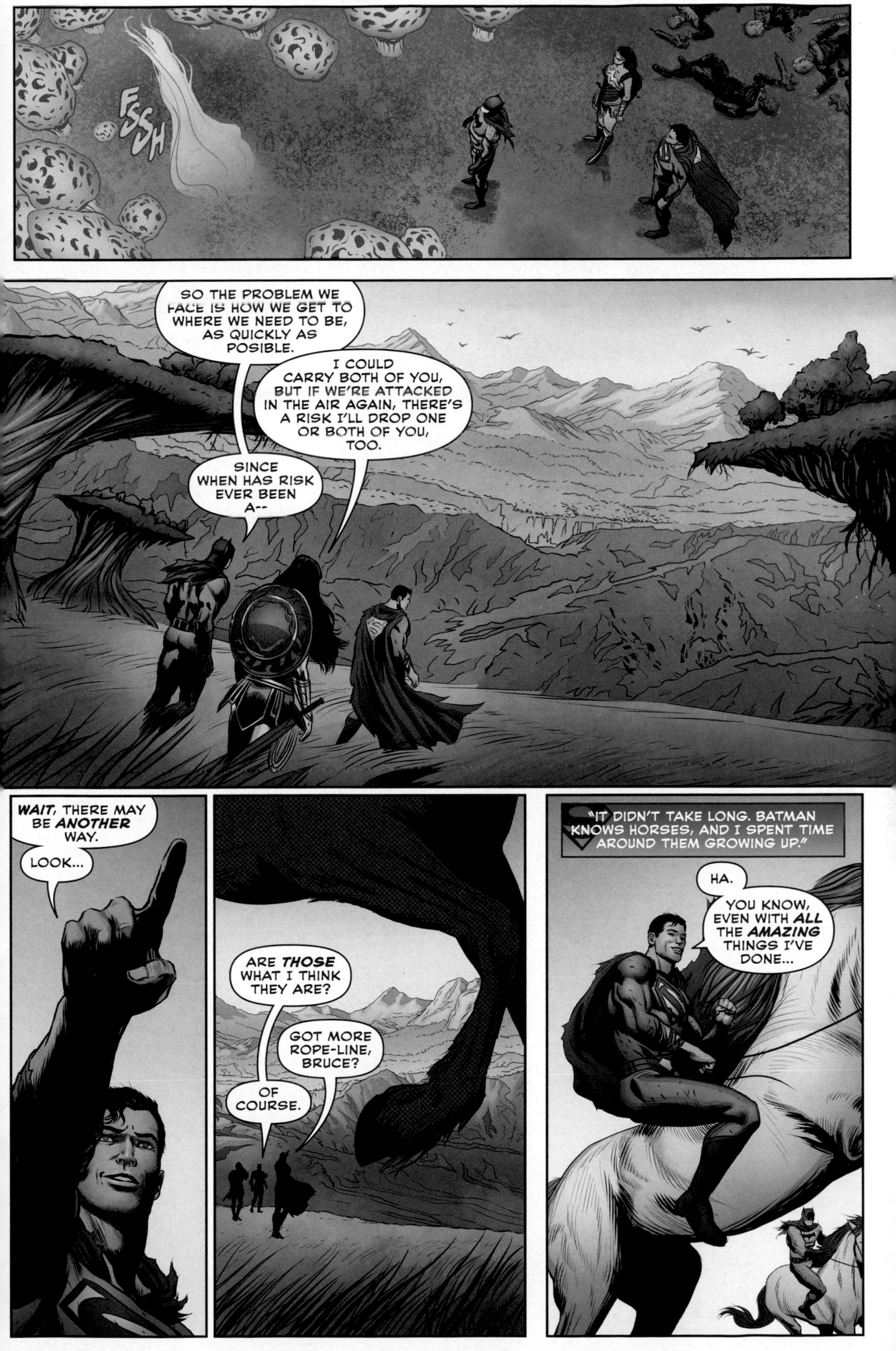
FSSH
SO THE PROBLEM WE FACE IS HOW WE GET TO WHERE WE NEED TO BE, AS QUICKLY AS POSIBLE.
I COULD CARRY BOTH OF YOU, BUT IF WE'RE ATTACKED IN THE AIR AGAIN, THERE'S A RISK I'LL DROP ONE OR BOTH OF YOU, TOO.
SINCE WHEN HAS RISK EVER BEEN A--
WAIT, THERE MAY BE ANOTHER WAY.
LOOK...
ARE THOSE WHAT I THINK THEY ARE?
GOT MORE ROPE-LINE, BRUCE?
OF COURSE.
"IT DIDN'T TAKE LONG. BATMAN KNOWS HORSES, AND I SPENT TIME AROUND THEM GROWING UP."
HA.
YOU KNOW, EVEN WITH ALL THE AMAZING THINGS I'VE DONE...

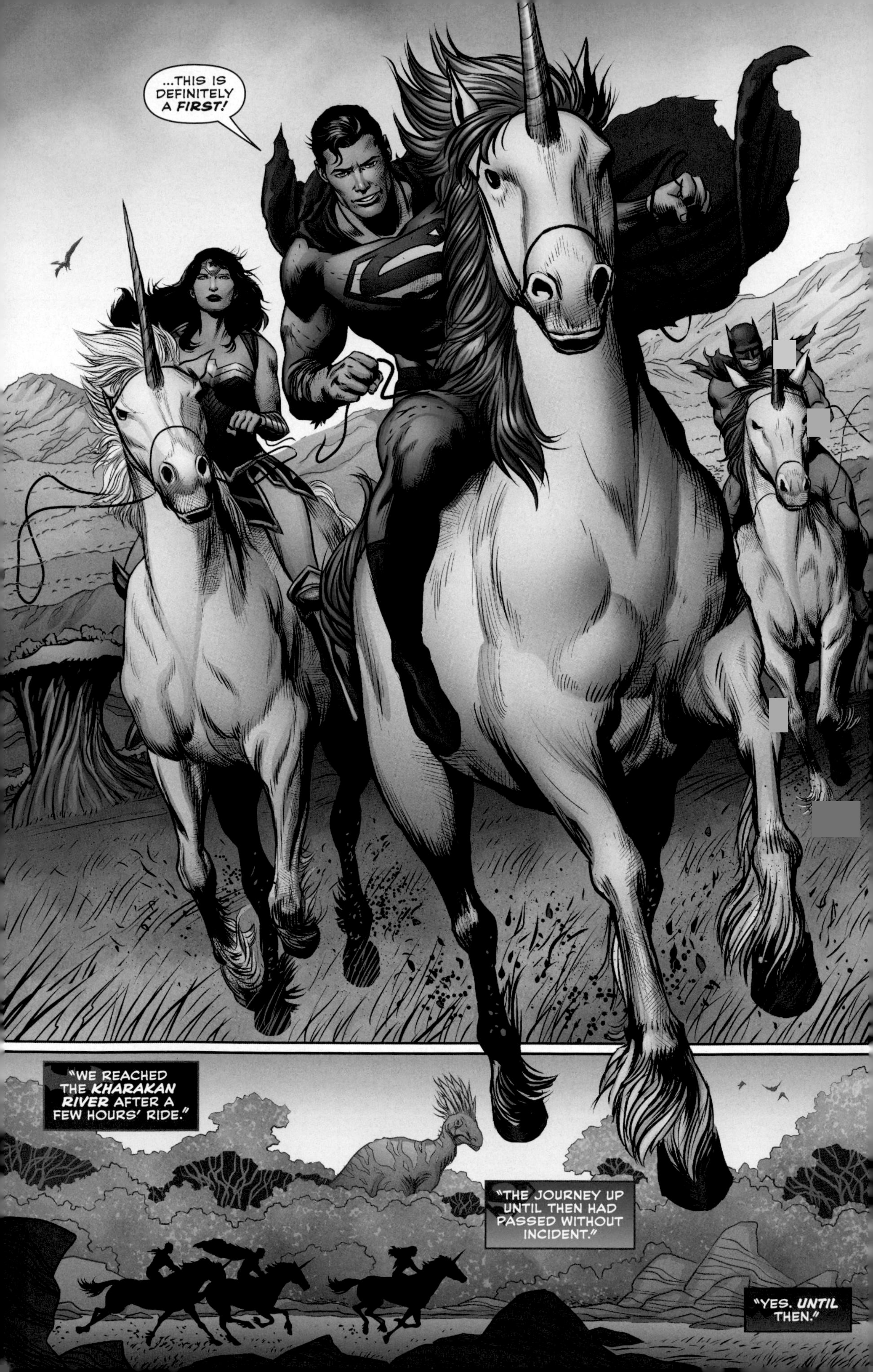
...THIS IS DEFINITELY A FIRST!
"WE REACHED THE KHARAKAN RIVER AFTER A FEW HOURS' RIDE."
"THE JOURNEY UP UNTIL THEN HAD PASSED WITHOUT INCIDENT."
"YES. UNTIL THEN."

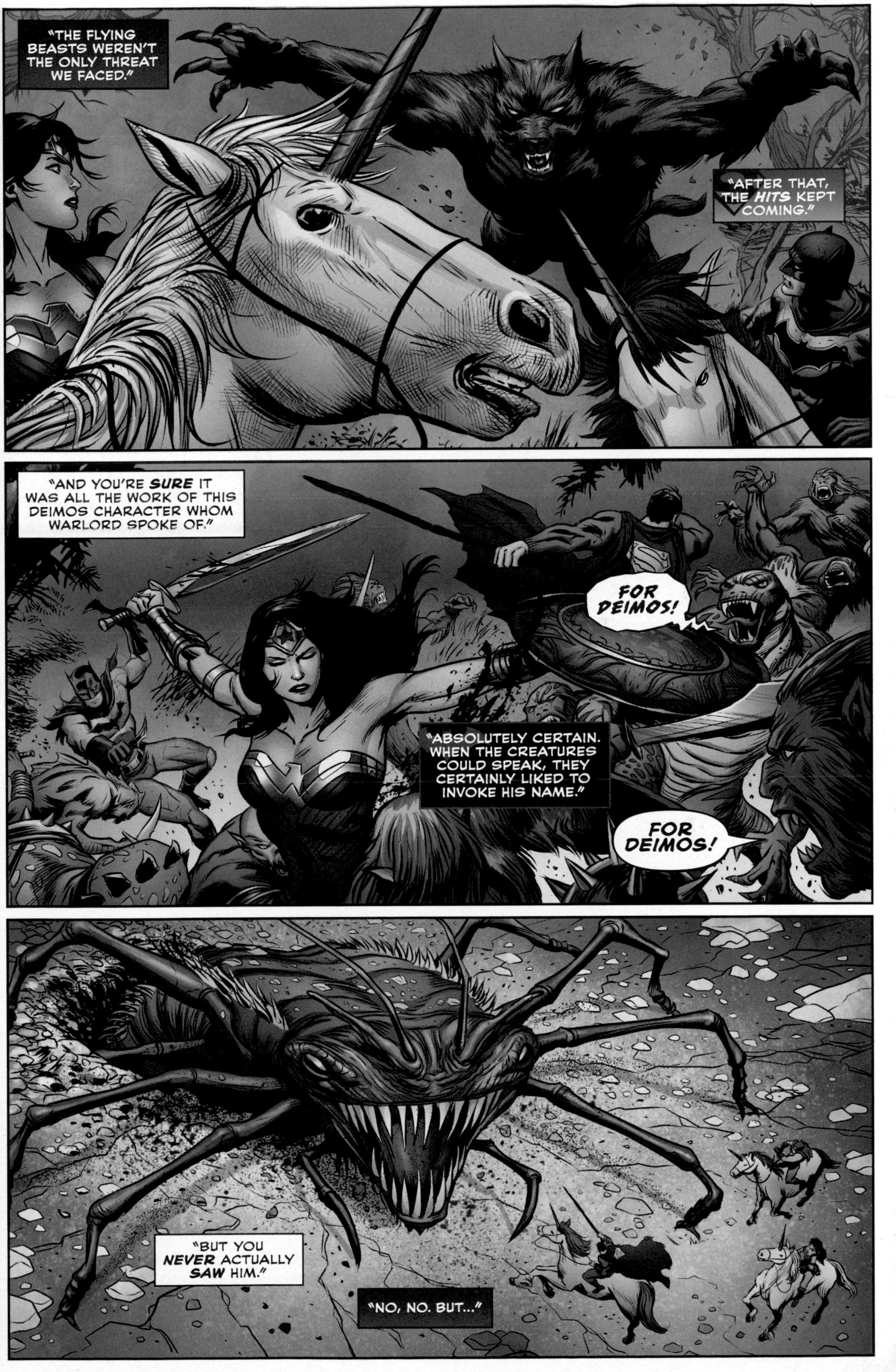
"THE FLYING BEASTS WEREN'T THE ONLY THREAT WE FACED."
"AFTER THAT, THE HITS KEPT COMING."
"AND YOU'RE SURE IT WAS ALL THE WORK OF THIS DEIMOS CHARACTER WHOM WARLORD SPOKE OF."
FOR DEIMOS!
"ABSOLUTELY CERTAIN. WHEN THE CREATURES COULD SPEAK, THEY CERTAINLY LIKED TO INVOKE HIS NAME."
FOR DEIMOS!
"BUT YOU NEVER ACTUALLY SAW HIM."
"NO, NO. BUT..."

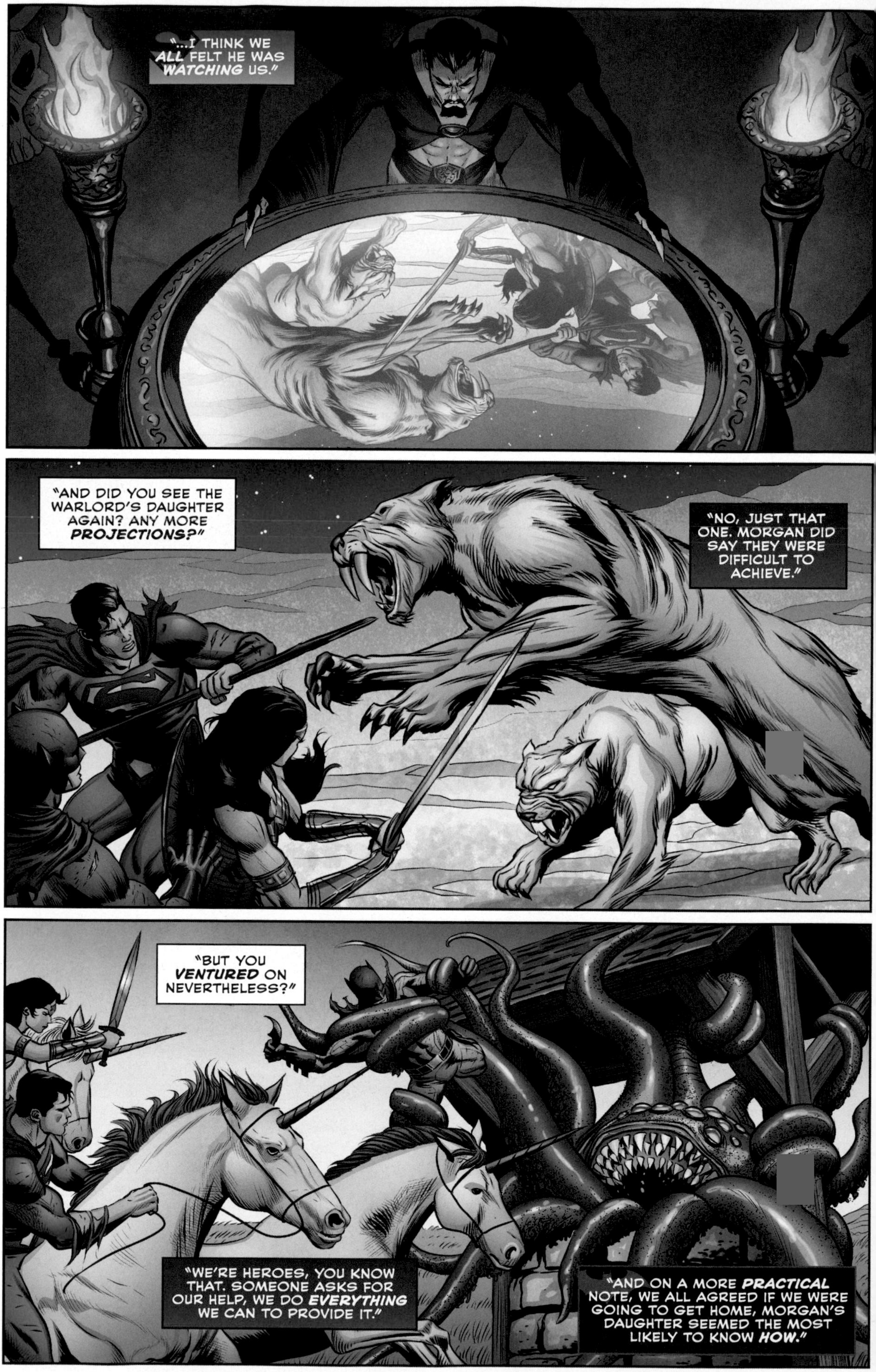
"...I THINK WE ALL FELT HE WAS WATCHING US."
"AND DID YOU SEE THE WARLORD'S DAUGHTER AGAIN? ANY MORE PROJECTIONS?"
"NO, JUST THAT ONE. MORGAN DID SAY THEY WERE DIFFICULT TO ACHIEVE."
"BUT YOU VENTURED ON NEVERTHELESS?"
"WE'RE HEROES, YOU KNOW THAT. SOMEONE ASKS FOR OUR HELP, WE DO EVERYTHING WE CAN TO PROVIDE IT."
"AND ON A MORE PRACTICAL NOTE, WE ALL AGREED IF WE WERE GOING TO GET HOME, MORGAN'S DAUGHTER SEEMED THE MOST LIKELY TO KNOW HOW."

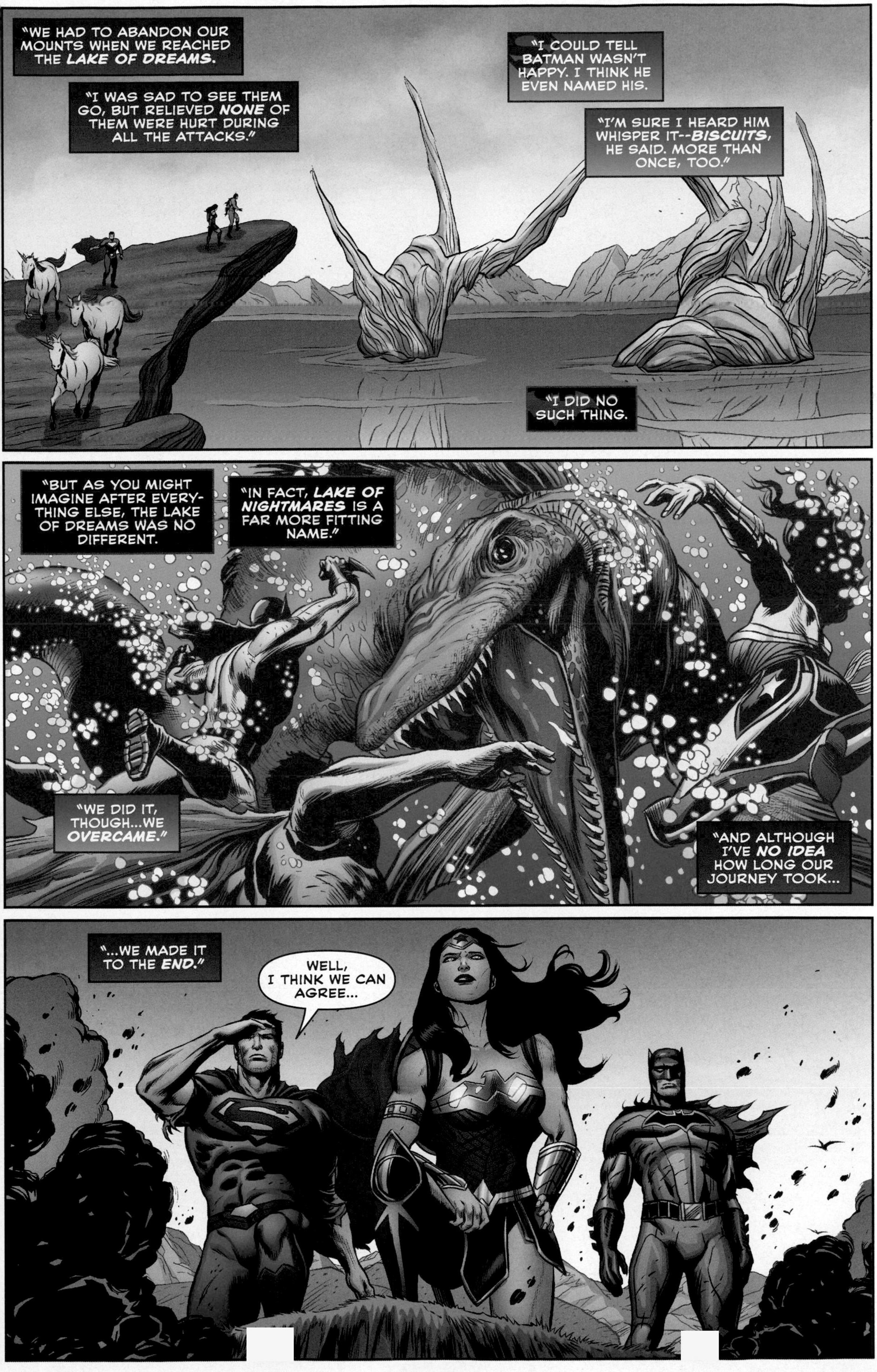
"WE HAD TO ABANDON OUR MOUNTS WHEN WE REACHED THE LAKE OF DREAMS.
"I WAS SAD TO SEE THEM GO, BUT RELIEVED NONE OF THEM WERE HURT DURING ALL THE ATTACKS."
"I COULD TELL BATMAN WASN'T HAPPY. I THINK HE EVEN NAMED HIS.
"I'M SURE I HEARD HIM WHISPER IT--BISCUITS, HE SAID. MORE THAN ONCE, TOO."
"I DID NO SUCH THING.
"BUT AS YOU MIGHT IMAGINE AFTER EVERY-THING ELSE, THE LAKE OF DREAMS WAS NO DIFFERENT.
"IN FACT, LAKE OF NIGHTMARES IS A FAR MORE FITTING NAME."
"WE DID IT, THOUGH...WE OVERCAME."
"AND ALTHOUGH I'VE NO IDEA HOW LONG OUR JOURNEY TOOK...
"...WE MADE IT TO THE END."
WELL, I THINK WE CAN AGREE...

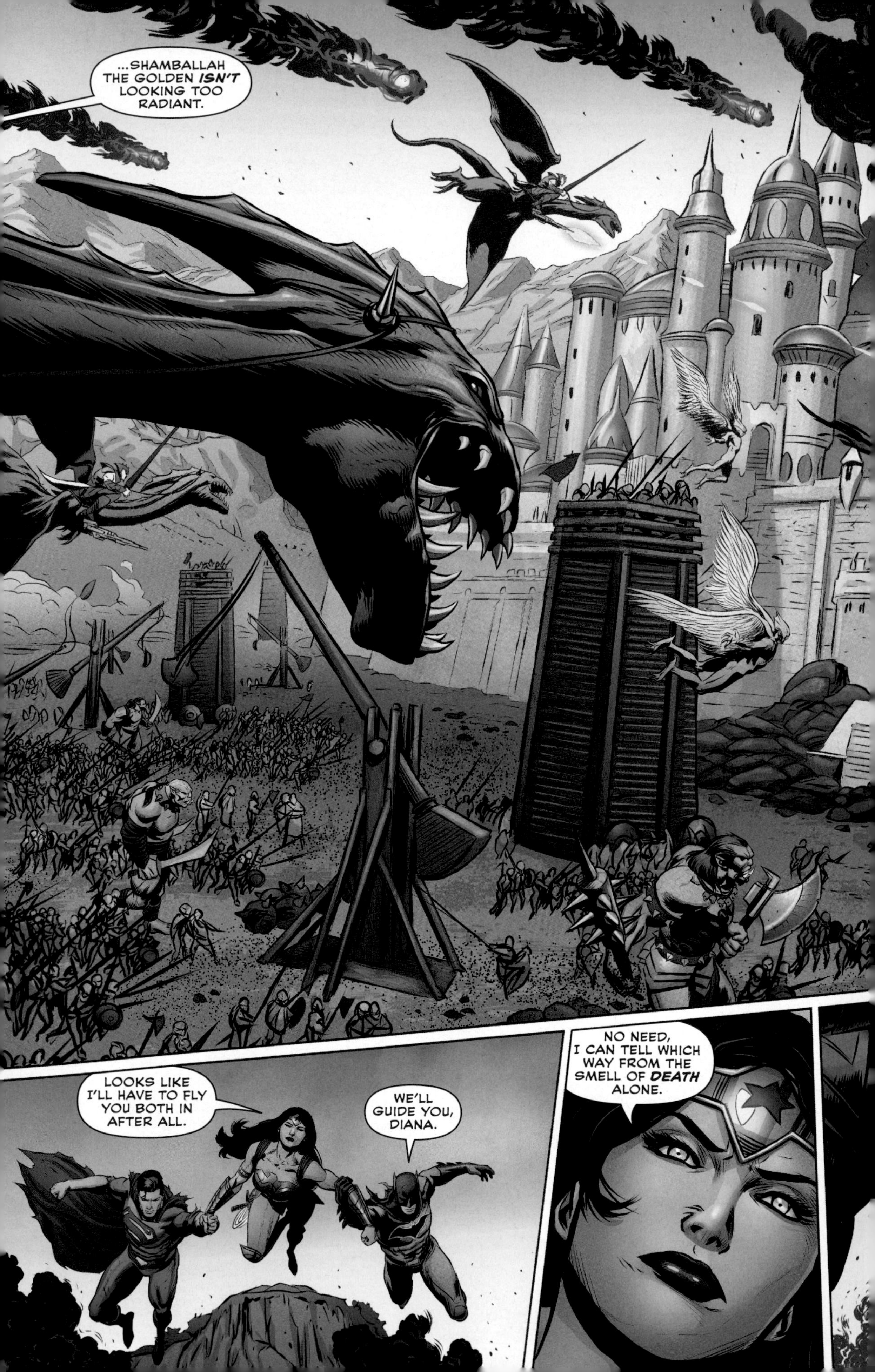
...SHAMBALLAH THE GOLDEN ISN'T LOOKING TOO RADIANT.
LOOKS LIKE I'LL HAVE TO FLY YOU BOTH IN AFTER ALL.
WE'LL GUIDE YOU, DIANA.
NO NEED, I CAN TELL WHICH WAY FROM THE SMELL OF DEATH ALONE.

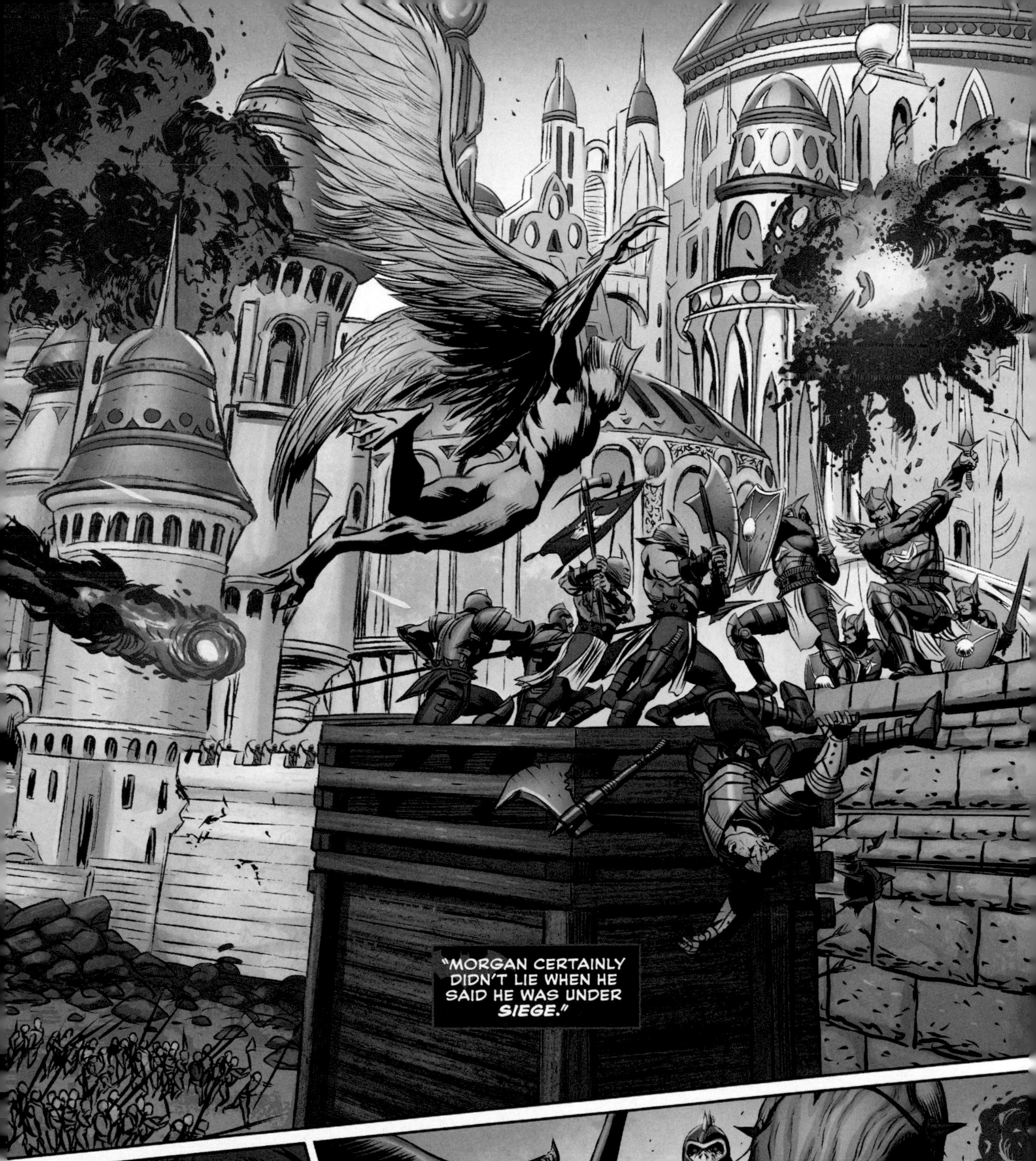
"MORGAN CERTAINLY DIDN'T LIE WHEN HE SAID HE WAS UNDER SIEGE."

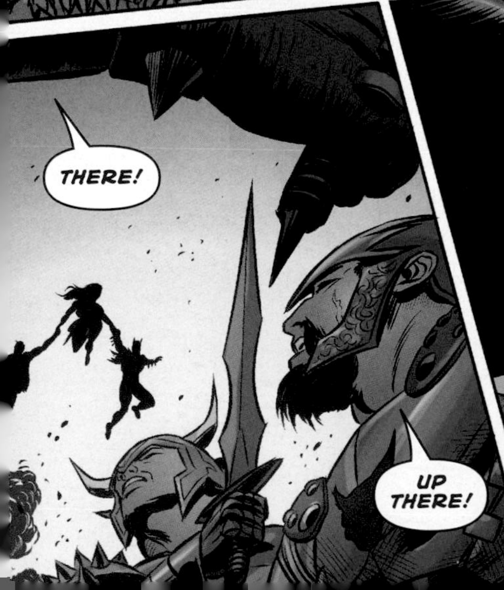
THERE!
UP THERE!

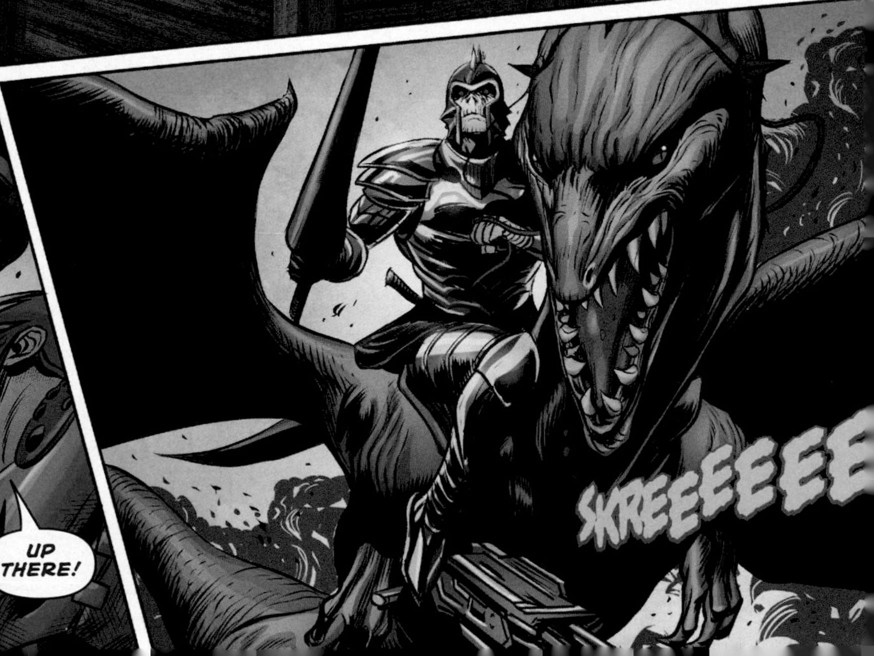
SKREEEEEEE

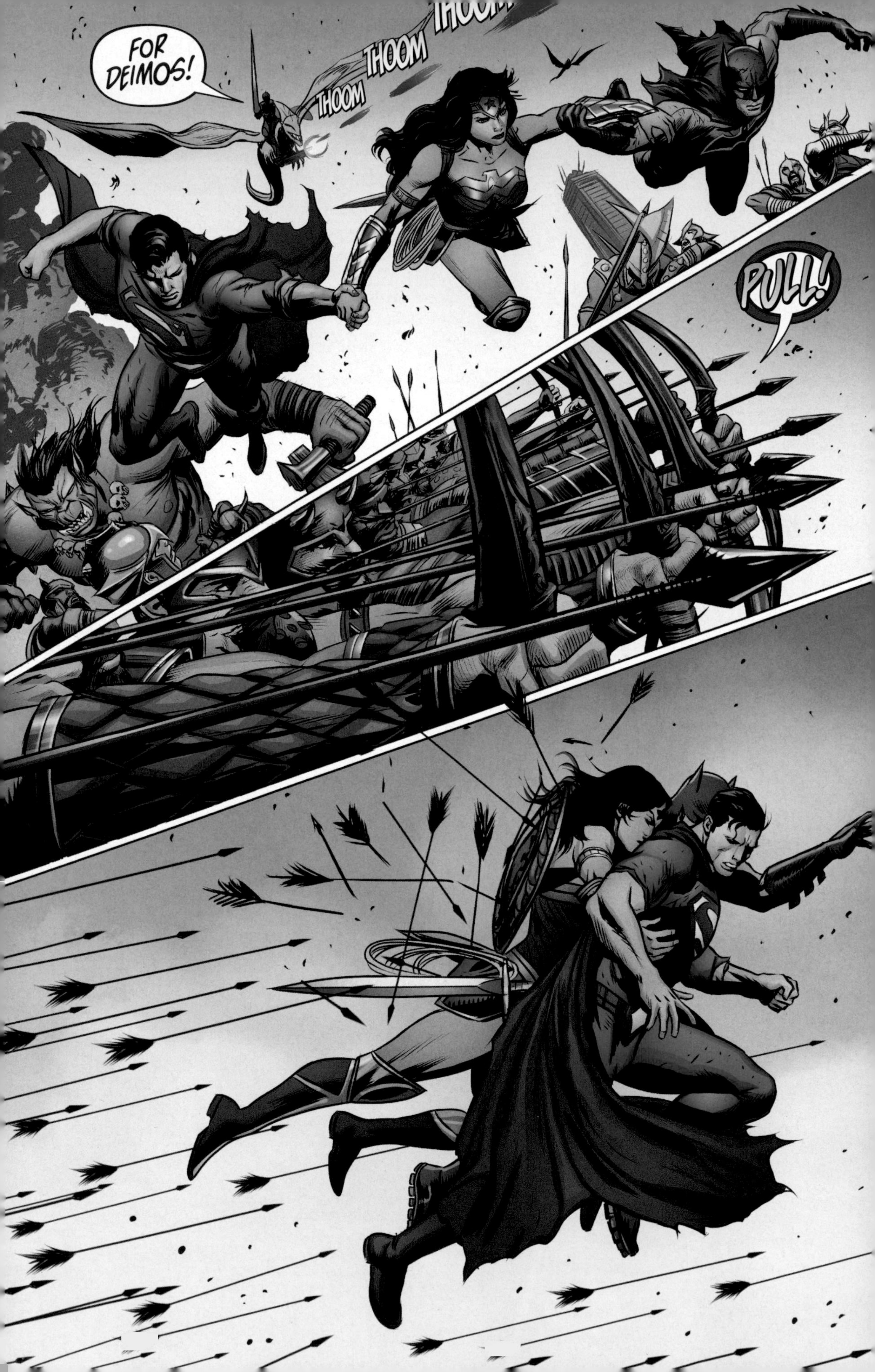
FOR DEIMOS!
THOOM THOOM THOOM
PULL!

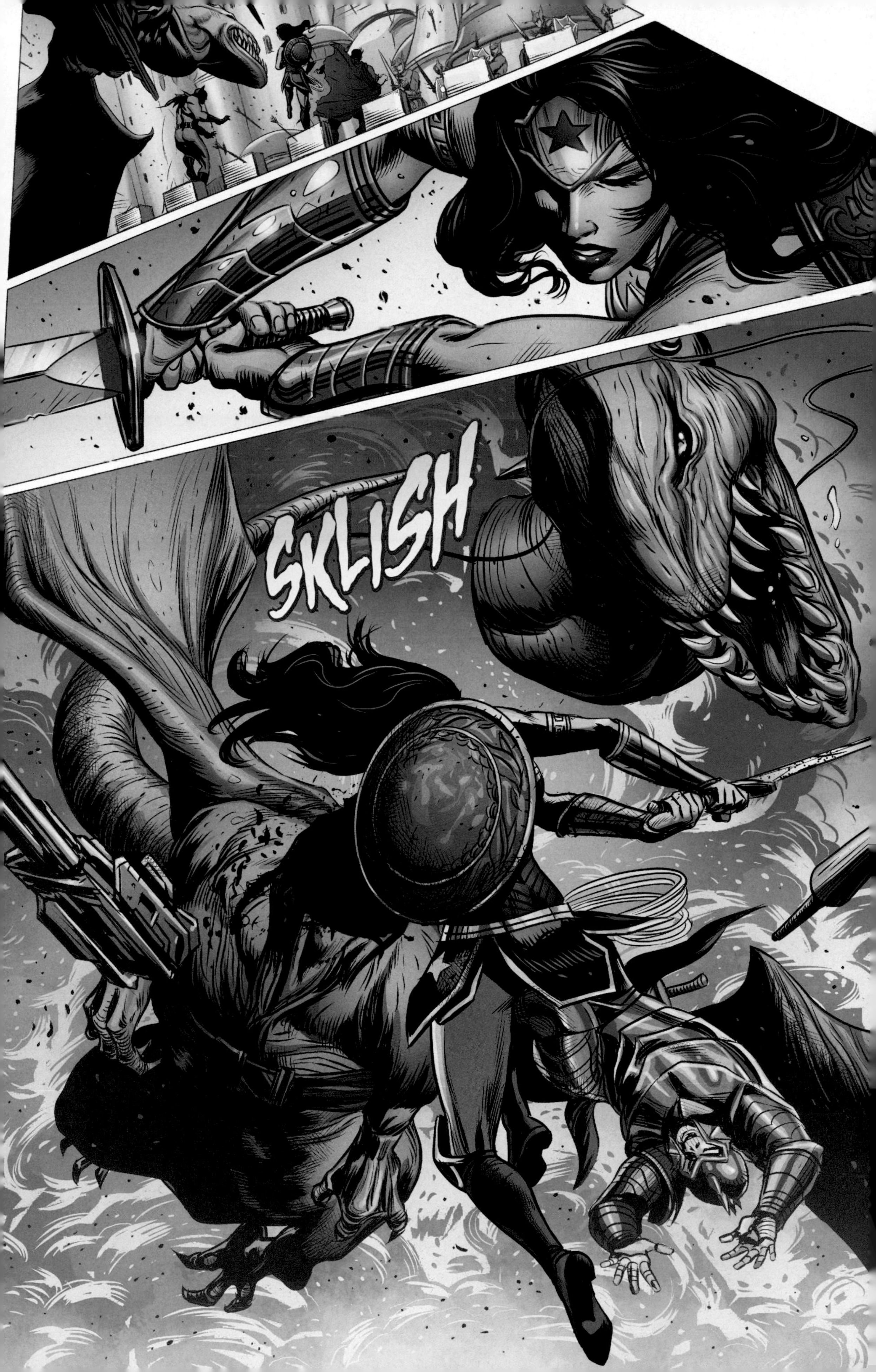
SKLISH

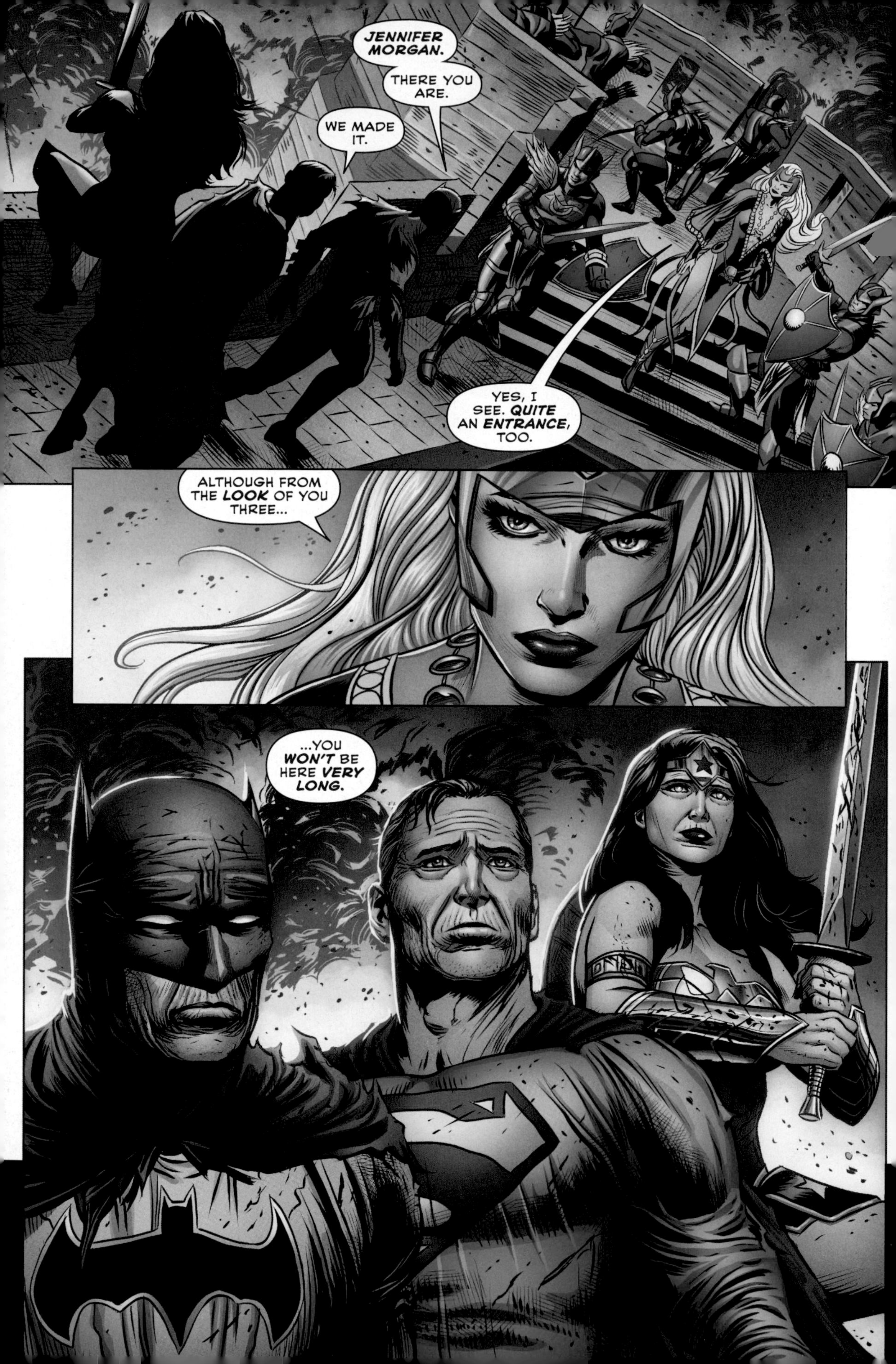
JENNIFER MORGAN.
THERE YOU ARE.
WE MADE IT.
YES, I SEE. QUITE AN ENTRANCE, TOO.
ALTHOUGH FROM THE LOOK OF YOU THREE...
...YOU WON'T BE HERE VERY LONG.

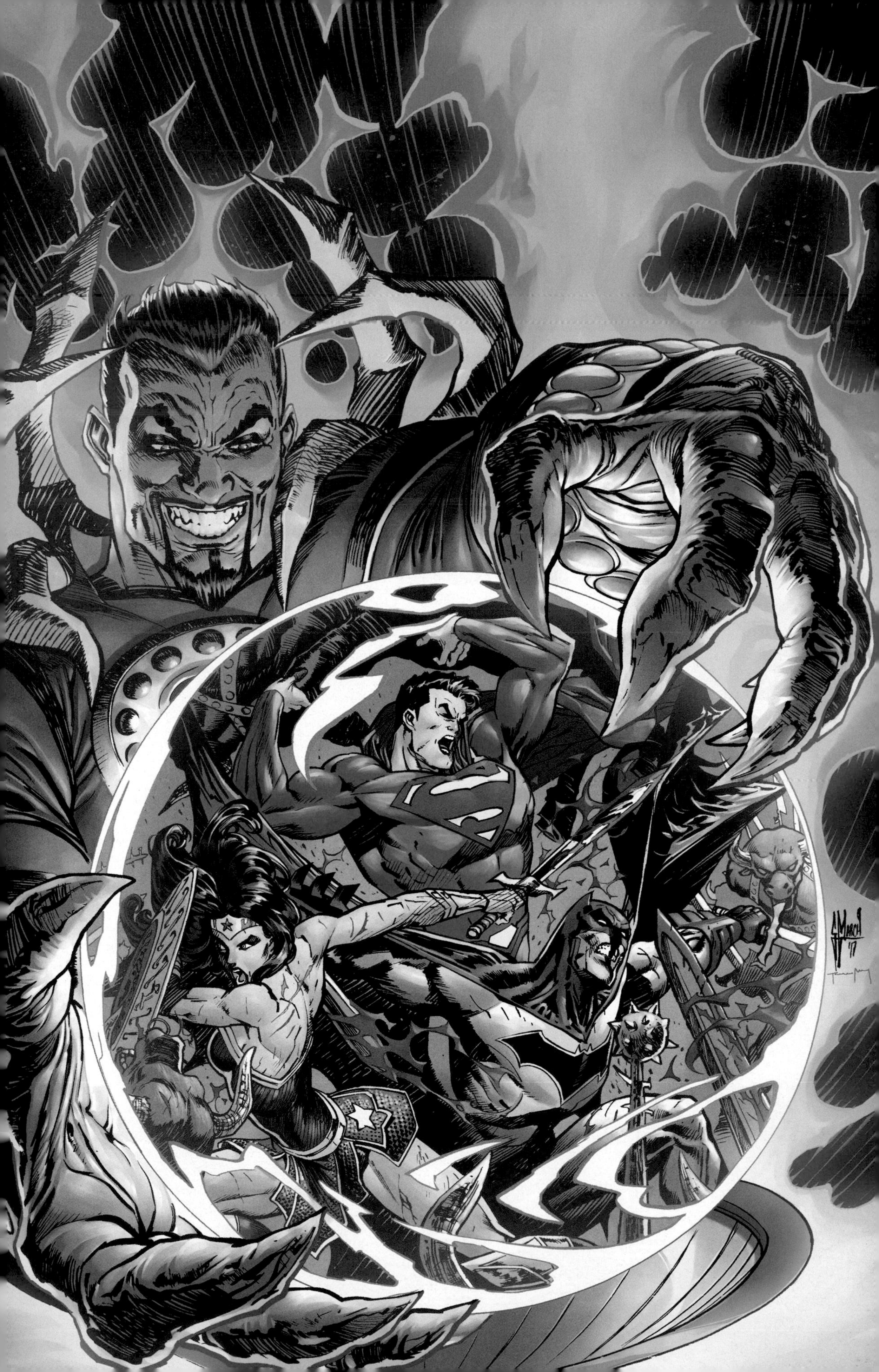

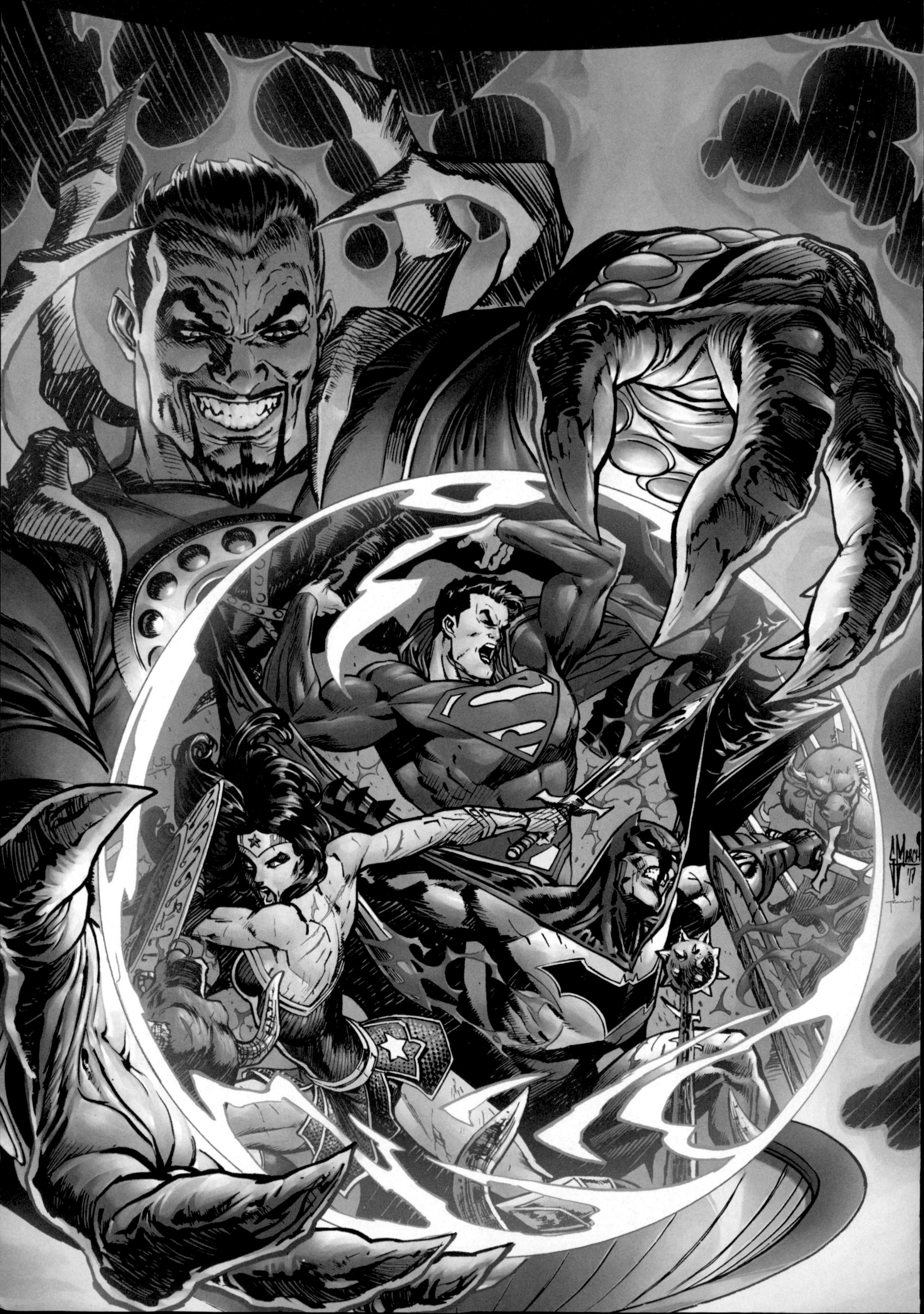

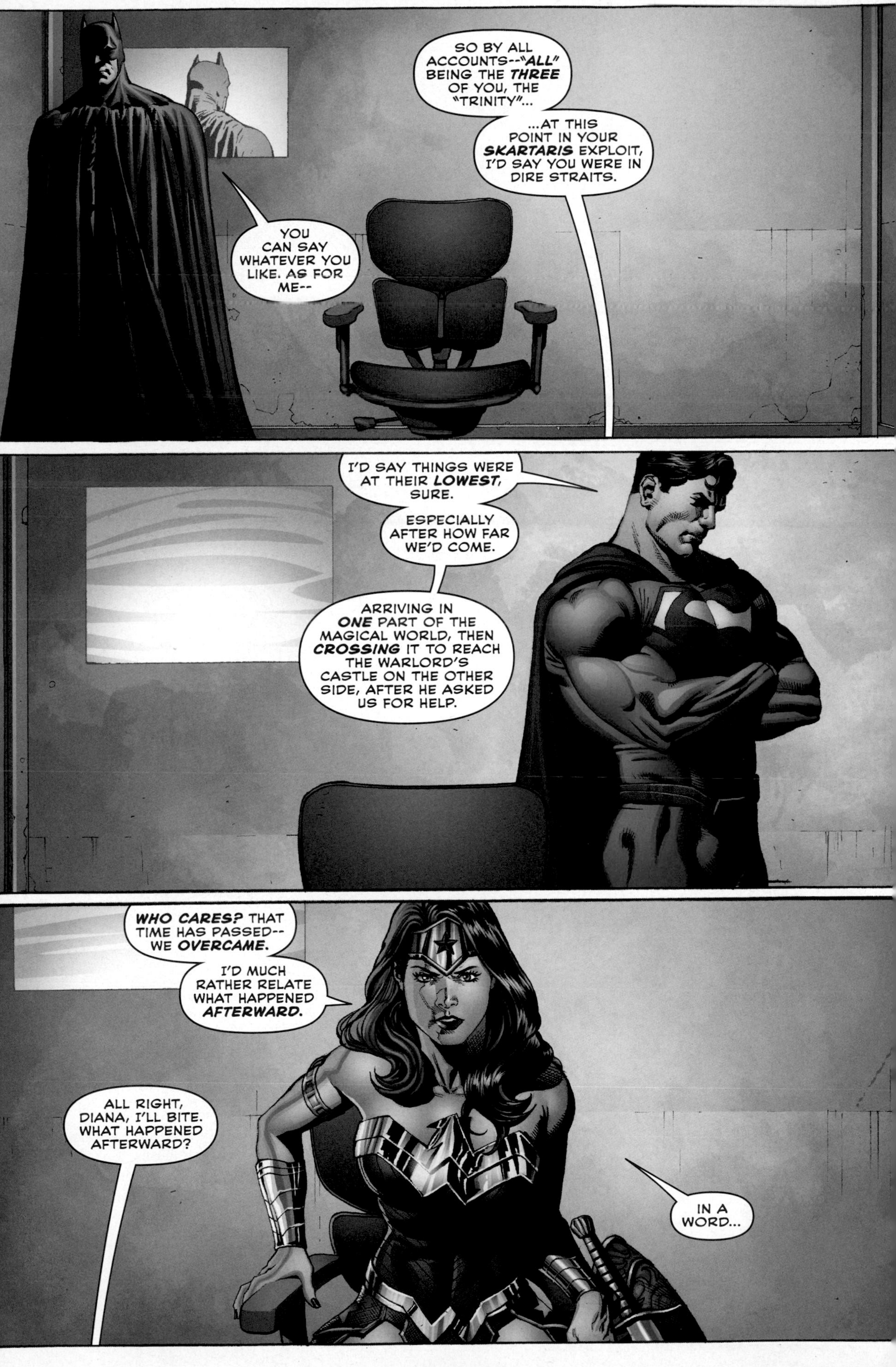
SO BY ALL ACCOUNTS--"ALL" BEING THE THREE OF YOU, THE "TRINITY"...
...AT THIS POINT IN YOUR SKARTARIS EXPLOIT, I'D SAY YOU WERE IN DIRE STRAITS.
YOU CAN SAY WHATEVER YOU LIKE. AS FOR ME--
I'D SAY THINGS WERE AT THEIR LOWEST, SURE.
ESPECIALLY AFTER HOW FAR WE'D COME.
ARRIVING IN ONE PART OF THE MAGICAL WORLD, THEN CROSSING IT TO REACH THE WARLORD'S CASTLE ON THE OTHER SIDE, AFTER HE ASKED US FOR HELP.
WHO CARES? THAT TIME HAS PASSED--WE OVERCAME.
I'D MUCH RATHER RELATE WHAT HAPPENED AFTERWARD.
ALL RIGHT, DIANA, I'LL BITE. WHAT HAPPENED AFTERWARD?
IN A WORD...

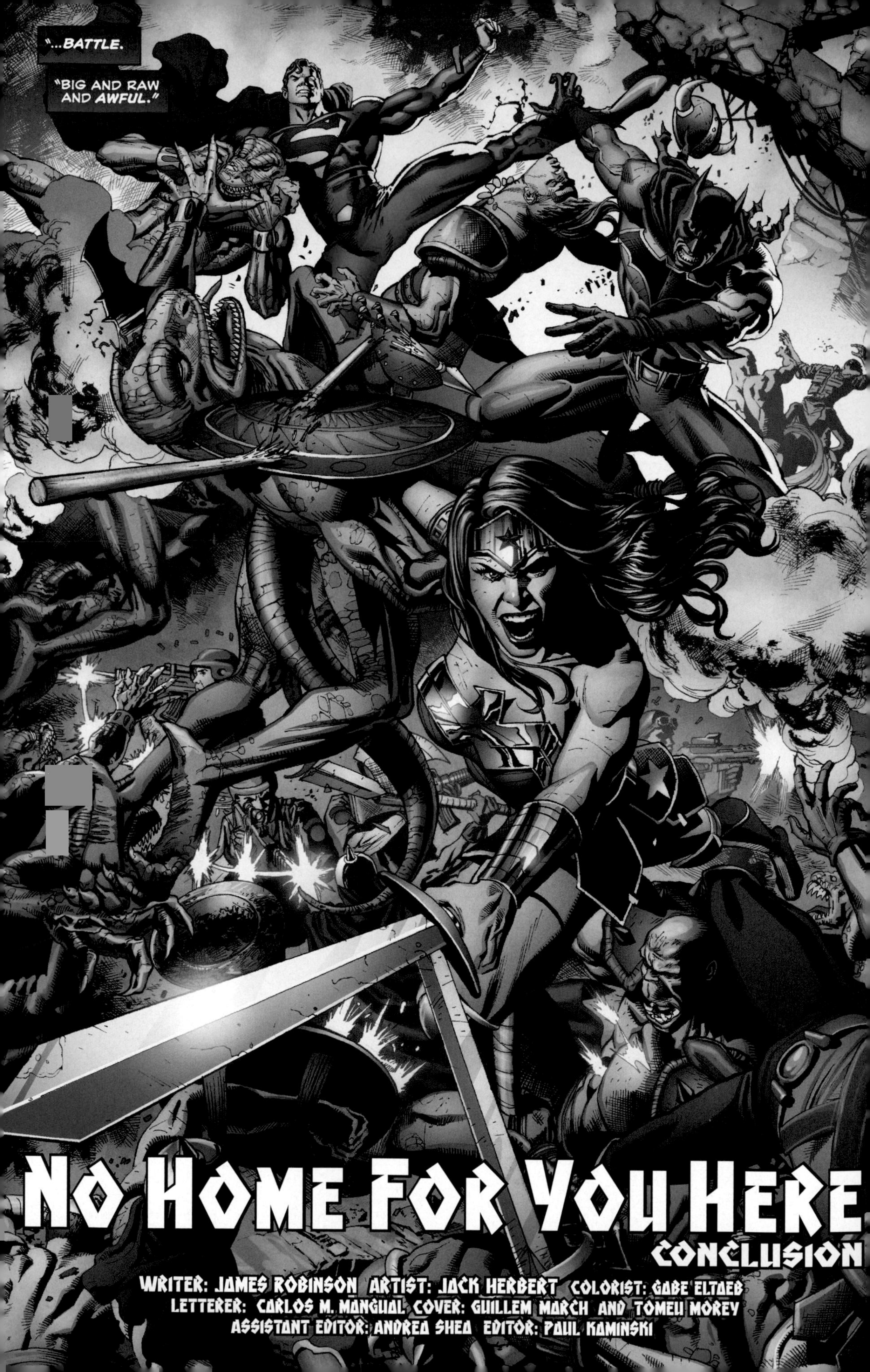
"...BATTLE.
"BIG AND RAW AND AWFUL."
NO HOME FOR YOU HERE
CONCLUSION
WRITER: JAMES ROBINSON ARTIST: JACK HERBERT COLORIST: GABE ELTAEB
LETTERER: CARLOS M. MANGUAL COVER: GUILLEM MARCH AND TOMEU MOREY
ASSISTANT EDITOR: ANDREA SHEA EDITOR: PAUL KAMINSKI

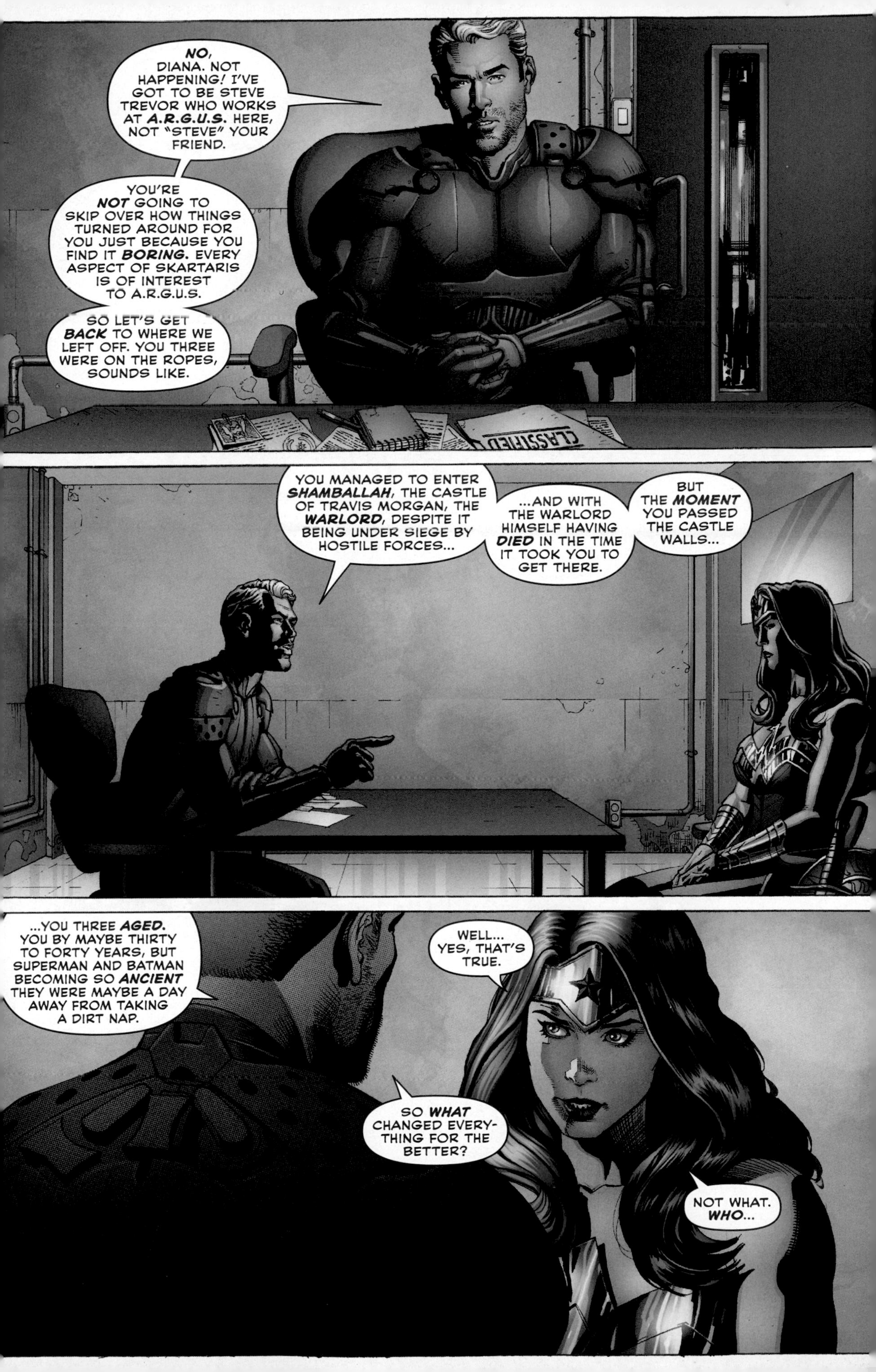
NO, DIANA. NOT HAPPENING! I'VE GOT TO BE STEVE TREVOR WHO WORKS AT A.R.G.U.S. HERE, NOT "STEVE" YOUR FRIEND.
YOU'RE NOT GOING TO SKIP OVER HOW THINGS TURNED AROUND FOR YOU JUST BECAUSE YOU FIND IT BORING. EVERY ASPECT OF SKARTARIS IS OF INTEREST TO A.R.G.U.S.
SO LET'S GET BACK TO WHERE WE LEFT OFF. YOU THREE WERE ON THE ROPES, SOUNDS LIKE.
CLASSIFIED
YOU MANAGED TO ENTER SHAMBALLAH, THE CASTLE OF TRAVIS MORGAN, THE WARLORD, DESPITE IT BEING UNDER SIEGE BY HOSTILE FORCES...
...AND WITH THE WARLORD HIMSELF HAVING DIED IN THE TIME IT TOOK YOU TO GET THERE.
BUT THE MOMENT YOU PASSED THE CASTLE WALLS...
...YOU THREE AGED. YOU BY MAYBE THIRTY TO FORTY YEARS, BUT SUPERMAN AND BATMAN BECOMING SO ANCIENT THEY WERE MAYBE A DAY AWAY FROM TAKING A DIRT NAP.
WELL... YES, THAT'S TRUE.
SO WHAT CHANGED EVERYTHING FOR THE BETTER?
NOT WHAT. WHO...

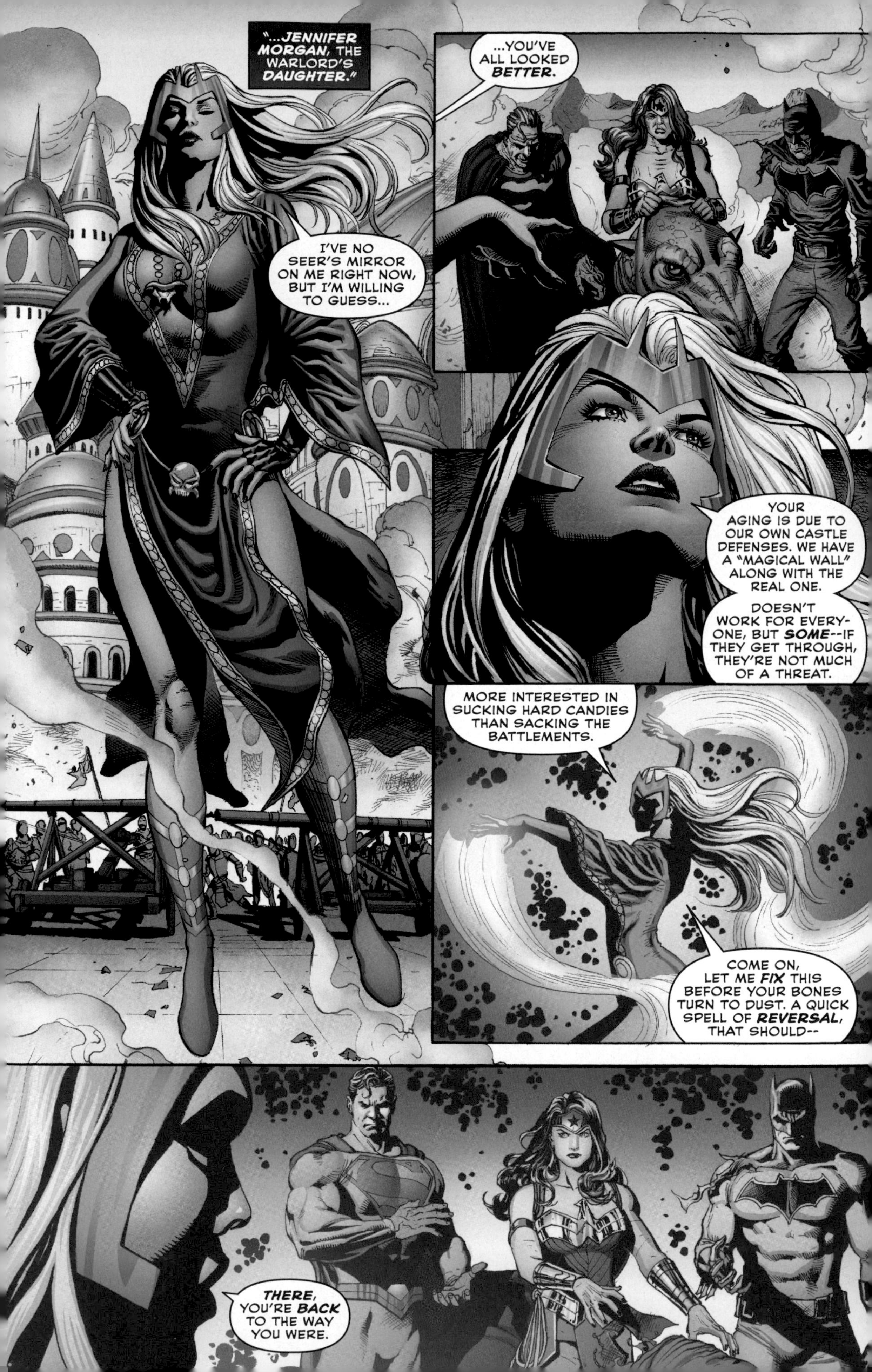
"...JENNIFER MORGAN, THE WARLORD'S DAUGHTER."
I'VE NO SEER'S MIRROR ON ME RIGHT NOW, BUT I'M WILLING TO GUESS...
...YOU'VE ALL LOOKED BETTER.
YOUR AGING IS DUE TO OUR OWN CASTLE DEFENSES. WE HAVE A "MAGICAL WALL" ALONG WITH THE REAL ONE.
DOESN'T WORK FOR EVERY-ONE, BUT SOME--IF THEY GET THROUGH, THEY'RE NOT MUCH OF A THREAT.
MORE INTERESTED IN SUCKING HARD CANDIES THAN SACKING THE BATTLEMENTS.
COME ON, LET ME FIX THIS BEFORE YOUR BONES TURN TO DUST. A QUICK SPELL OF REVERSAL, THAT SHOULD--
THERE, YOU'RE BACK TO THE WAY YOU WERE.

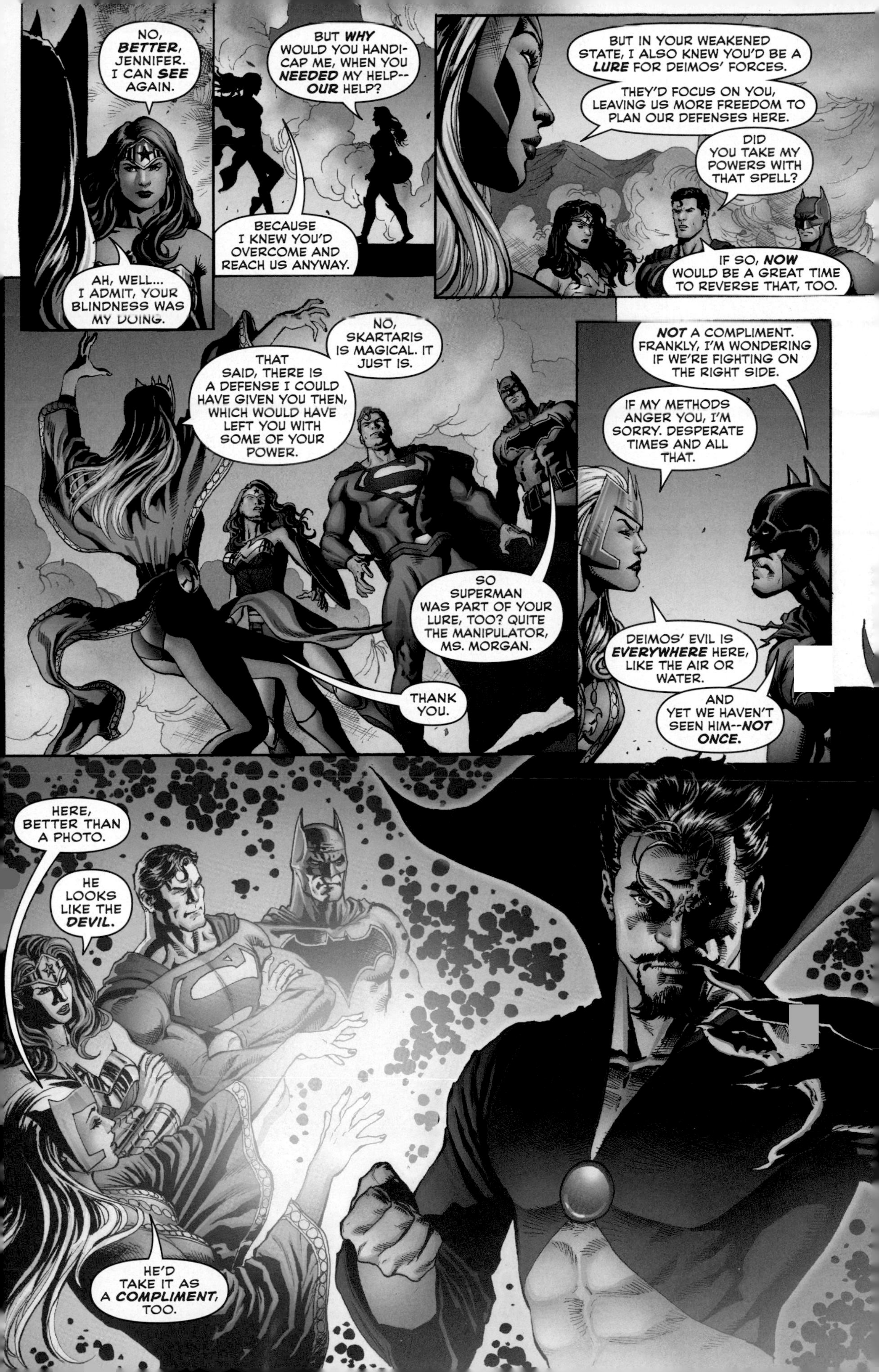

NO, **BETTER**, JENNIFER. I CAN **SEE** AGAIN.
AH, WELL... I ADMIT, YOUR BLINDNESS WAS MY DOING.
BUT **WHY** WOULD YOU HANDI-CAP ME, WHEN YOU **NEEDED** MY HELP-- **OUR** HELP?
BECAUSE I KNEW YOU'D OVERCOME AND REACH US ANYWAY.
BUT IN YOUR WEAKENED STATE, I ALSO KNEW YOU'D BE A **LURE** FOR DEIMOS' FORCES.
THEY'D FOCUS ON YOU, LEAVING US MORE FREEDOM TO PLAN OUR DEFENSES HERE.
DID YOU TAKE MY POWERS WITH THAT SPELL?
IF SO, **NOW** WOULD BE A GREAT TIME TO REVERSE THAT, TOO.
NO, SKARTARIS IS MAGICAL. IT JUST IS.
THAT SAID, THERE IS A DEFENSE I COULD HAVE GIVEN YOU THEN, WHICH WOULD HAVE LEFT YOU WITH SOME OF YOUR POWER.
SO SUPERMAN WAS PART OF YOUR LURE, TOO? QUITE THE MANIPULATOR, MS. MORGAN.
THANK YOU.
NOT A COMPLIMENT. FRANKLY, I'M WONDERING IF WE'RE FIGHTING ON THE RIGHT SIDE.
IF MY METHODS ANGER YOU, I'M SORRY. DESPERATE TIMES AND ALL THAT.
DEIMOS' EVIL IS **EVERYWHERE** HERE, LIKE THE AIR OR WATER.
AND YET WE HAVEN'T SEEN HIM--**NOT ONCE.**
HERE, BETTER THAN A PHOTO.
HE LOOKS LIKE THE **DEVIL**.
HE'D TAKE IT AS A **COMPLIMENT**, TOO.

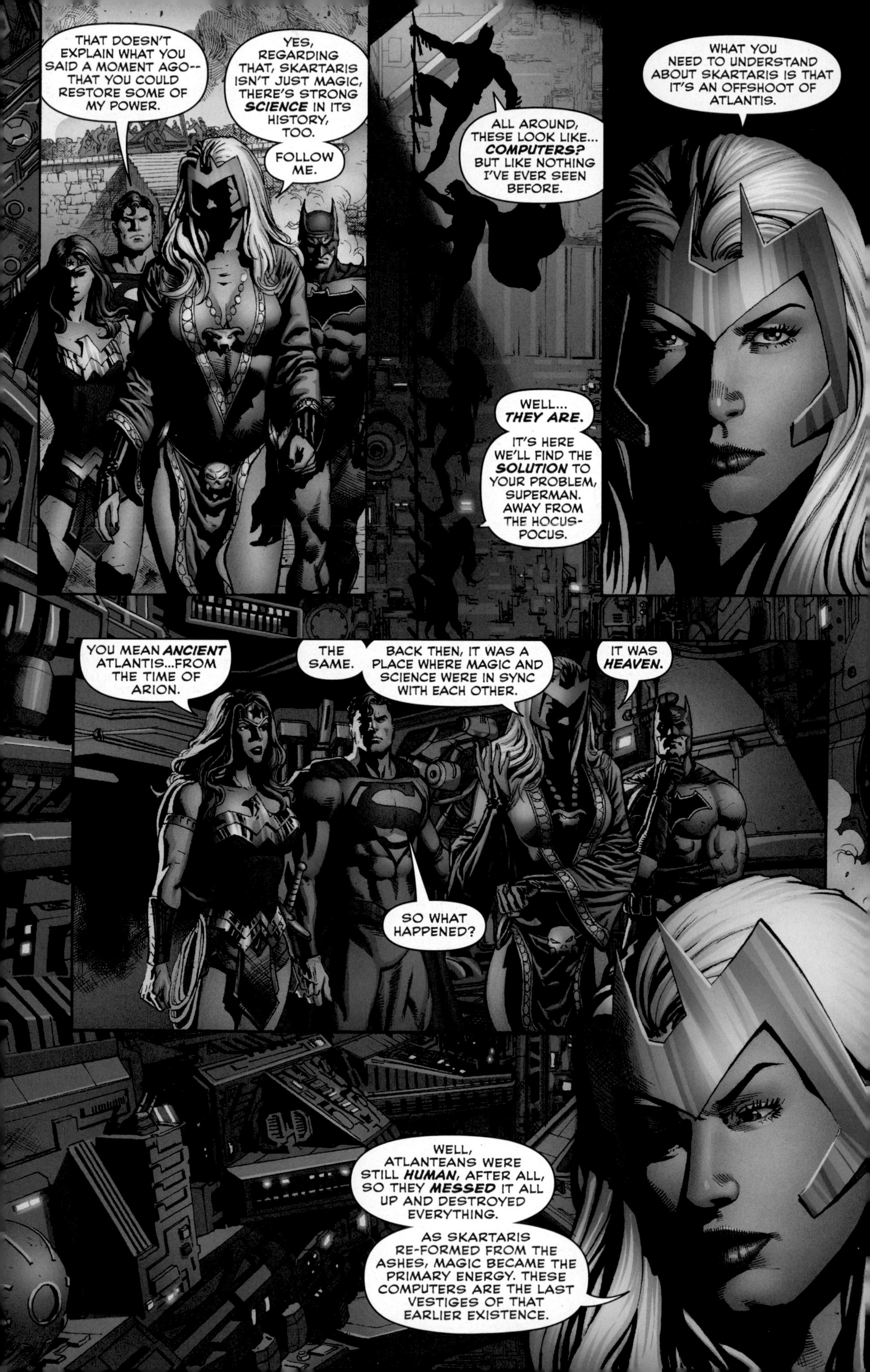
THAT DOESN'T EXPLAIN WHAT YOU SAID A MOMENT AGO-- THAT YOU COULD RESTORE SOME OF MY POWER.
YES, REGARDING THAT, SKARTARIS ISN'T JUST MAGIC, THERE'S STRONG SCIENCE IN ITS HISTORY, TOO.
FOLLOW ME.
ALL AROUND, THESE LOOK LIKE... COMPUTERS? BUT LIKE NOTHING I'VE EVER SEEN BEFORE.
WELL... THEY ARE.
IT'S HERE WE'LL FIND THE SOLUTION TO YOUR PROBLEM, SUPERMAN. AWAY FROM THE HOCUS-POCUS.
WHAT YOU NEED TO UNDERSTAND ABOUT SKARTARIS IS THAT IT'S AN OFFSHOOT OF ATLANTIS.
YOU MEAN ANCIENT ATLANTIS...FROM THE TIME OF ARION.
THE SAME.
BACK THEN, IT WAS A PLACE WHERE MAGIC AND SCIENCE WERE IN SYNC WITH EACH OTHER.
IT WAS HEAVEN.
SO WHAT HAPPENED?
WELL, ATLANTEANS WERE STILL HUMAN, AFTER ALL, SO THEY MESSED IT ALL UP AND DESTROYED EVERYTHING.
AS SKARTARIS RE-FORMED FROM THE ASHES, MAGIC BECAME THE PRIMARY ENERGY. THESE COMPUTERS ARE THE LAST VESTIGES OF THAT EARLIER EXISTENCE.

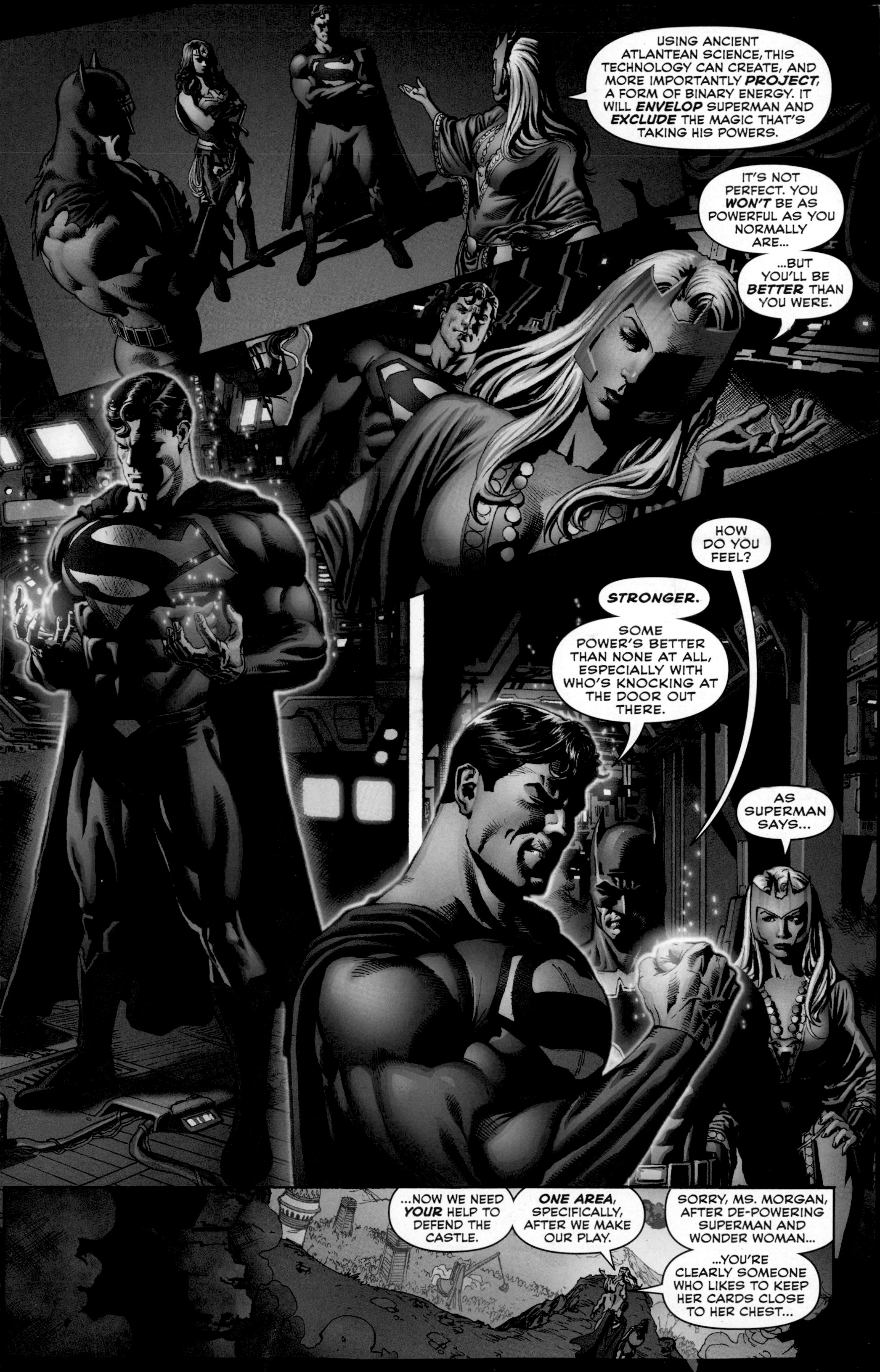
USING ANCIENT ATLANTEAN SCIENCE, THIS TECHNOLOGY CAN CREATE, AND MORE IMPORTANTLY PROJECT, A FORM OF BINARY ENERGY. IT WILL ENVELOP SUPERMAN AND EXCLUDE THE MAGIC THAT'S TAKING HIS POWERS.
IT'S NOT PERFECT. YOU WON'T BE AS POWERFUL AS YOU NORMALLY ARE...
...BUT YOU'LL BE BETTER THAN YOU WERE.
HOW DO YOU FEEL?
STRONGER.
SOME POWER'S BETTER THAN NONE AT ALL, ESPECIALLY WITH WHO'S KNOCKING AT THE DOOR OUT THERE.
AS SUPERMAN SAYS...
...NOW WE NEED YOUR HELP TO DEFEND THE CASTLE.
ONE AREA, SPECIFICALLY, AFTER WE MAKE OUR PLAY.
SORRY, MS. MORGAN, AFTER DE-POWERING SUPERMAN AND WONDER WOMAN...
...YOU'RE CLEARLY SOMEONE WHO LIKES TO KEEP HER CARDS CLOSE TO HER CHEST...

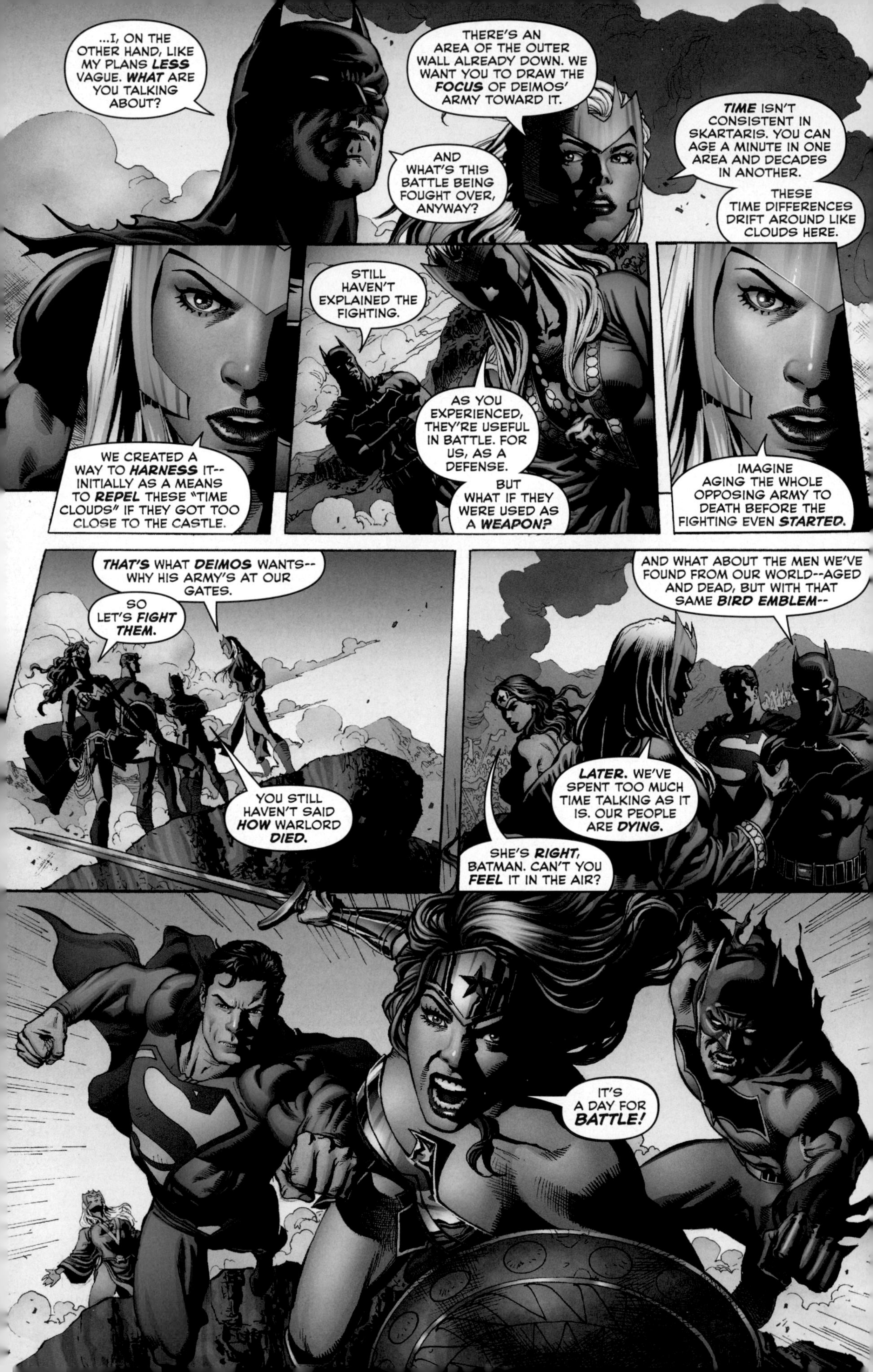
...I, ON THE OTHER HAND, LIKE MY PLANS LESS VAGUE. WHAT ARE YOU TALKING ABOUT?
THERE'S AN AREA OF THE OUTER WALL ALREADY DOWN. WE WANT YOU TO DRAW THE FOCUS OF DEIMOS' ARMY TOWARD IT.
AND WHAT'S THIS BATTLE BEING FOUGHT OVER, ANYWAY?
TIME ISN'T CONSISTENT IN SKARTARIS. YOU CAN AGE A MINUTE IN ONE AREA AND DECADES IN ANOTHER.
THESE TIME DIFFERENCES DRIFT AROUND LIKE CLOUDS HERE.
WE CREATED A WAY TO HARNESS IT-- INITIALLY AS A MEANS TO REPEL THESE "TIME CLOUDS" IF THEY GOT TOO CLOSE TO THE CASTLE.
STILL HAVEN'T EXPLAINED THE FIGHTING.
AS YOU EXPERIENCED, THEY'RE USEFUL IN BATTLE. FOR US, AS A DEFENSE.
BUT WHAT IF THEY WERE USED AS A WEAPON?
IMAGINE AGING THE WHOLE OPPOSING ARMY TO DEATH BEFORE THE FIGHTING EVEN STARTED.
THAT'S WHAT DEIMOS WANTS-- WHY HIS ARMY'S AT OUR GATES.
SO LET'S FIGHT THEM.
YOU STILL HAVEN'T SAID HOW WARLORD DIED.
AND WHAT ABOUT THE MEN WE'VE FOUND FROM OUR WORLD--AGED AND DEAD, BUT WITH THAT SAME BIRD EMBLEM--
LATER. WE'VE SPENT TOO MUCH TIME TALKING AS IT IS. OUR PEOPLE ARE DYING.
SHE'S RIGHT, BATMAN. CAN'T YOU FEEL IT IN THE AIR?
IT'S A DAY FOR BATTLE!

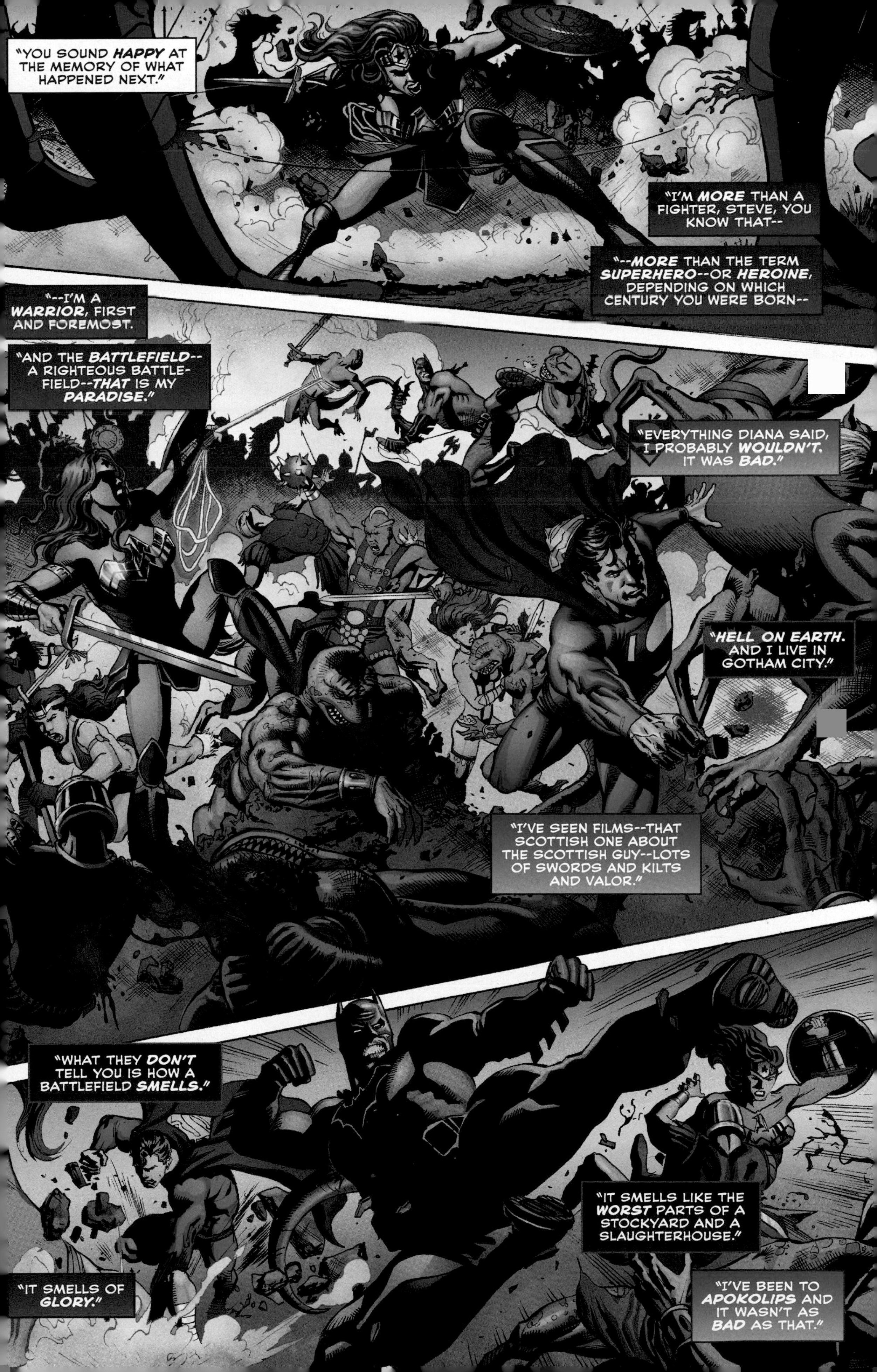
"YOU SOUND HAPPY AT THE MEMORY OF WHAT HAPPENED NEXT."
"I'M MORE THAN A FIGHTER, STEVE, YOU KNOW THAT--
"--MORE THAN THE TERM SUPERHERO--OR HEROINE, DEPENDING ON WHICH CENTURY YOU WERE BORN--
"--I'M A WARRIOR, FIRST AND FOREMOST.
"AND THE BATTLEFIELD--A RIGHTEOUS BATTLE-FIELD--THAT IS MY PARADISE."
"EVERYTHING DIANA SAID, I PROBABLY WOULDN'T. IT WAS BAD."
"HELL ON EARTH. AND I LIVE IN GOTHAM CITY."
"I'VE SEEN FILMS--THAT SCOTTISH ONE ABOUT THE SCOTTISH GUY--LOTS OF SWORDS AND KILTS AND VALOR."
"WHAT THEY DON'T TELL YOU IS HOW A BATTLEFIELD SMELLS."
"IT SMELLS LIKE THE WORST PARTS OF A STOCKYARD AND A SLAUGHTERHOUSE."
"IT SMELLS OF GLORY."
"I'VE BEEN TO APOKOLIPS AND IT WASN'T AS BAD AS THAT."

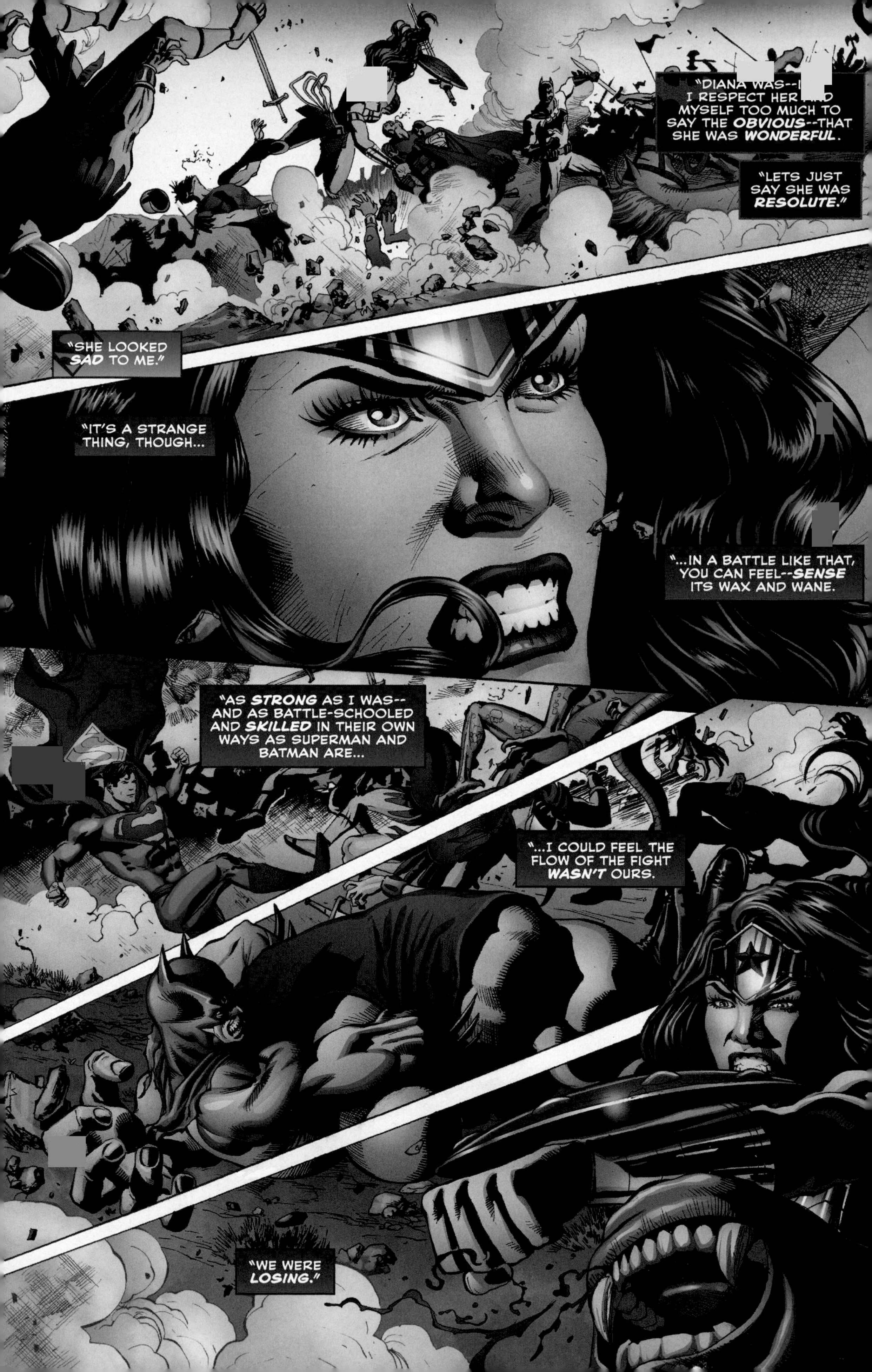
“DIANA WAS--I
I RESPECT HER AND MYSELF TOO MUCH TO SAY THE OBVIOUS--THAT SHE WAS WONDERFUL.
“LETS JUST SAY SHE WAS RESOLUTE.”
“SHE LOOKED SAD TO ME.”
“IT'S A STRANGE THING, THOUGH...
“...IN A BATTLE LIKE THAT, YOU CAN FEEL--SENSE ITS WAX AND WANE.
“AS STRONG AS I WAS--AND AS BATTLE-SCHOOLED AND SKILLED IN THEIR OWN WAYS AS SUPERMAN AND BATMAN ARE...
“...I COULD FEEL THE FLOW OF THE FIGHT WASN'T OURS.
“WE WERE LOSING.”

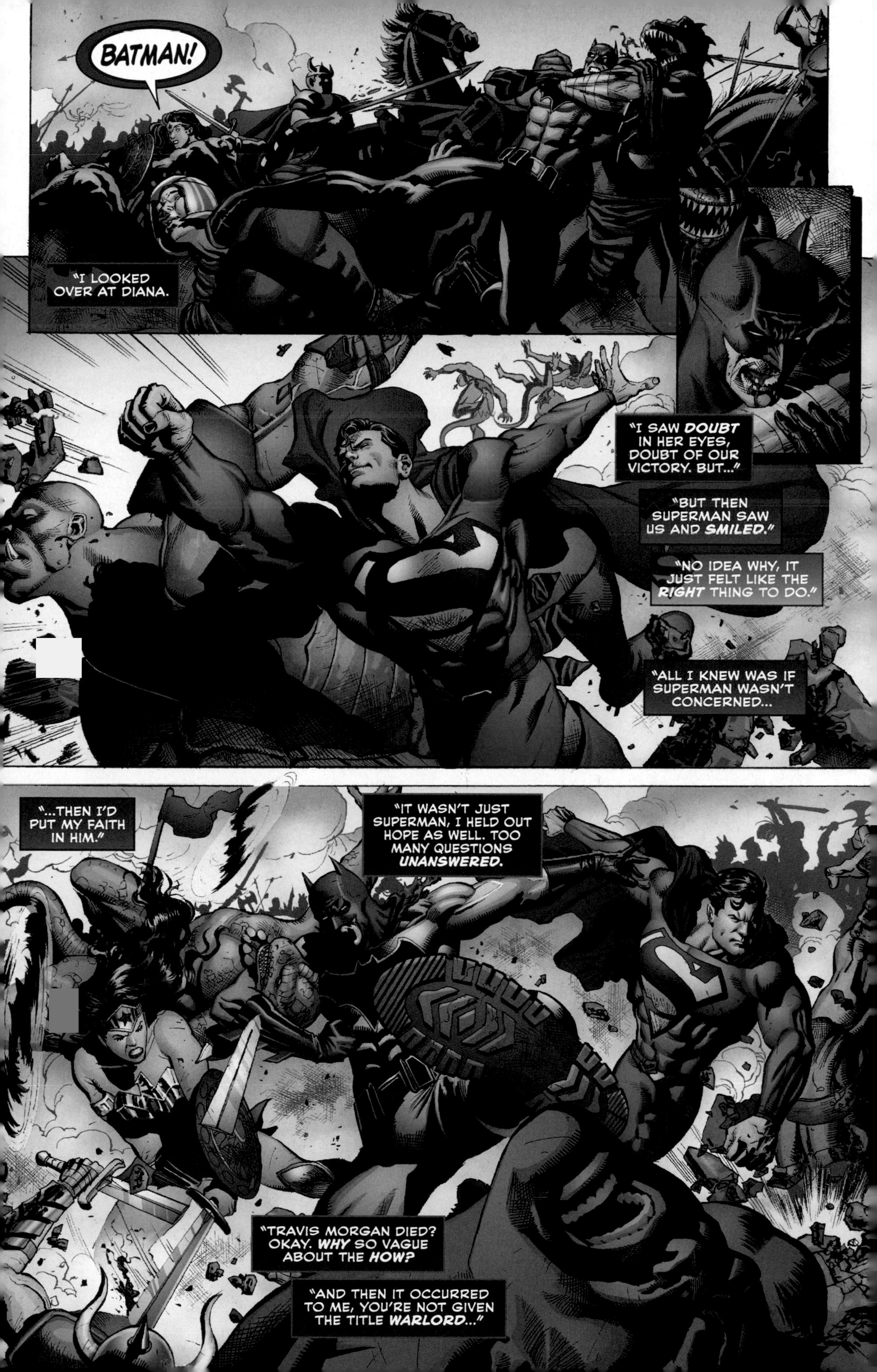
BATMAN!
"I LOOKED OVER AT DIANA.
"I SAW DOUBT IN HER EYES, DOUBT OF OUR VICTORY. BUT..."
"BUT THEN SUPERMAN SAW US AND SMILED."
"NO IDEA WHY, IT JUST FELT LIKE THE RIGHT THING TO DO."
"ALL I KNEW WAS IF SUPERMAN WASN'T CONCERNED...
"...THEN I'D PUT MY FAITH IN HIM."
"IT WASN'T JUST SUPERMAN, I HELD OUT HOPE AS WELL. TOO MANY QUESTIONS UNANSWERED.
"TRAVIS MORGAN DIED? OKAY. WHY SO VAGUE ABOUT THE HOW?
"AND THEN IT OCCURRED TO ME, YOU'RE NOT GIVEN THE TITLE WARLORD..."

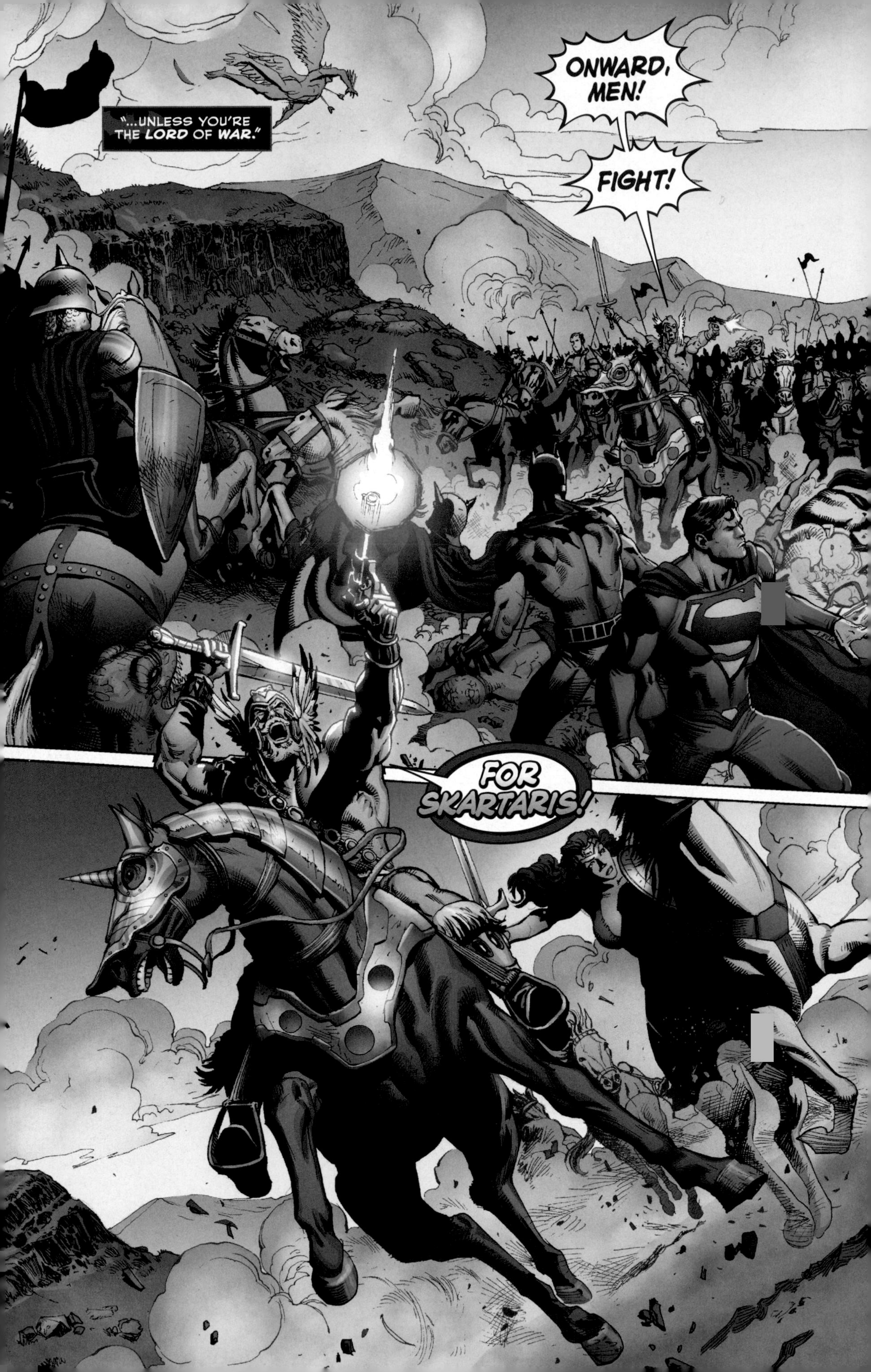
"...UNLESS YOU'RE THE LORD OF WAR."
ONWARD, MEN!
FIGHT!
FOR SKARTARIS!

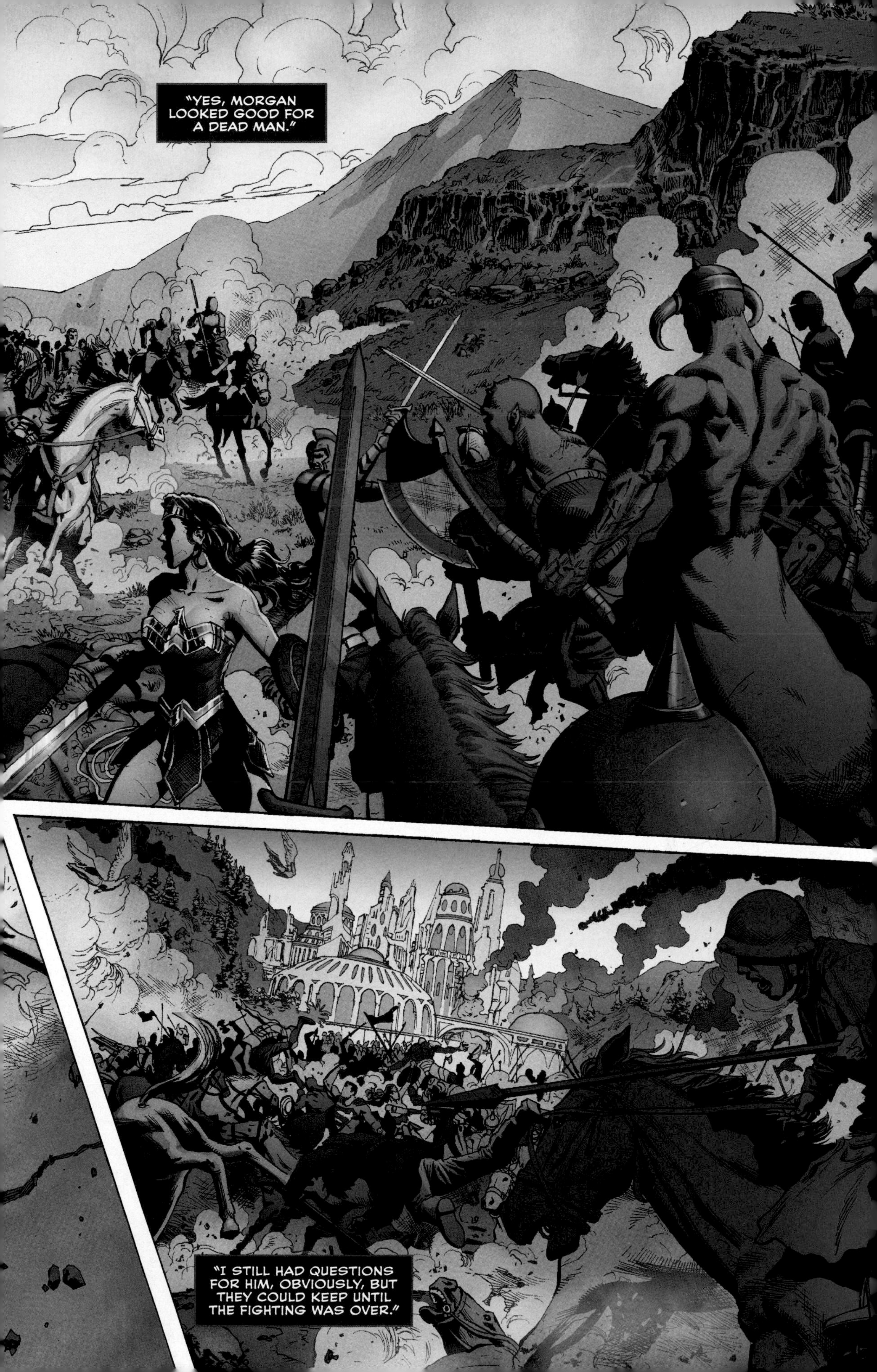
"YES, MORGAN LOOKED GOOD FOR A DEAD MAN."
"I STILL HAD QUESTIONS FOR HIM, OBVIOUSLY, BUT THEY COULD KEEP UNTIL THE FIGHTING WAS OVER."

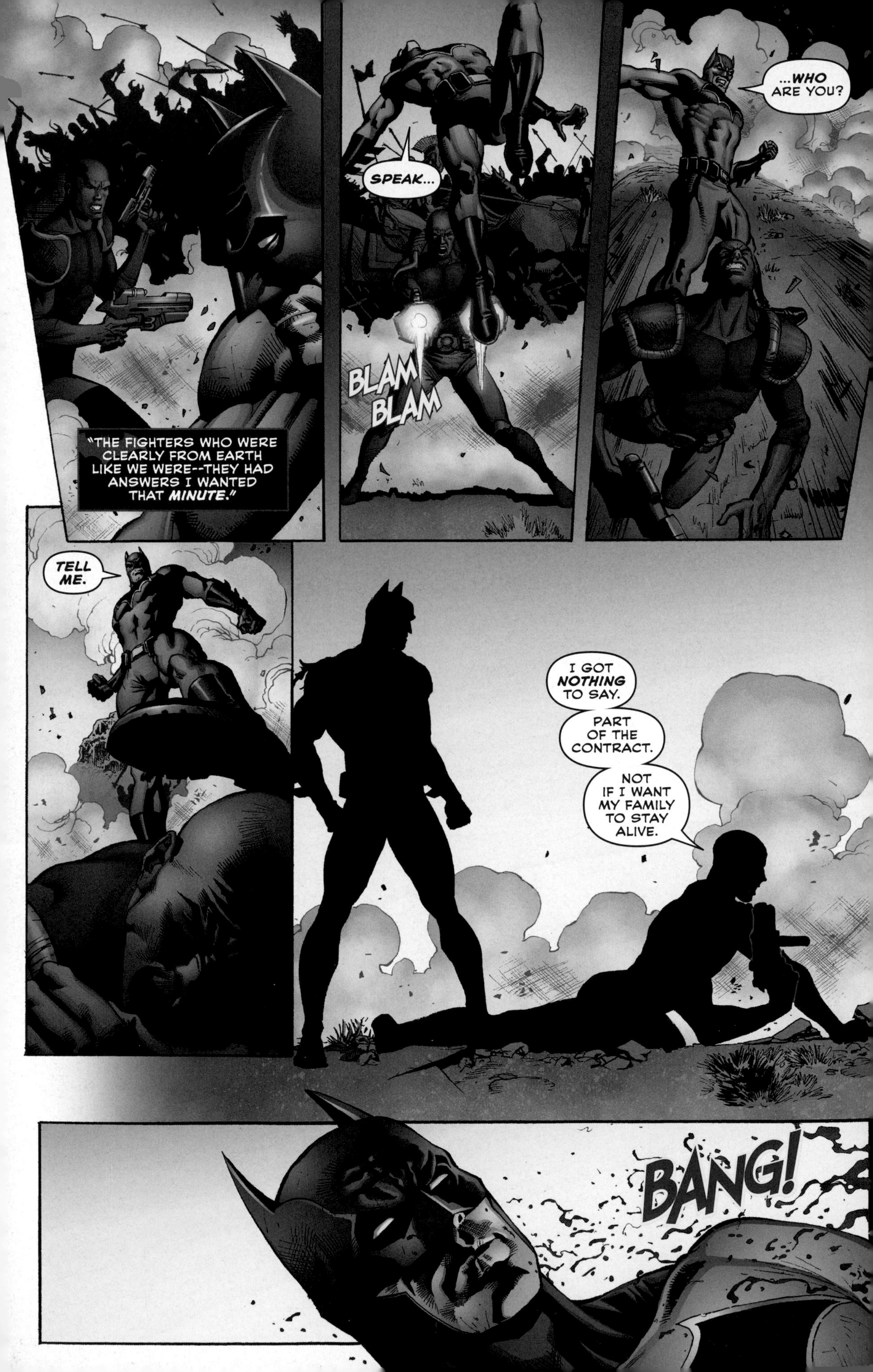
"THE FIGHTERS WHO WERE CLEARLY FROM EARTH LIKE WE WERE--THEY HAD ANSWERS I WANTED THAT *MINUTE.*"
SPEAK...
BLAM BLAM
...*WHO* ARE YOU?
TELL ME.
I GOT *NOTHING* TO SAY.
PART OF THE CONTRACT.
NOT IF I WANT MY FAMILY TO STAY ALIVE.
BANG!

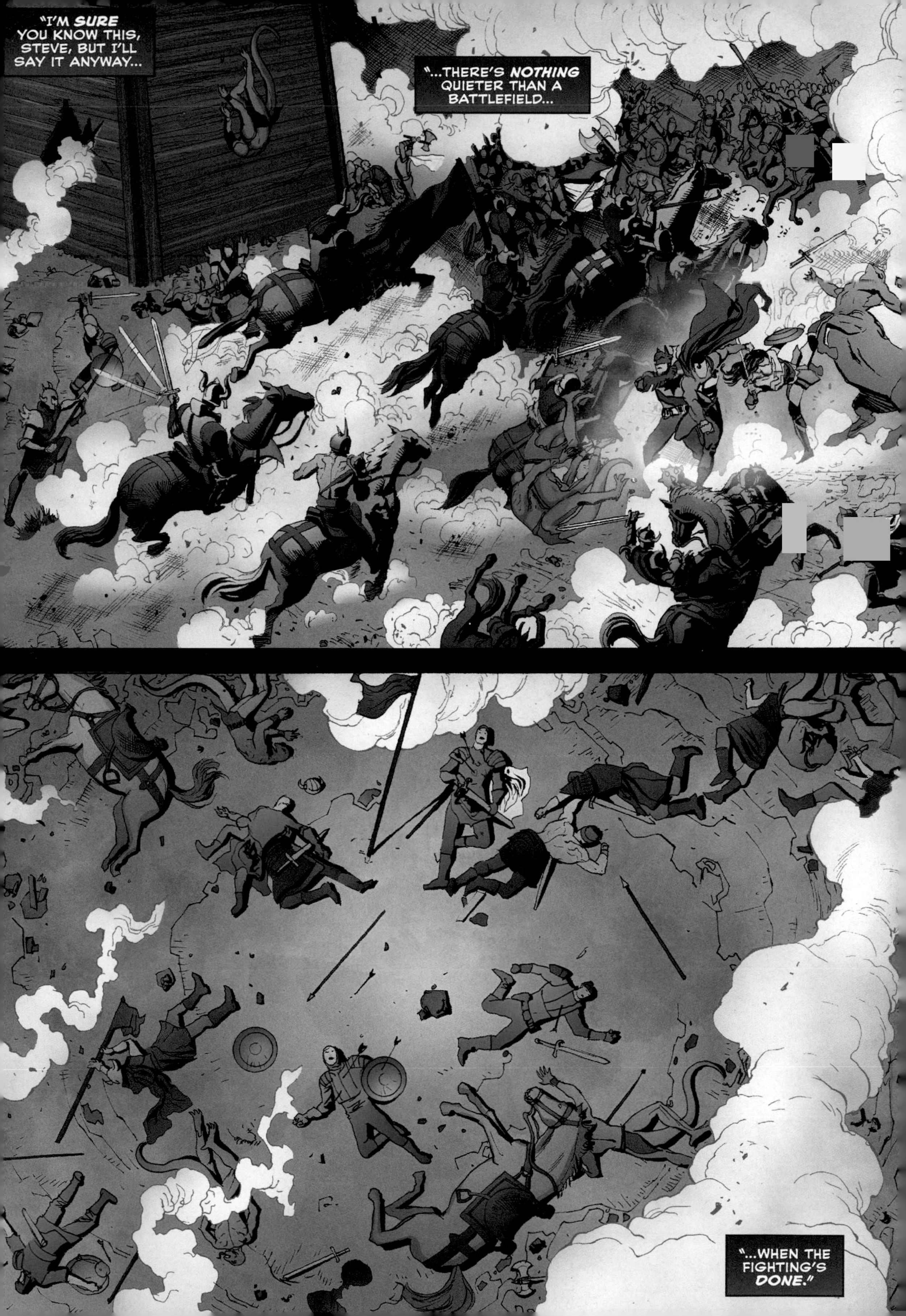
"I'M SURE YOU KNOW THIS, STEVE, BUT I'LL SAY IT ANYWAY...
"...THERE'S NOTHING QUIETER THAN A BATTLEFIELD...
"...WHEN THE FIGHTING'S DONE."

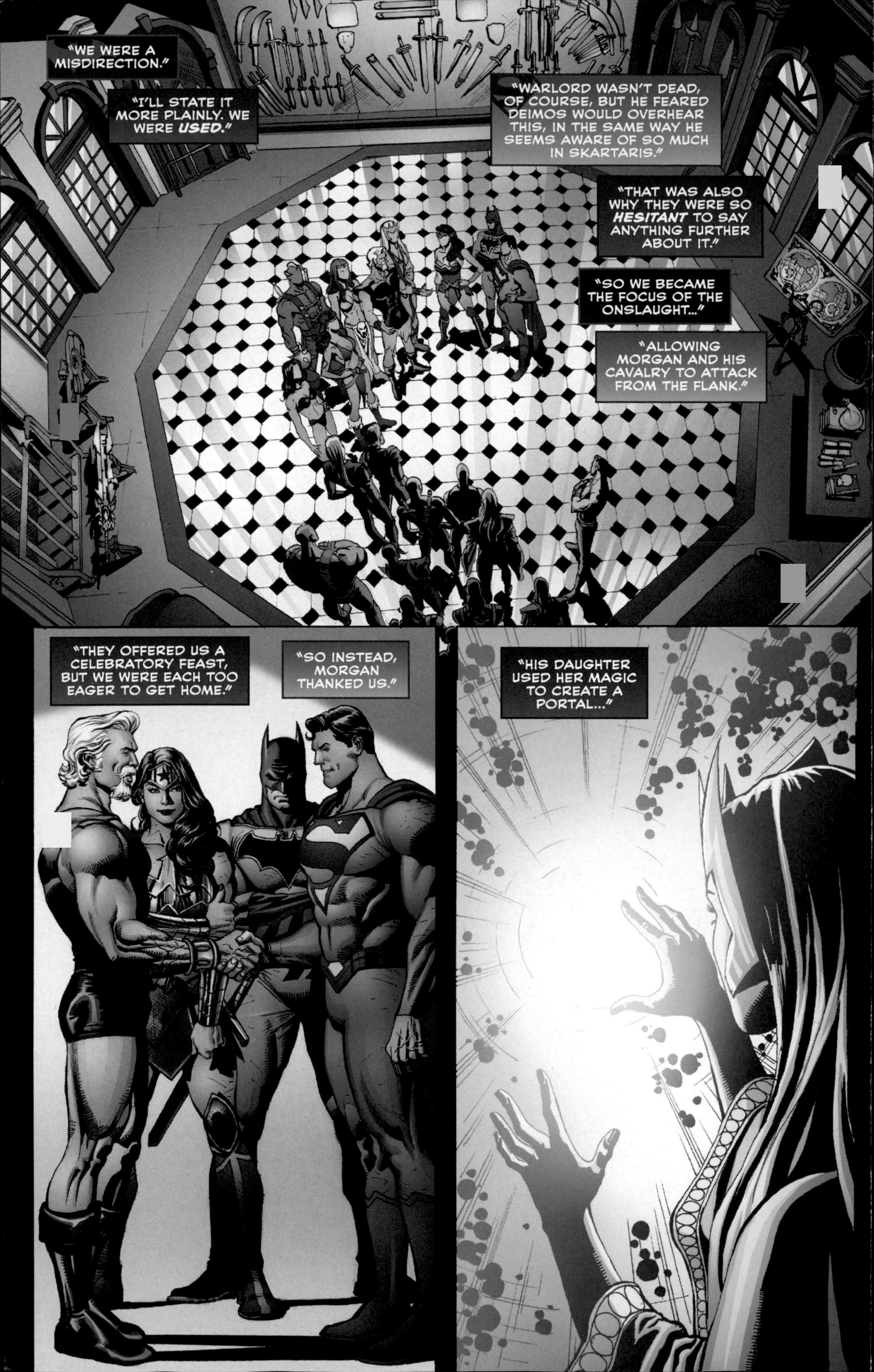
"WE WERE A MISDIRECTION."
"I'LL STATE IT MORE PLAINLY. WE WERE USED."
"WARLORD WASN'T DEAD, OF COURSE, BUT HE FEARED DEIMOS WOULD OVERHEAR THIS, IN THE SAME WAY HE SEEMS AWARE OF SO MUCH IN SKARTARIS."
"THAT WAS ALSO WHY THEY WERE SO HESITANT TO SAY ANYTHING FURTHER ABOUT IT."
"SO WE BECAME THE FOCUS OF THE ONSLAUGHT..."
"ALLOWING MORGAN AND HIS CAVALRY TO ATTACK FROM THE FLANK."
"THEY OFFERED US A CELEBRATORY FEAST, BUT WE WERE EACH TOO EAGER TO GET HOME."
"SO INSTEAD, MORGAN THANKED US."
"HIS DAUGHTER USED HER MAGIC TO CREATE A PORTAL..."

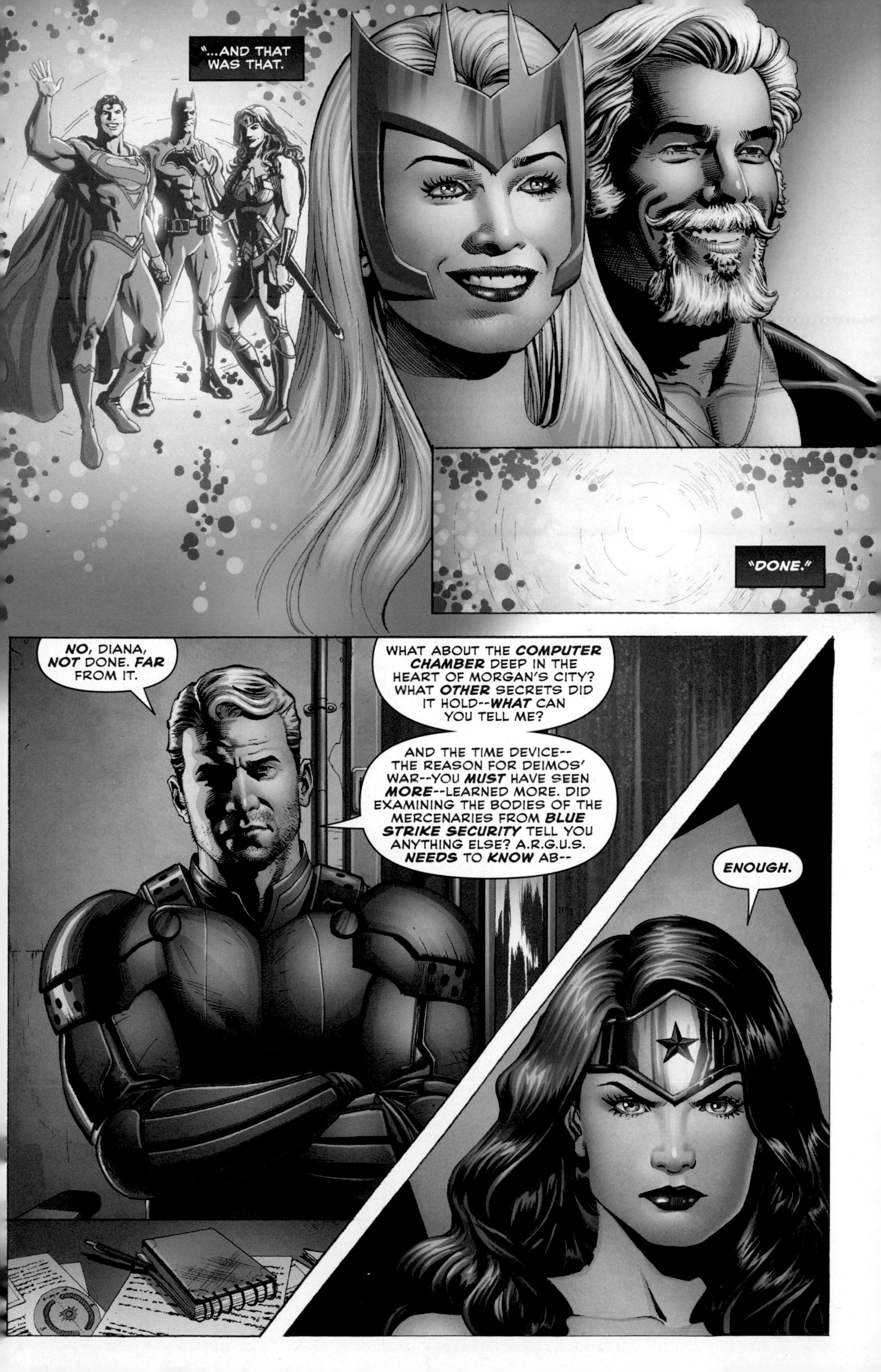
"...AND THAT WAS THAT.
"DONE."
NO, DIANA, NOT DONE. FAR FROM IT.
WHAT ABOUT THE COMPUTER CHAMBER DEEP IN THE HEART OF MORGAN'S CITY? WHAT OTHER SECRETS DID IT HOLD--WHAT CAN YOU TELL ME?
AND THE TIME DEVICE-- THE REASON FOR DEIMOS' WAR--YOU MUST HAVE SEEN MORE--LEARNED MORE. DID EXAMINING THE BODIES OF THE MERCENARIES FROM BLUE STRIKE SECURITY TELL YOU ANYTHING ELSE? A.R.G.U.S. NEEDS TO KNOW AB--
ENOUGH.

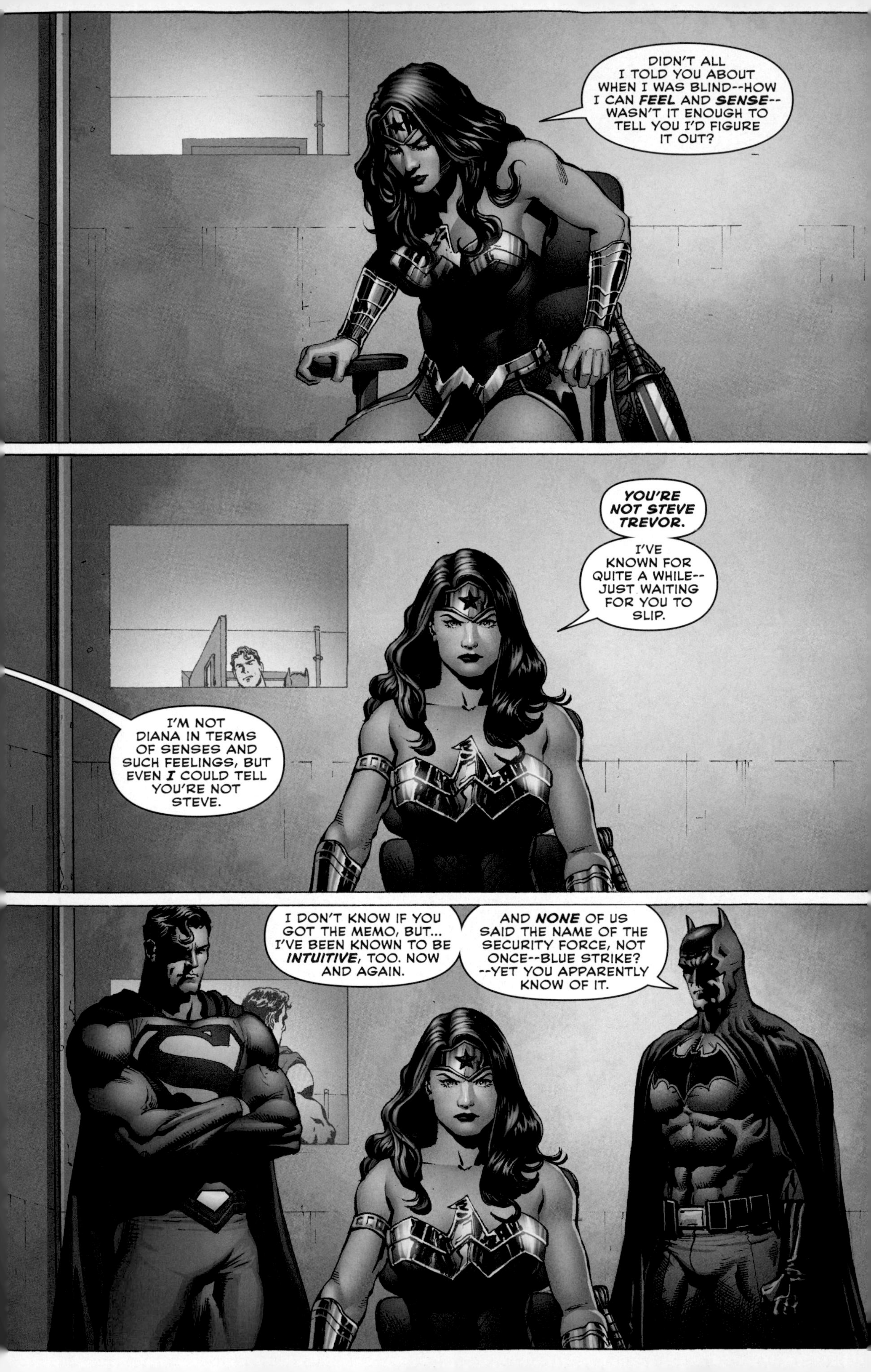
DIDN'T ALL I TOLD YOU ABOUT WHEN I WAS BLIND--HOW I CAN FEEL AND SENSE--WASN'T IT ENOUGH TO TELL YOU I'D FIGURE IT OUT?
YOU'RE NOT STEVE TREVOR.
I'VE KNOWN FOR QUITE A WHILE--JUST WAITING FOR YOU TO SLIP.
I'M NOT DIANA IN TERMS OF SENSES AND SUCH FEELINGS, BUT EVEN I COULD TELL YOU'RE NOT STEVE.
I DON'T KNOW IF YOU GOT THE MEMO, BUT... I'VE BEEN KNOWN TO BE INTUITIVE, TOO. NOW AND AGAIN.
AND NONE OF US SAID THE NAME OF THE SECURITY FORCE, NOT ONCE--BLUE STRIKE? --YET YOU APPARENTLY KNOW OF IT.

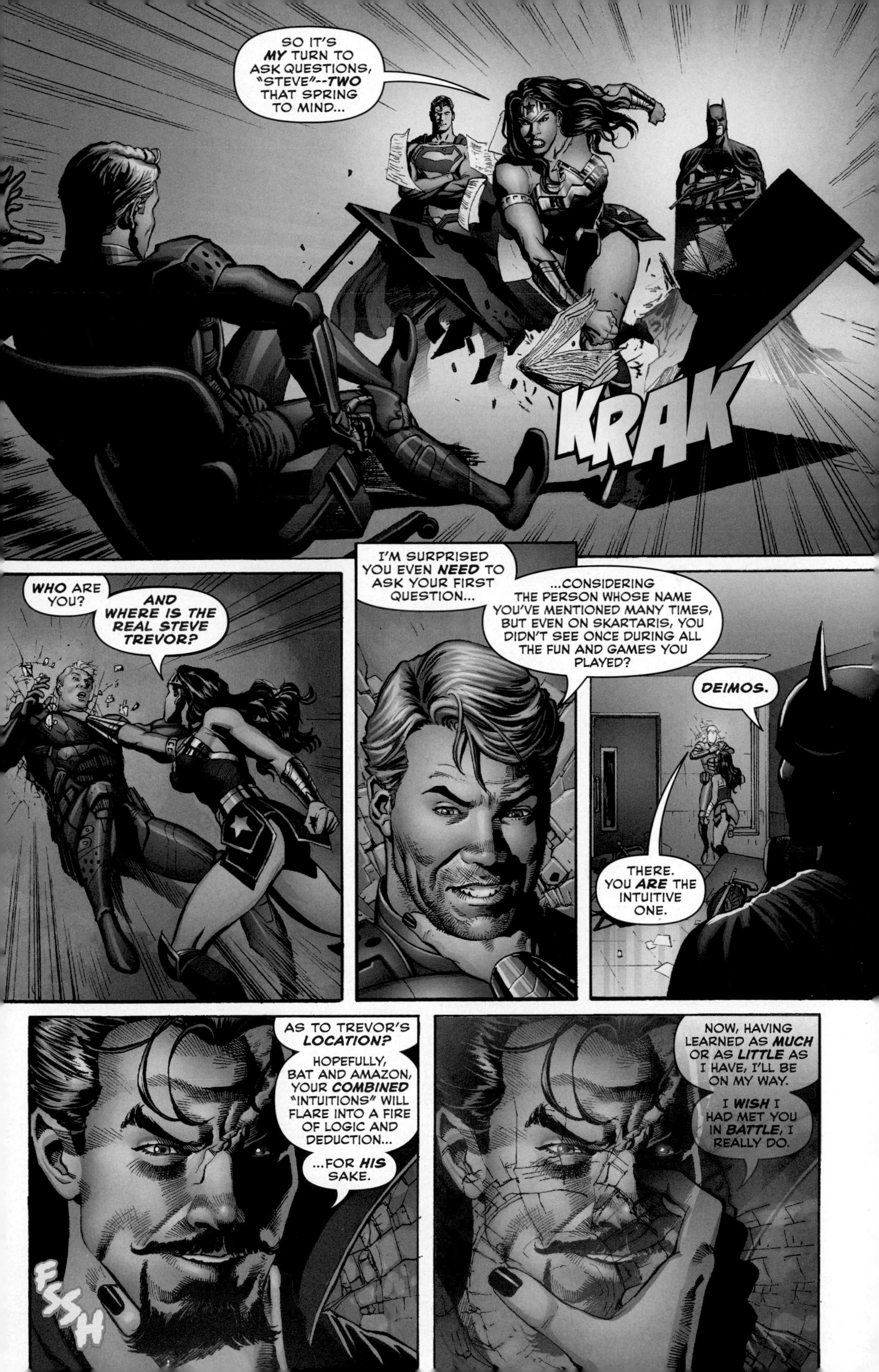
SO IT'S *MY* TURN TO ASK QUESTIONS, "STEVE"--*TWO* THAT SPRING TO MIND...
KRAK
WHO ARE YOU?
AND WHERE IS THE REAL STEVE TREVOR?
I'M SURPRISED YOU EVEN *NEED* TO ASK YOUR FIRST QUESTION...
...CONSIDERING THE PERSON WHOSE NAME YOU'VE MENTIONED MANY TIMES, BUT EVEN ON SKARTARIS, YOU DIDN'T SEE ONCE DURING ALL THE FUN AND GAMES YOU PLAYED?
DEIMOS.
THERE. YOU *ARE* THE INTUITIVE ONE.
AS TO TREVOR'S *LOCATION?*
HOPEFULLY, BAT AND AMAZON, YOUR *COMBINED* "INTUITIONS" WILL FLARE INTO A FIRE OF LOGIC AND DEDUCTION...
...FOR *HIS* SAKE.
FSSH
NOW, HAVING LEARNED AS *MUCH* OR AS *LITTLE* AS I HAVE, I'LL BE ON MY WAY.
I *WISH* I HAD MET YOU IN *BATTLE,* I REALLY DO.

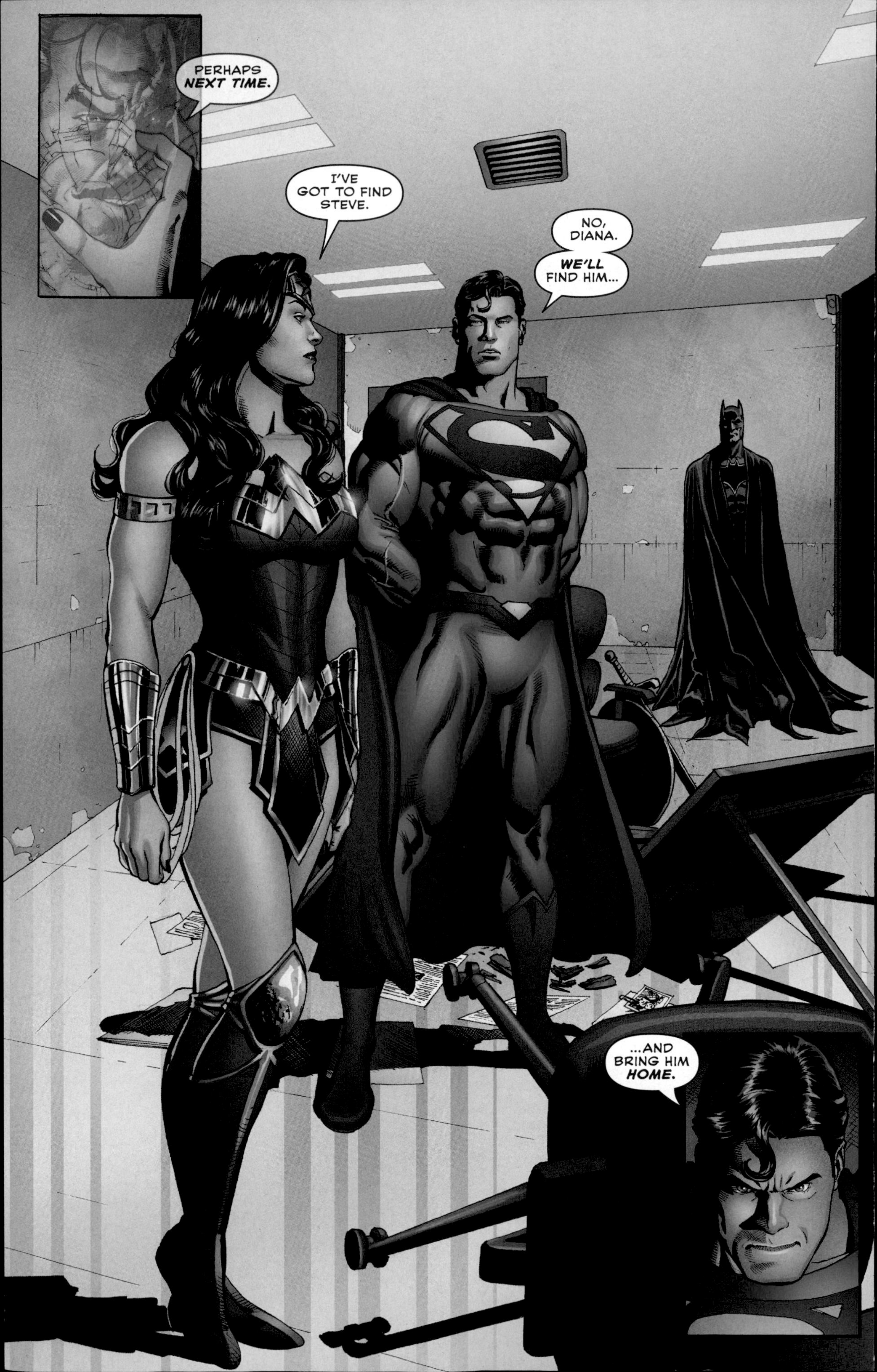
PERHAPS NEXT TIME.
I'VE GOT TO FIND STEVE.
NO, DIANA.
WE'LL FIND HIM...
...AND BRING HIM HOME.

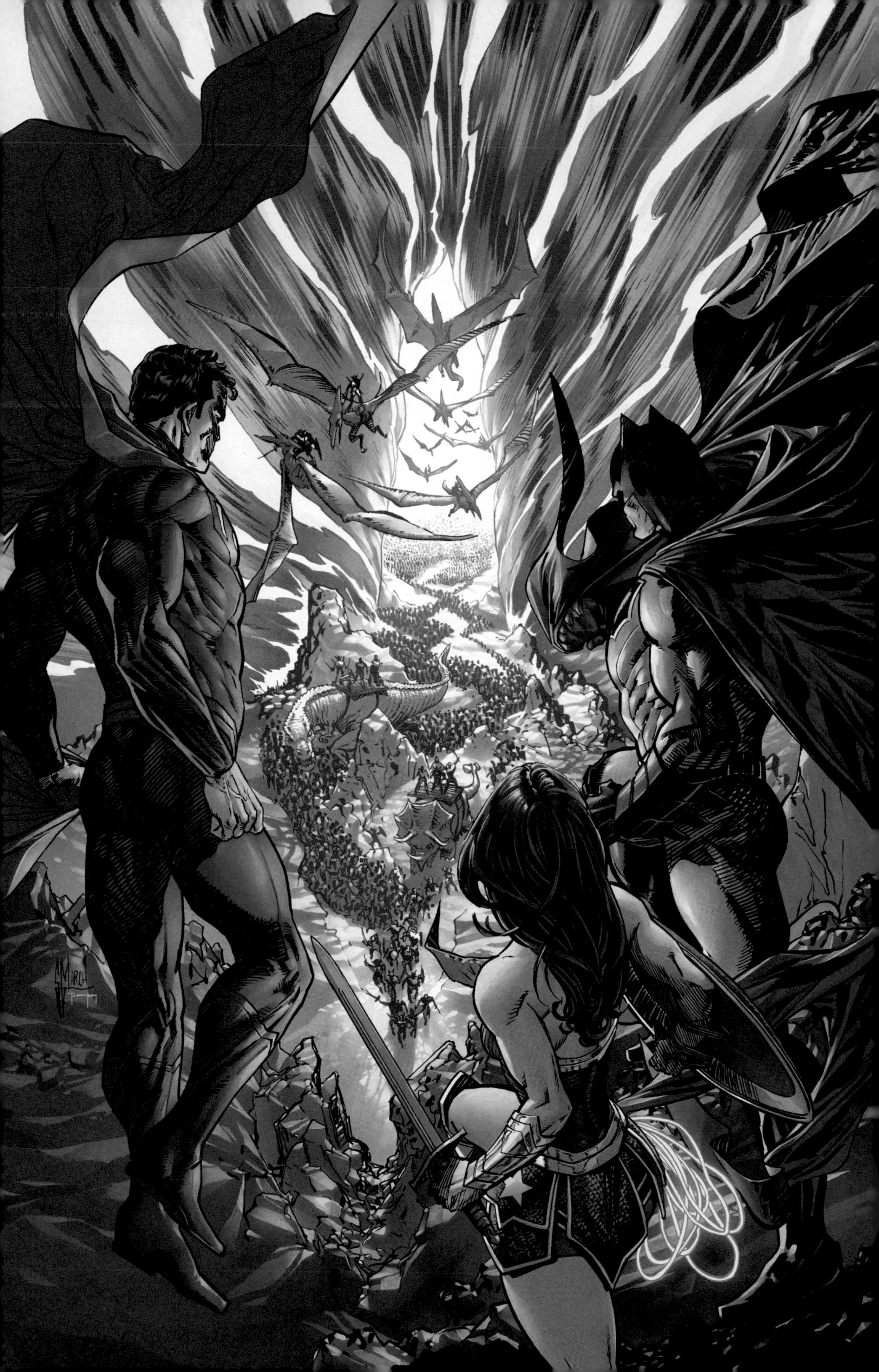

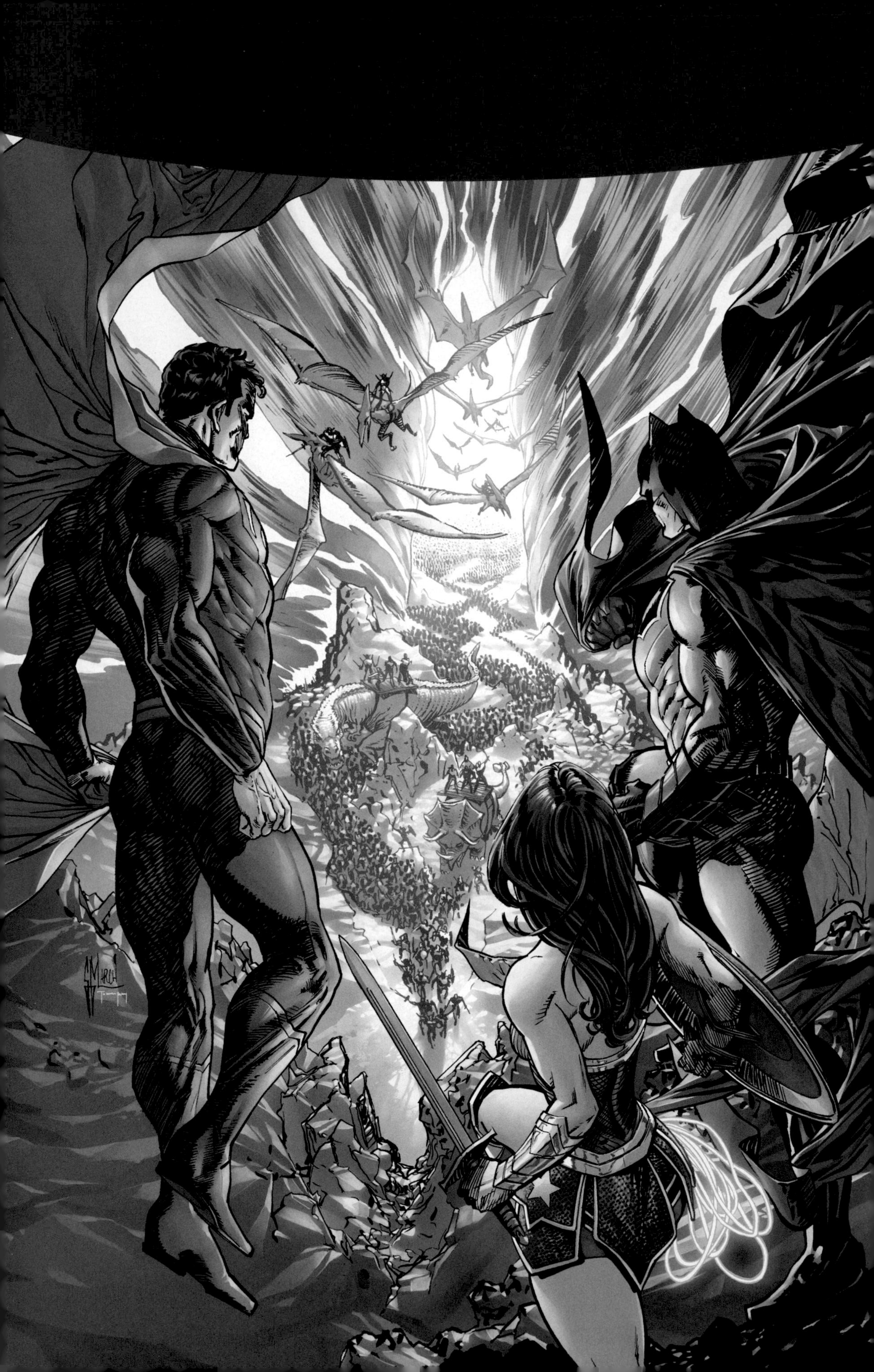

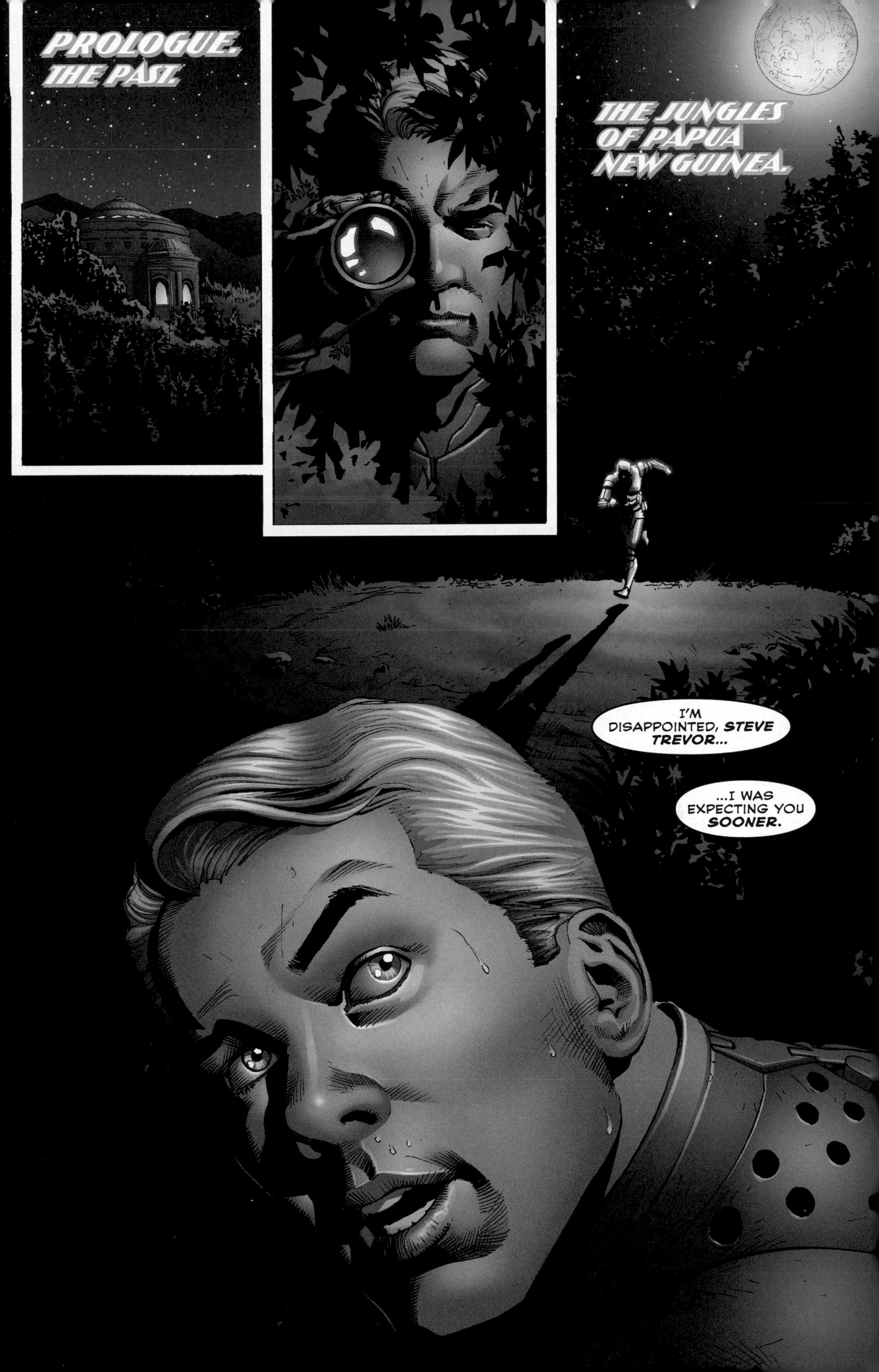
PROLOGUE.
THE PAST.
THE JUNGLES OF PAPUA NEW GUINEA.
I'M DISAPPOINTED, STEVE TREVOR...
...I WAS EXPECTING YOU SOONER.

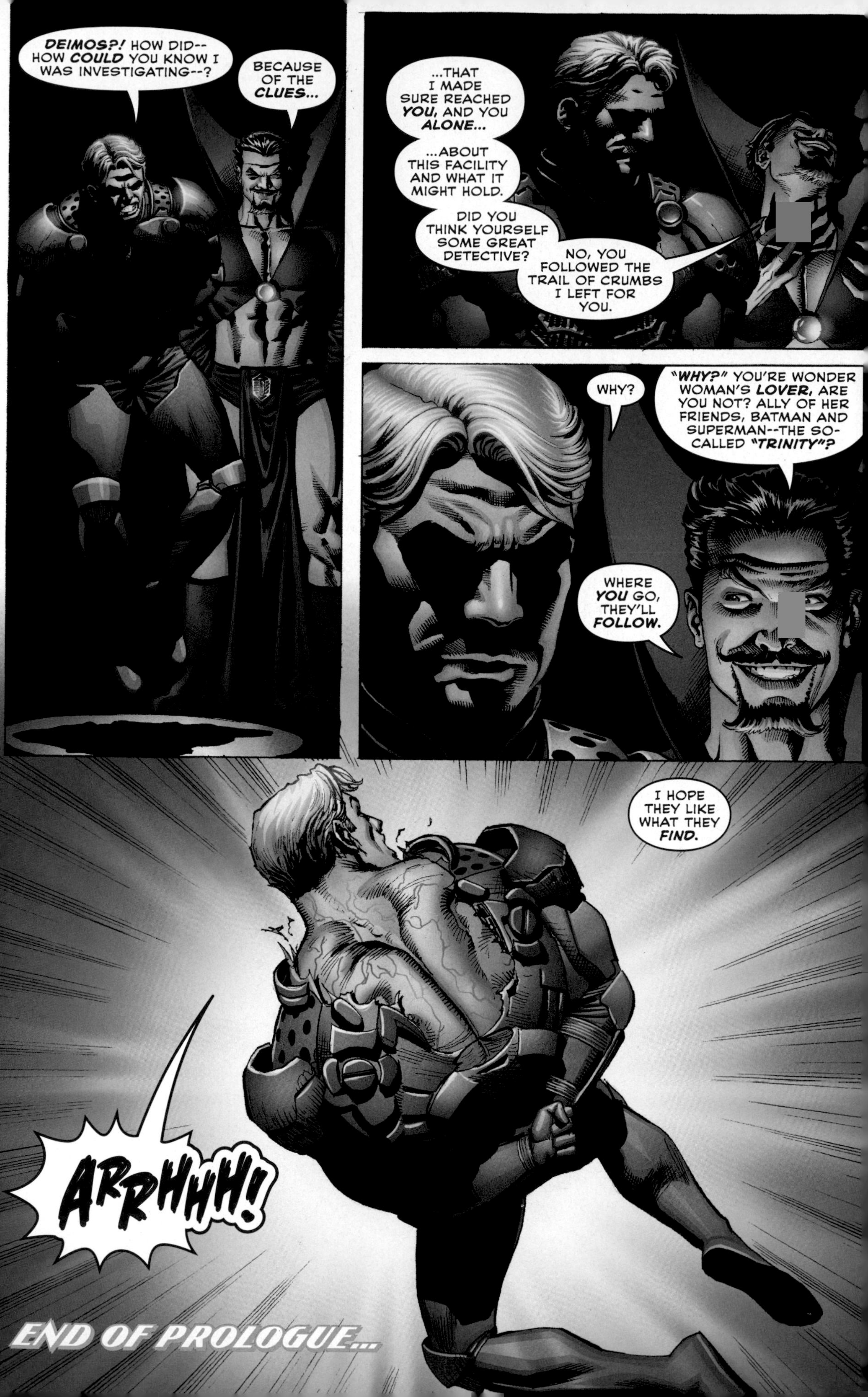
DEIMOS?! HOW DID-- HOW COULD YOU KNOW I WAS INVESTIGATING--?
BECAUSE OF THE CLUES...
...THAT I MADE SURE REACHED YOU, AND YOU ALONE...
...ABOUT THIS FACILITY AND WHAT IT MIGHT HOLD.
DID YOU THINK YOURSELF SOME GREAT DETECTIVE?
NO, YOU FOLLOWED THE TRAIL OF CRUMBS I LEFT FOR YOU.
WHY?
"WHY?" YOU'RE WONDER WOMAN'S LOVER, ARE YOU NOT? ALLY OF HER FRIENDS, BATMAN AND SUPERMAN--THE SO-CALLED "TRINITY"?
WHERE YOU GO, THEY'LL FOLLOW.
I HOPE THEY LIKE WHAT THEY FIND.
ARRHHH!
END OF PROLOGUE...

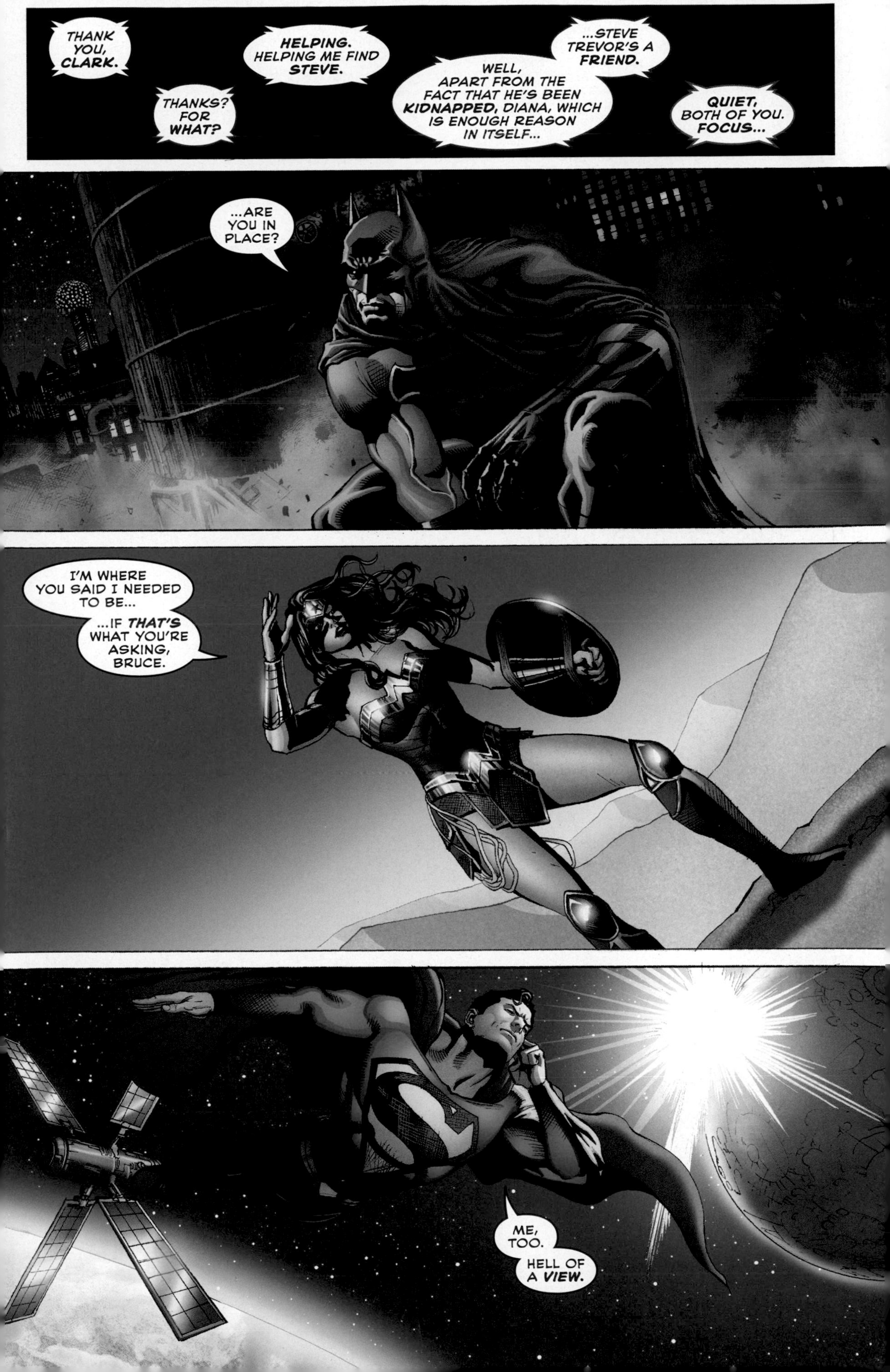

THANK YOU, CLARK.
THANKS? FOR WHAT?
HELPING. HELPING ME FIND STEVE.
WELL, APART FROM THE FACT THAT HE'S BEEN KIDNAPPED, DIANA, WHICH IS ENOUGH REASON IN ITSELF...
...STEVE TREVOR'S A FRIEND.
QUIET, BOTH OF YOU. FOCUS...
...ARE YOU IN PLACE?
I'M WHERE YOU SAID I NEEDED TO BE...
...IF THAT'S WHAT YOU'RE ASKING, BRUCE.
ME, TOO.
HELL OF A VIEW.

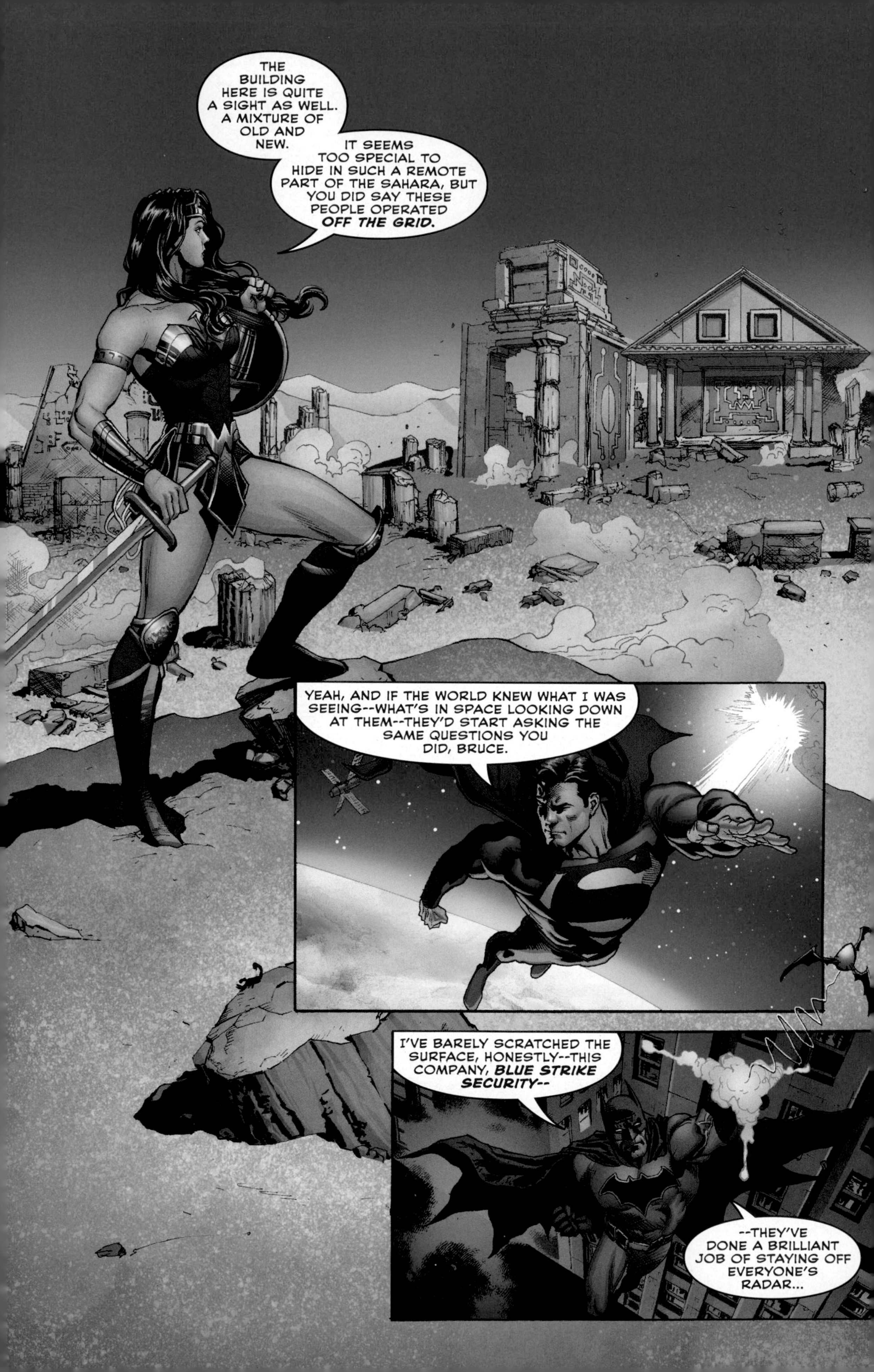
THE BUILDING HERE IS QUITE A SIGHT AS WELL. A MIXTURE OF OLD AND NEW.
IT SEEMS TOO SPECIAL TO HIDE IN SUCH A REMOTE PART OF THE SAHARA, BUT YOU DID SAY THESE PEOPLE OPERATED **OFF THE GRID.**
YEAH, AND IF THE WORLD KNEW WHAT I WAS SEEING--WHAT'S IN SPACE LOOKING DOWN AT THEM--THEY'D START ASKING THE SAME QUESTIONS YOU DID, BRUCE.
I'VE BARELY SCRATCHED THE SURFACE, HONESTLY--THIS COMPANY, **BLUE STRIKE SECURITY--**
--THEY'VE DONE A BRILLIANT JOB OF STAYING OFF EVERYONE'S RADAR...

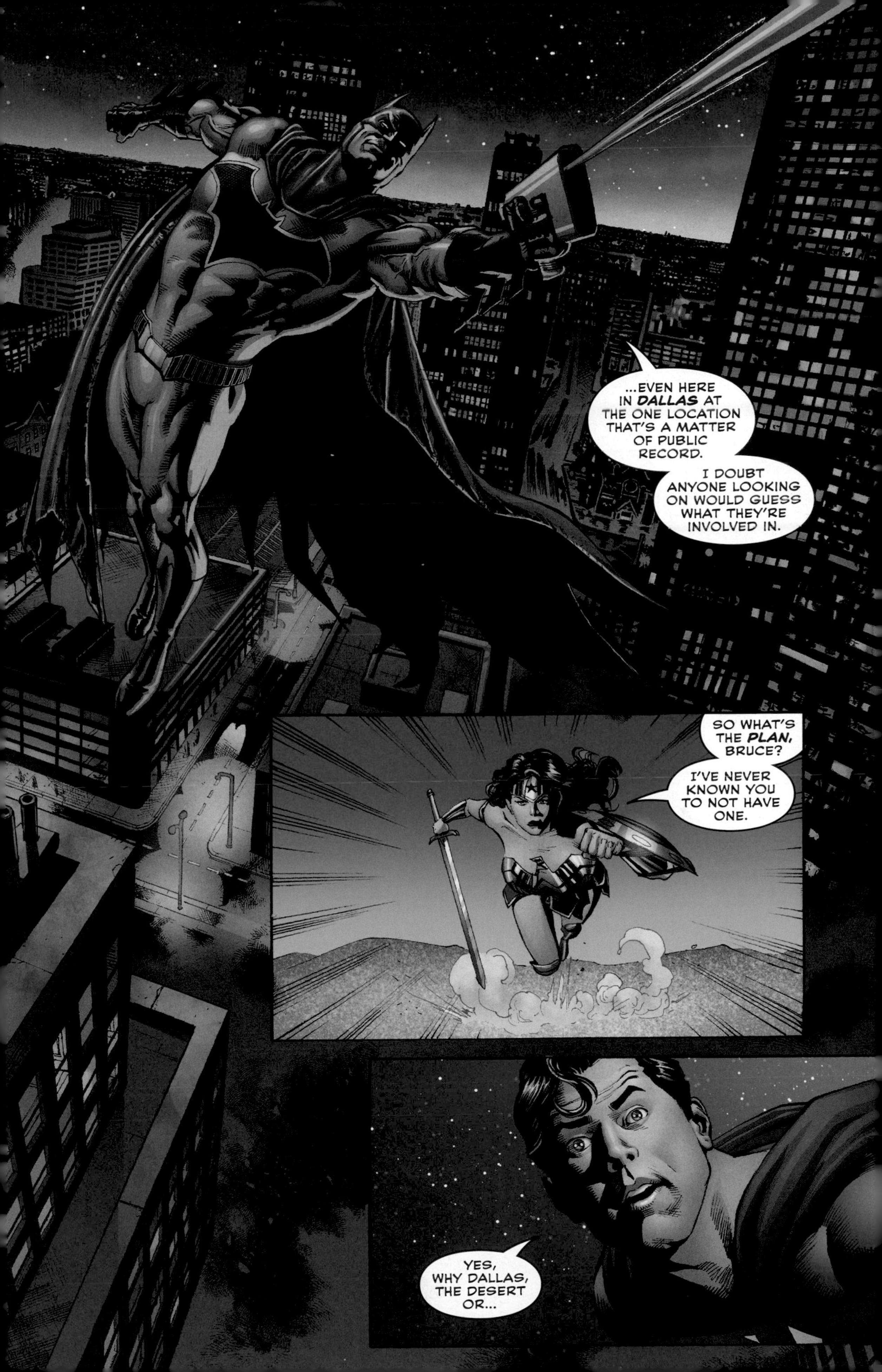
...EVEN HERE IN DALLAS AT THE ONE LOCATION THAT'S A MATTER OF PUBLIC RECORD.
I DOUBT ANYONE LOOKING ON WOULD GUESS WHAT THEY'RE INVOLVED IN.
SO WHAT'S THE PLAN, BRUCE?
I'VE NEVER KNOWN YOU TO NOT HAVE ONE.
YES, WHY DALLAS, THE DESERT OR...

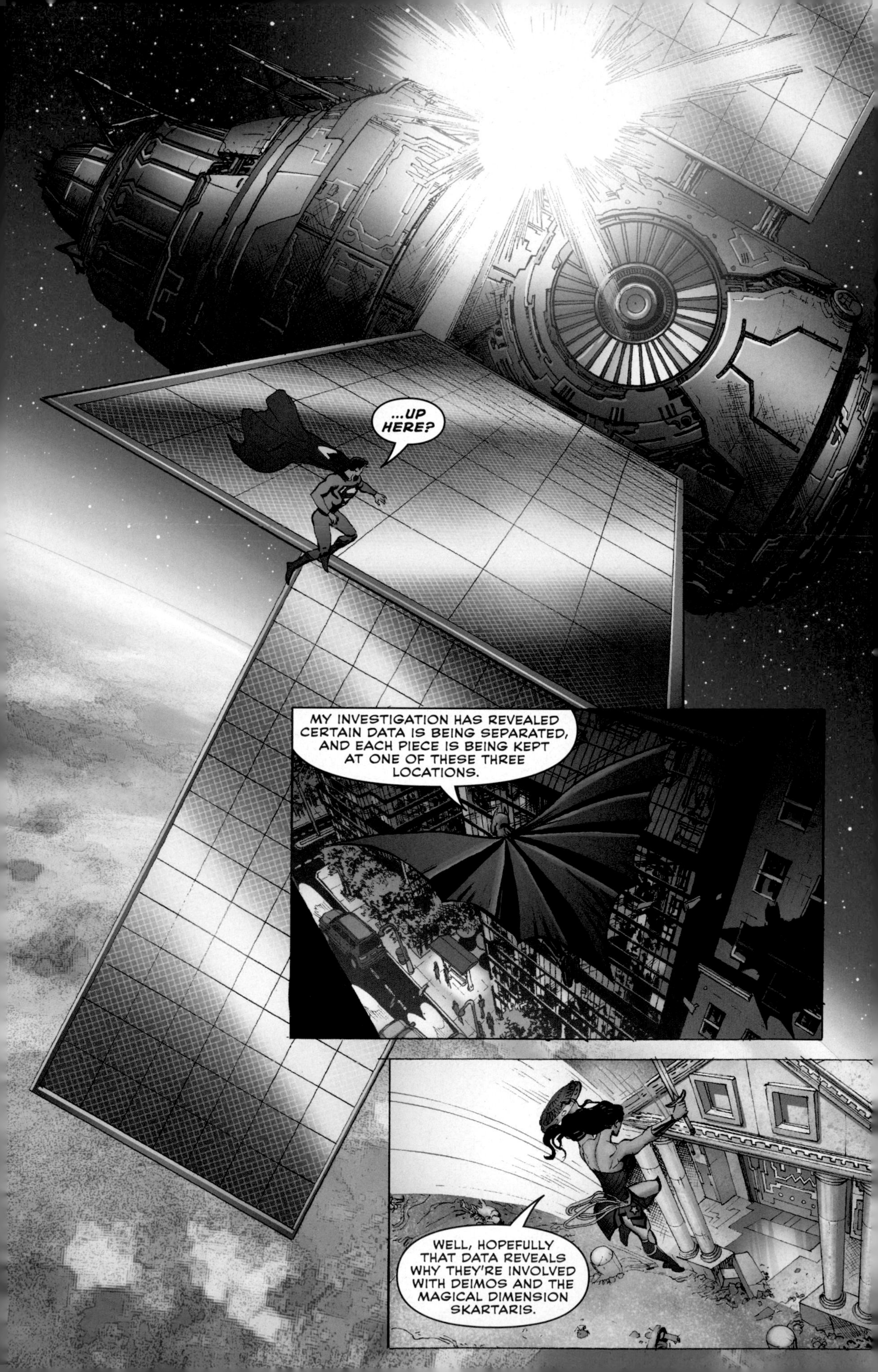
...UP HERE?
MY INVESTIGATION HAS REVEALED CERTAIN DATA IS BEING SEPARATED, AND EACH PIECE IS BEING KEPT AT ONE OF THESE THREE LOCATIONS.
WELL, HOPEFULLY THAT DATA REVEALS WHY THEY'RE INVOLVED WITH DEIMOS AND THE MAGICAL DIMENSION SKARTARIS.

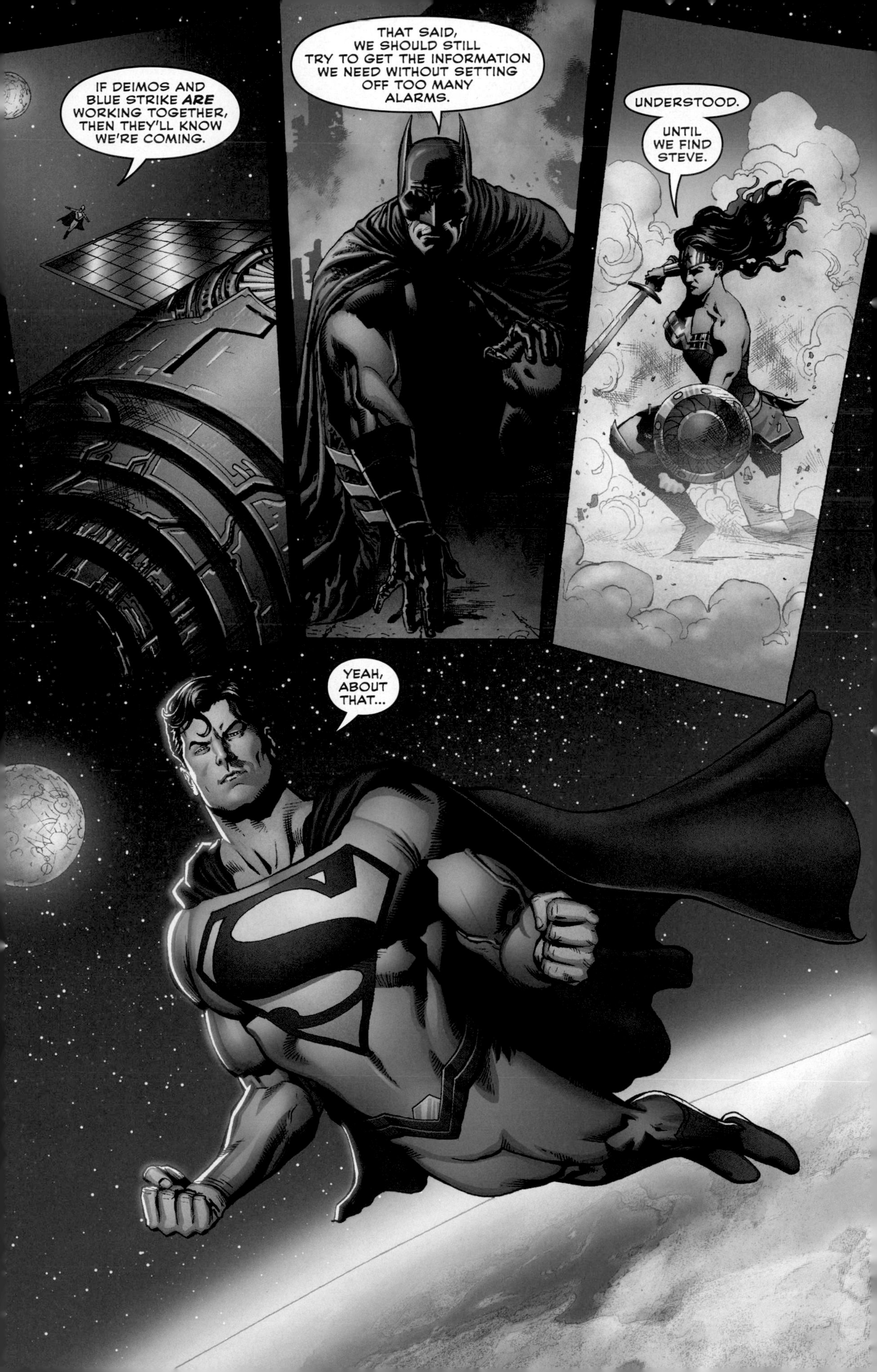
IF DEIMOS AND BLUE STRIKE ARE WORKING TOGETHER, THEN THEY'LL KNOW WE'RE COMING.
THAT SAID, WE SHOULD STILL TRY TO GET THE INFORMATION WE NEED WITHOUT SETTING OFF TOO MANY ALARMS.
UNDERSTOOD.
UNTIL WE FIND STEVE.
YEAH, ABOUT THAT...

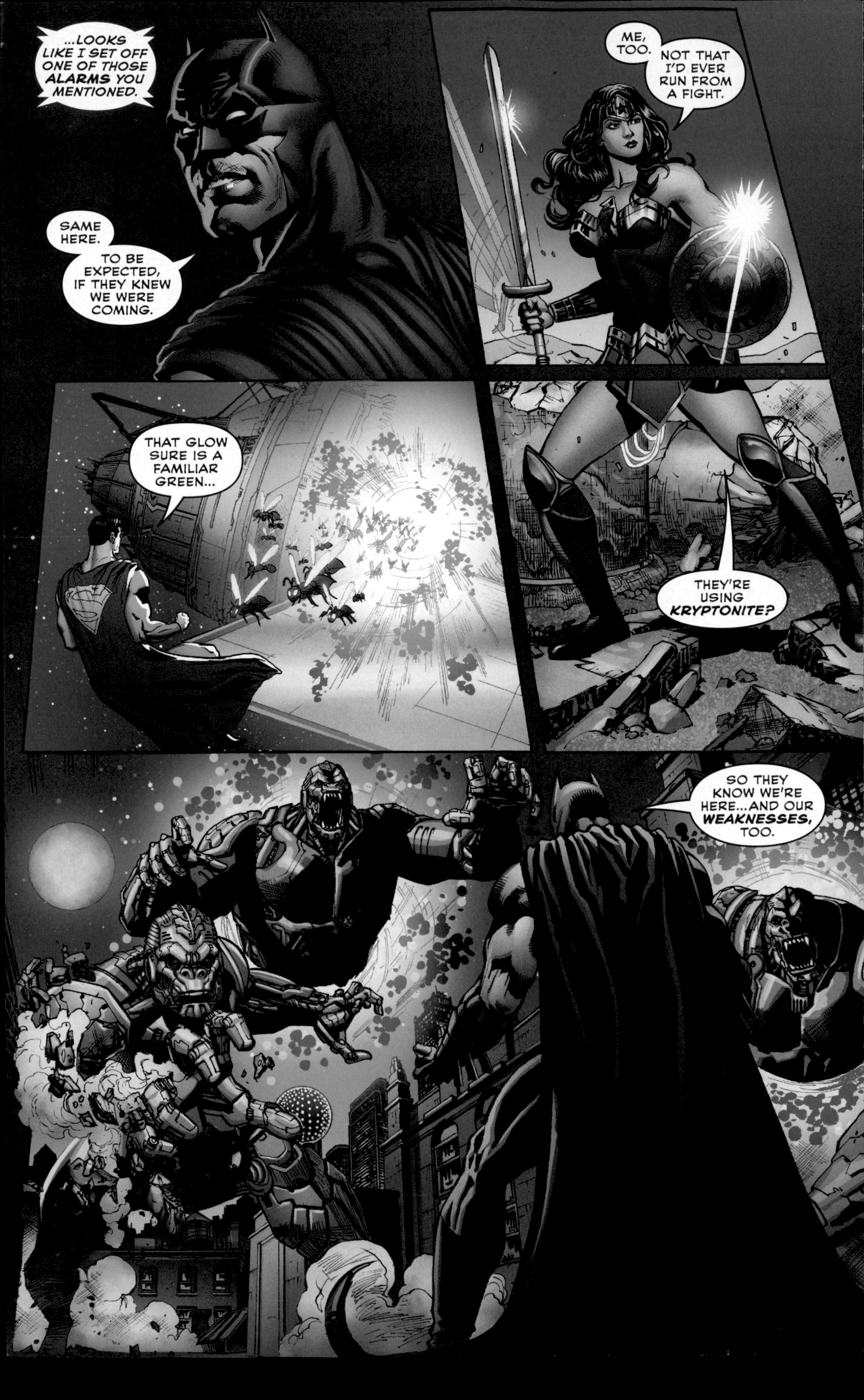
...LOOKS LIKE I SET OFF ONE OF THOSE ALARMS YOU MENTIONED.
ME, TOO.
NOT THAT I'D EVER RUN FROM A FIGHT.
SAME HERE.
TO BE EXPECTED, IF THEY KNEW WE WERE COMING.
THAT GLOW SURE IS A FAMILIAR GREEN...
THEY'RE USING KRYPTONITE?
SO THEY KNOW WE'RE HERE...AND OUR WEAKNESSES, TOO.

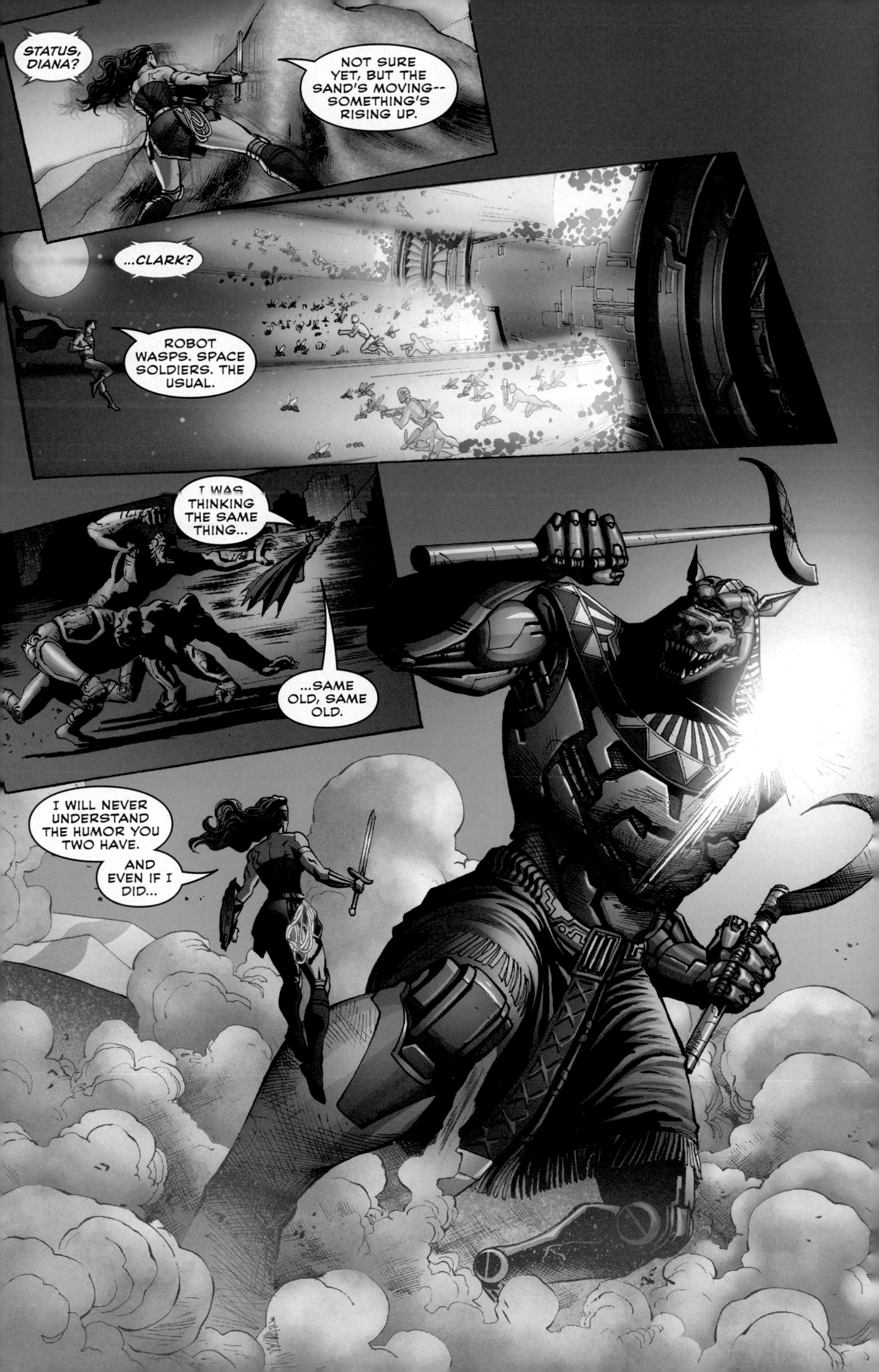
STATUS, DIANA?
NOT SURE YET, BUT THE SAND'S MOVING-- SOMETHING'S RISING UP.
...CLARK?
ROBOT WASPS. SPACE SOLDIERS. THE USUAL.
I WAS THINKING THE SAME THING...
...SAME OLD, SAME OLD.
I WILL NEVER UNDERSTAND THE HUMOR YOU TWO HAVE.
AND EVEN IF I DID...

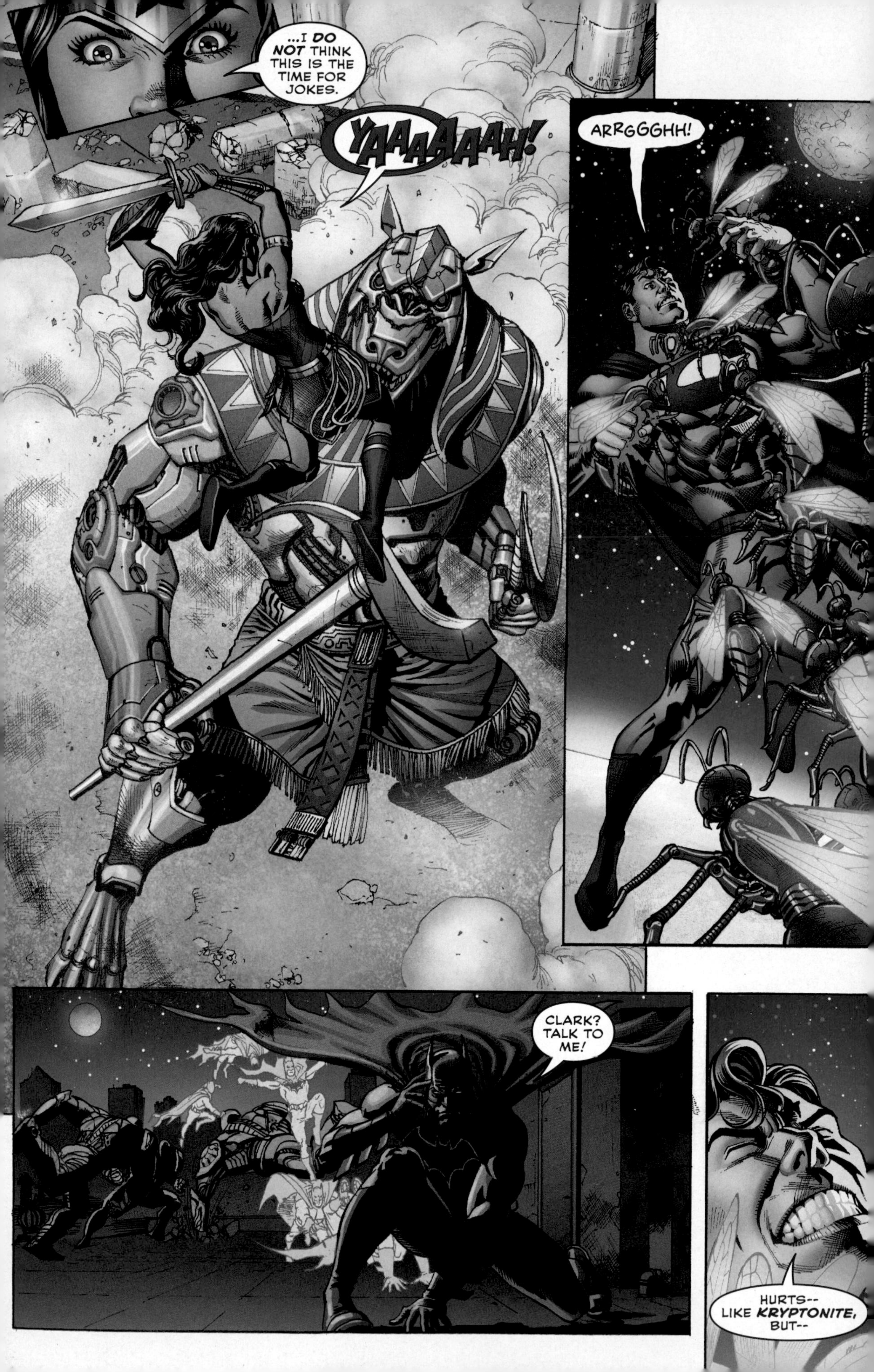
...I DO NOT THINK THIS IS THE TIME FOR JOKES.
YAAAAAAAH!
ARRGGGHH!
CLARK? TALK TO ME!
HURTS-- LIKE KRYPTONITE, BUT--

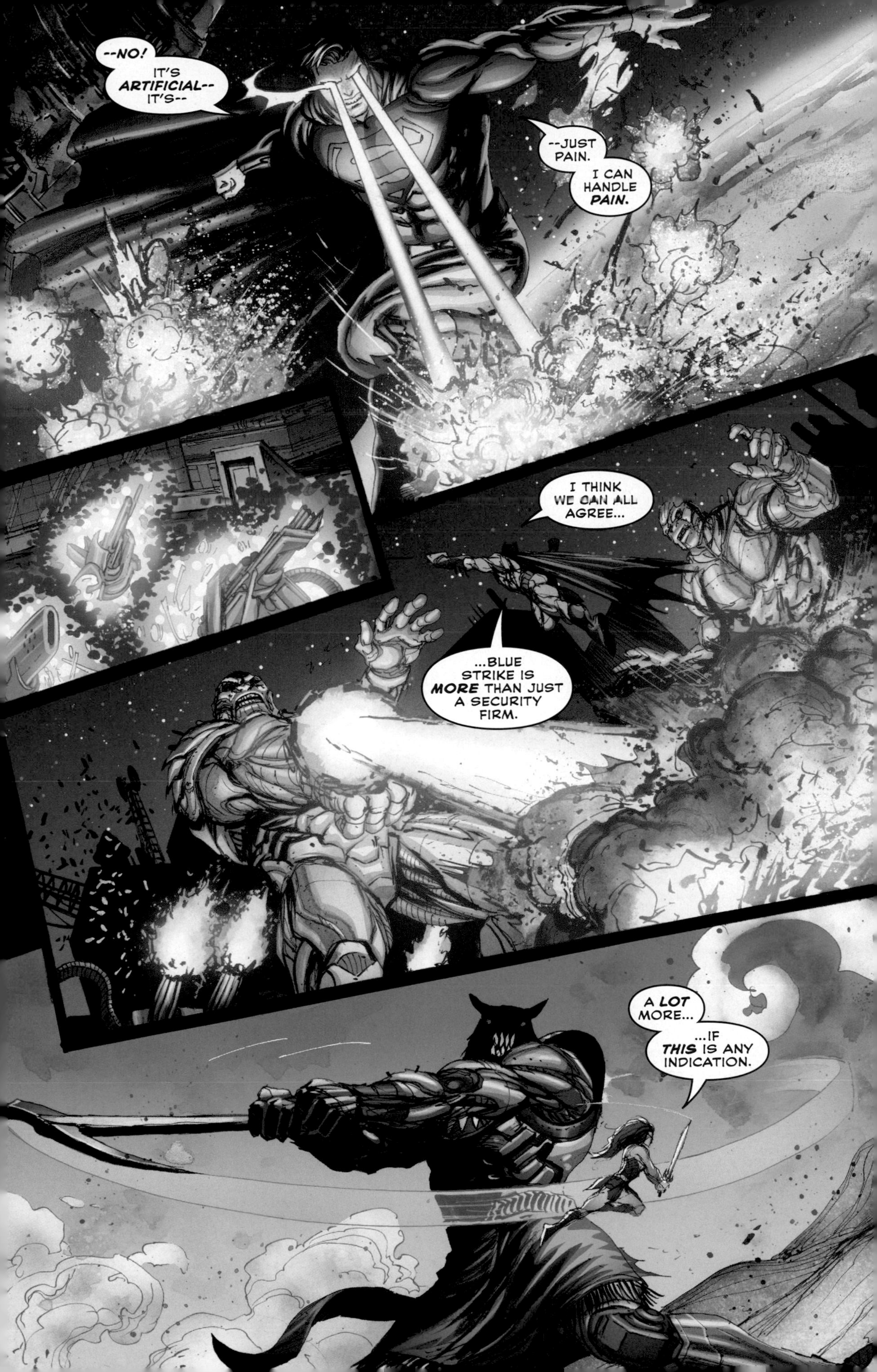
--NO!
IT'S ARTIFICIAL-- IT'S--
--JUST PAIN.
I CAN HANDLE PAIN.
I THINK WE CAN ALL AGREE...
...BLUE STRIKE IS MORE THAN JUST A SECURITY FIRM.
A LOT MORE...
...IF THIS IS ANY INDICATION.

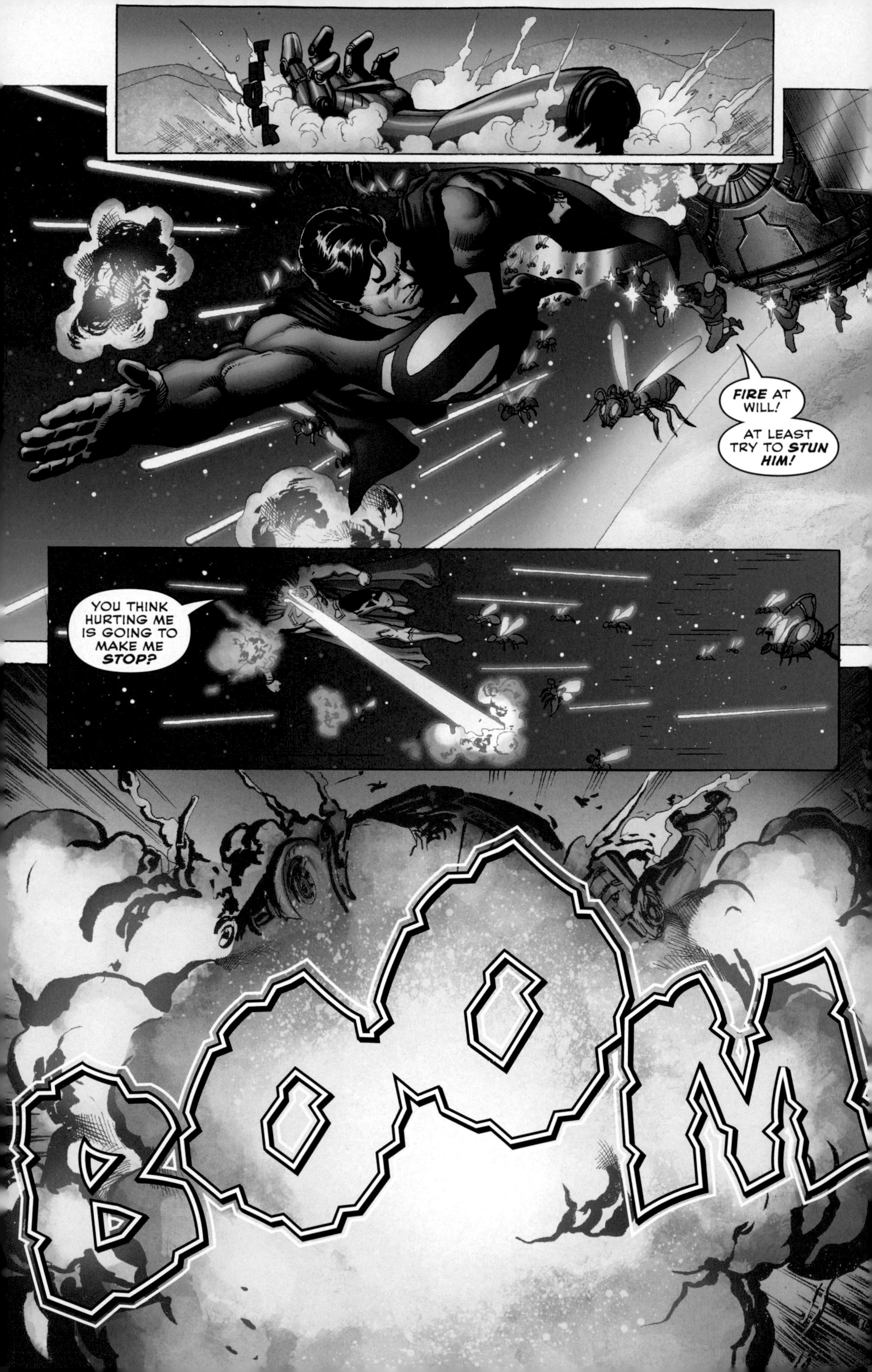
THUNK
FIRE AT WILL!
AT LEAST TRY TO STUN HIM!
YOU THINK HURTING ME IS GOING TO MAKE ME STOP?
BOOM

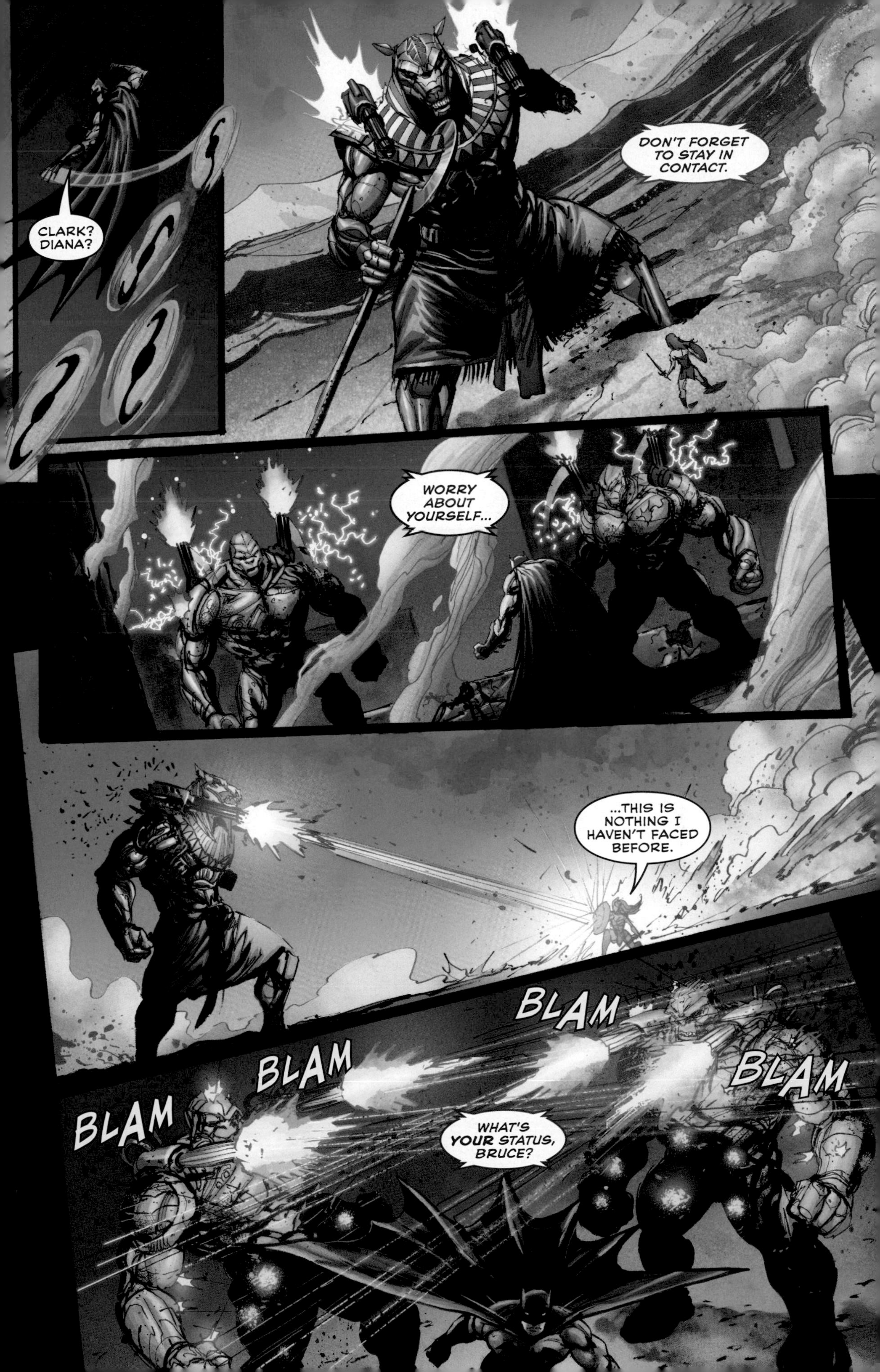
CLARK? DIANA?
DON'T FORGET TO STAY IN CONTACT.
WORRY ABOUT YOURSELF...
...THIS IS NOTHING I HAVEN'T FACED BEFORE.
BLAM
BLAM
BLAM
BLAM
WHAT'S YOUR STATUS, BRUCE?

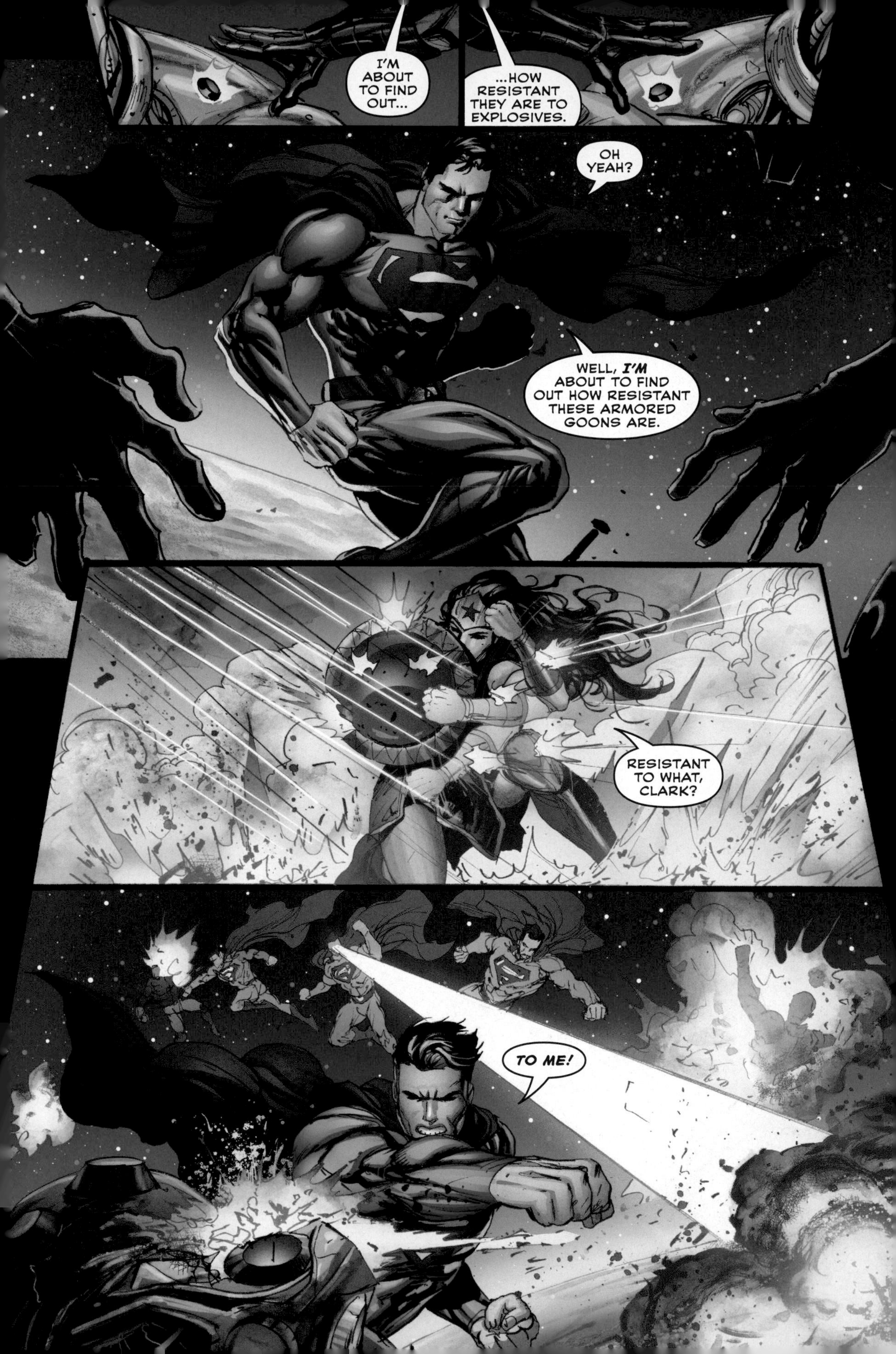
I'M ABOUT TO FIND OUT...
...HOW RESISTANT THEY ARE TO EXPLOSIVES.
OH YEAH?
WELL, ***I'M*** ABOUT TO FIND OUT HOW RESISTANT THESE ARMORED GOONS ARE.
RESISTANT TO WHAT, CLARK?
TO ME!

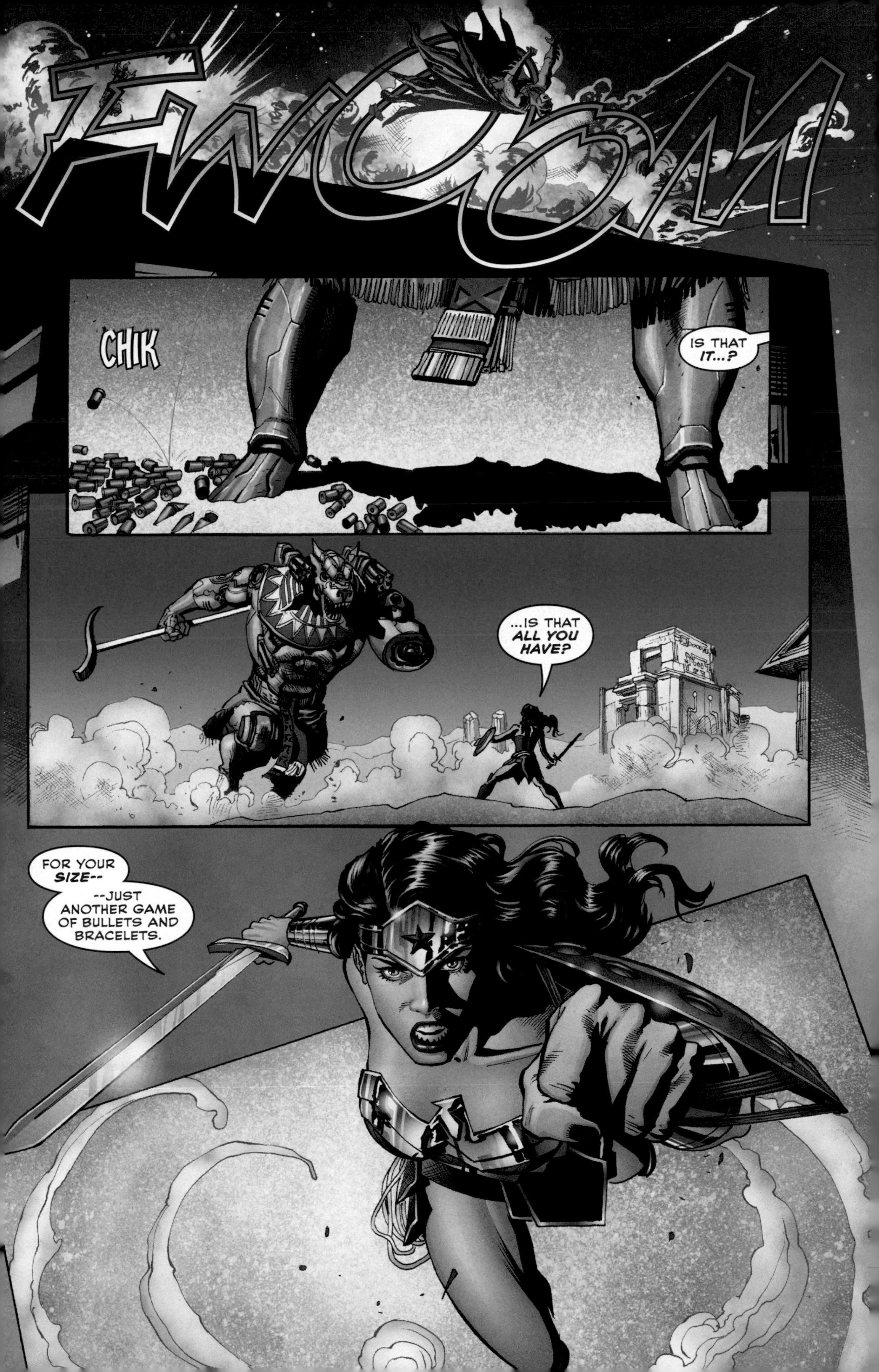
FWOOM
CHIK
IS THAT IT...?
...IS THAT ALL YOU HAVE?
FOR YOUR SIZE--
--JUST ANOTHER GAME OF BULLETS AND BRACELETS.

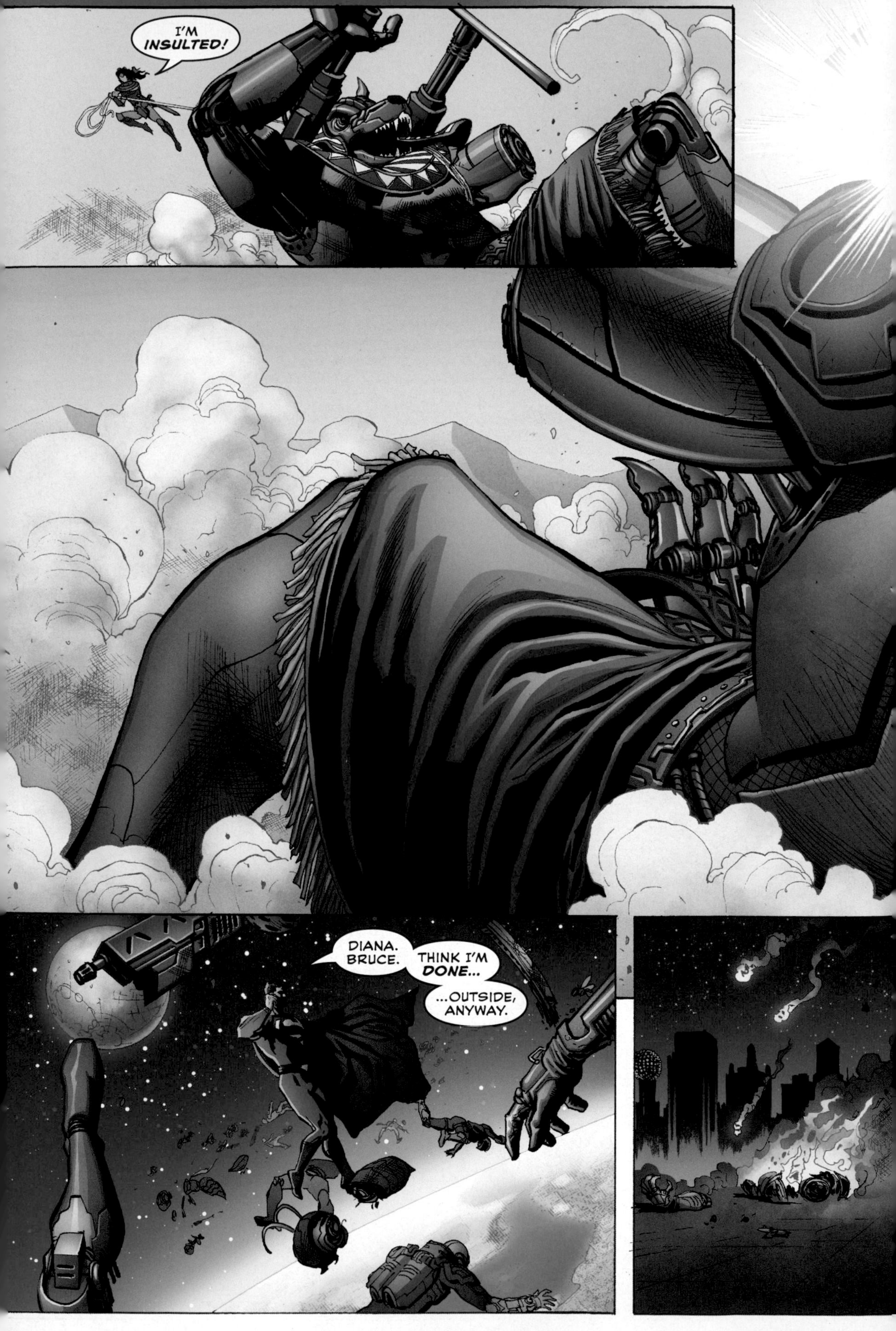
I'M INSULTED!
DIANA. BRUCE.
THINK I'M DONE...
...OUTSIDE, ANYWAY.

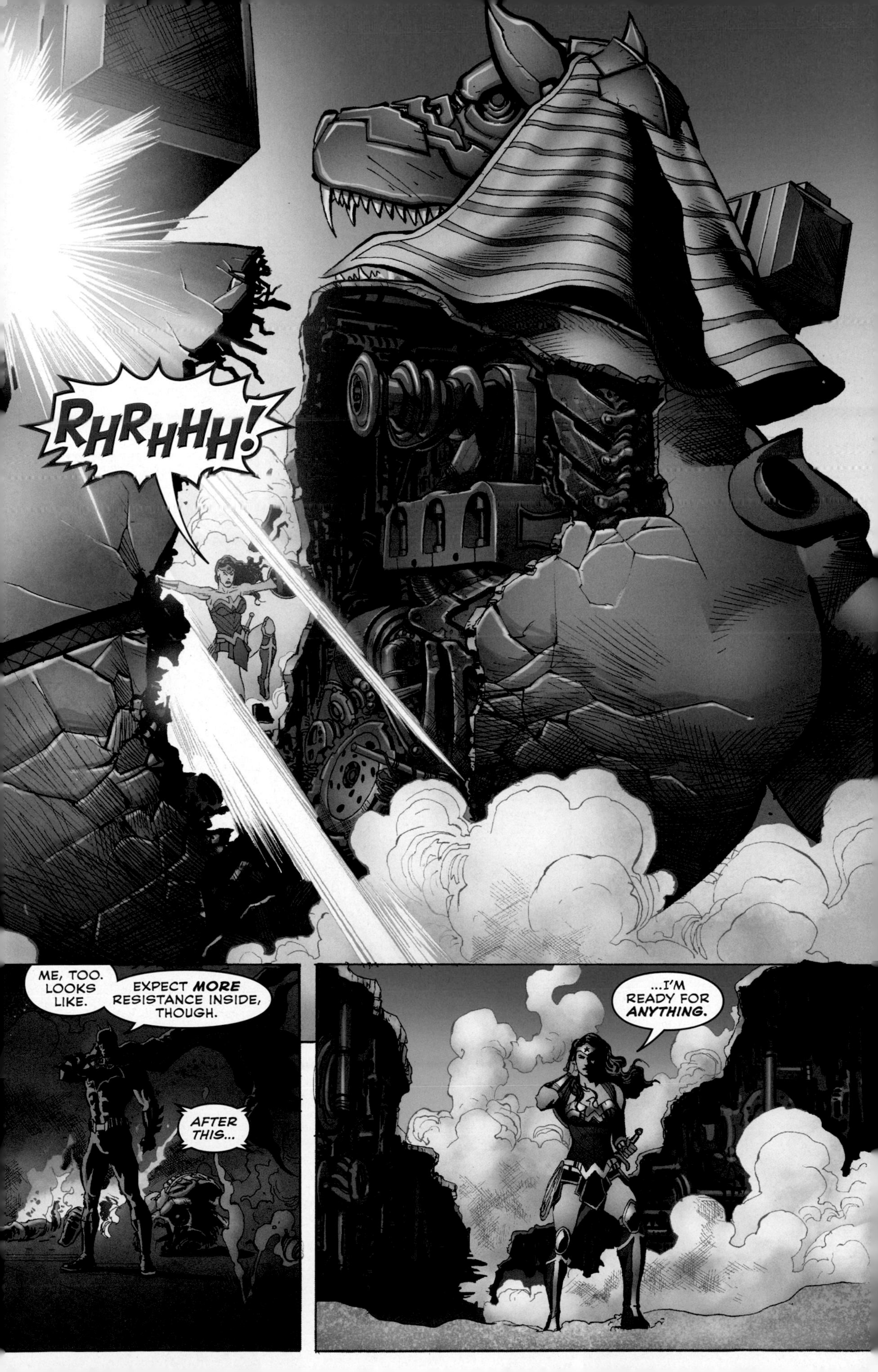
RHRHHH!
ME, TOO. LOOKS LIKE.
EXPECT MORE RESISTANCE INSIDE, THOUGH.
AFTER THIS...
...I'M READY FOR ANYTHING.

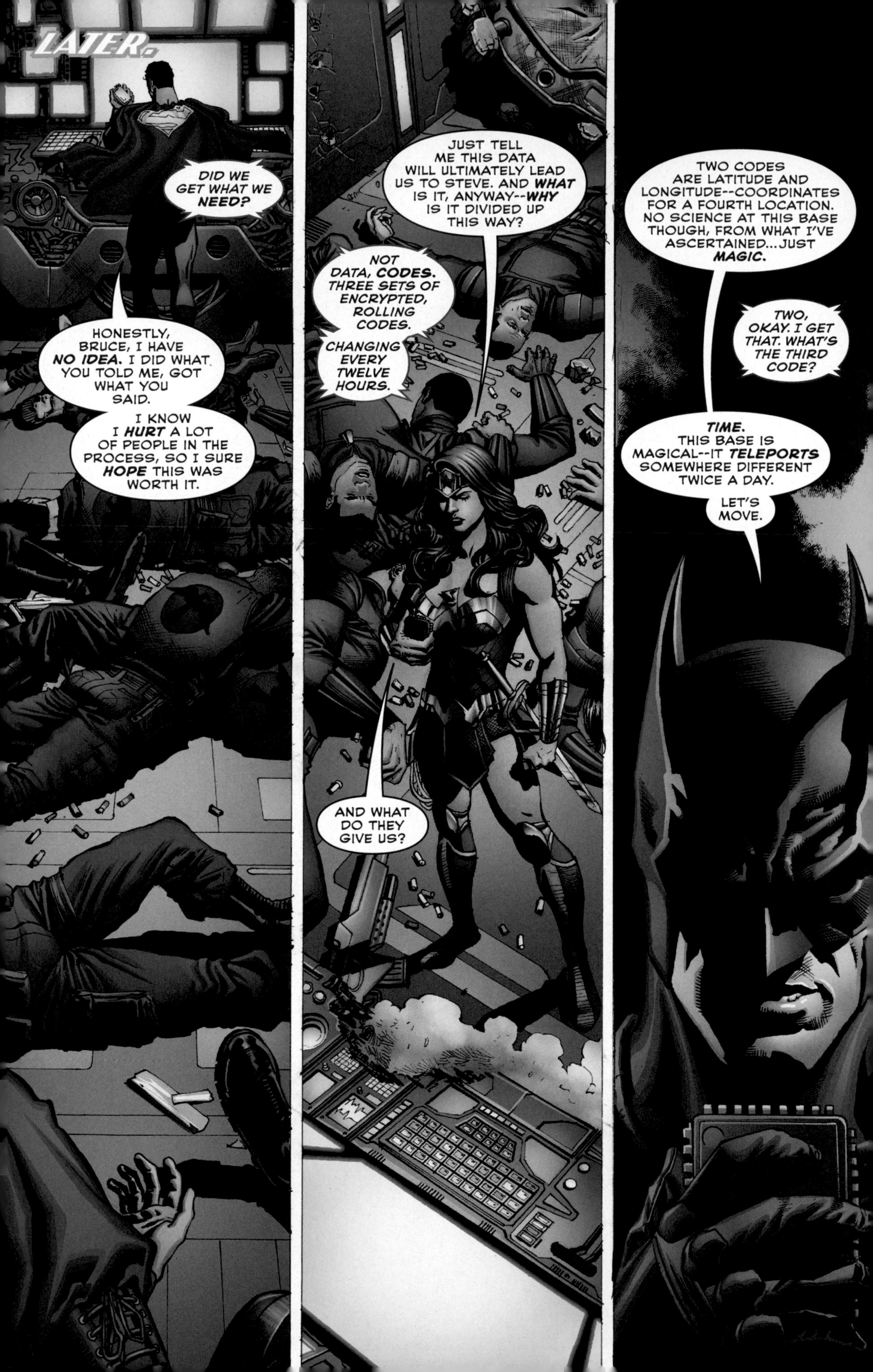
LATER.
DID WE GET WHAT WE NEED?
HONESTLY, BRUCE, I HAVE NO IDEA. I DID WHAT YOU TOLD ME, GOT WHAT YOU SAID.
I KNOW I HURT A LOT OF PEOPLE IN THE PROCESS, SO I SURE HOPE THIS WAS WORTH IT.
JUST TELL ME THIS DATA WILL ULTIMATELY LEAD US TO STEVE. AND WHAT IS IT, ANYWAY--WHY IS IT DIVIDED UP THIS WAY?
NOT DATA, CODES. THREE SETS OF ENCRYPTED, ROLLING CODES.
CHANGING EVERY TWELVE HOURS.
AND WHAT DO THEY GIVE US?
TWO CODES ARE LATITUDE AND LONGITUDE--COORDINATES FOR A FOURTH LOCATION. NO SCIENCE AT THIS BASE THOUGH, FROM WHAT I'VE ASCERTAINED...JUST MAGIC.
TWO, OKAY. I GET THAT. WHAT'S THE THIRD CODE?
TIME. THIS BASE IS MAGICAL--IT TELEPORTS SOMEWHERE DIFFERENT TWICE A DAY.
LET'S MOVE.

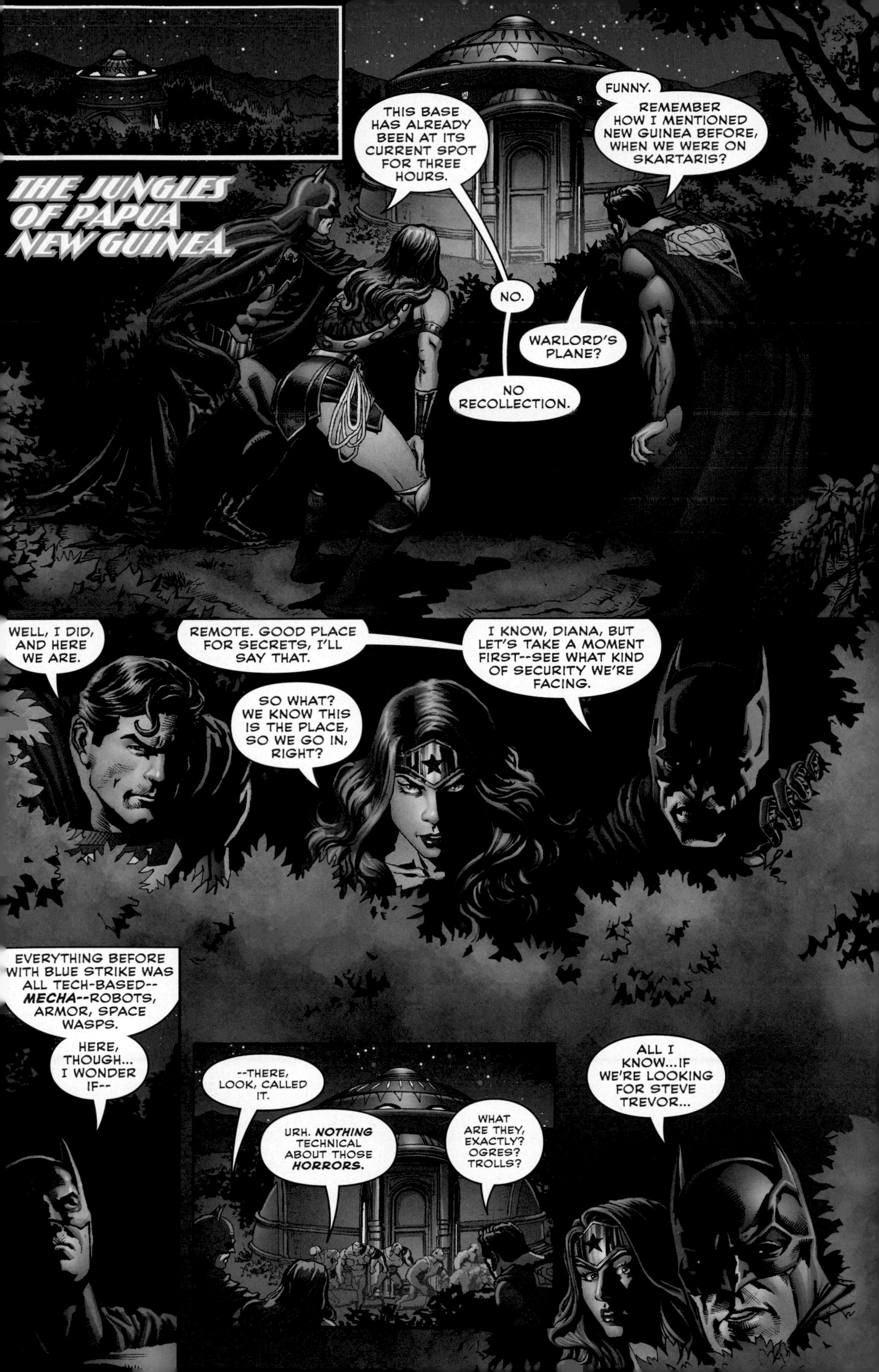
THE JUNGLES OF PAPUA NEW GUINEA.
THIS BASE HAS ALREADY BEEN AT ITS CURRENT SPOT FOR THREE HOURS.
FUNNY.
REMEMBER HOW I MENTIONED NEW GUINEA BEFORE, WHEN WE WERE ON SKARTARIS?
NO.
WARLORD'S PLANE?
NO RECOLLECTION.
WELL, I DID, AND HERE WE ARE.
REMOTE. GOOD PLACE FOR SECRETS, I'LL SAY THAT.
SO WHAT? WE KNOW THIS IS THE PLACE, SO WE GO IN, RIGHT?
I KNOW, DIANA, BUT LET'S TAKE A MOMENT FIRST--SEE WHAT KIND OF SECURITY WE'RE FACING.
EVERYTHING BEFORE WITH BLUE STRIKE WAS ALL TECH-BASED--MECHA--ROBOTS, ARMOR, SPACE WASPS.
HERE, THOUGH... I WONDER IF--
--THERE, LOOK, CALLED IT.
URH. NOTHING TECHNICAL ABOUT THOSE HORRORS.
WHAT ARE THEY, EXACTLY? OGRES? TROLLS?
ALL I KNOW...IF WE'RE LOOKING FOR STEVE TREVOR...

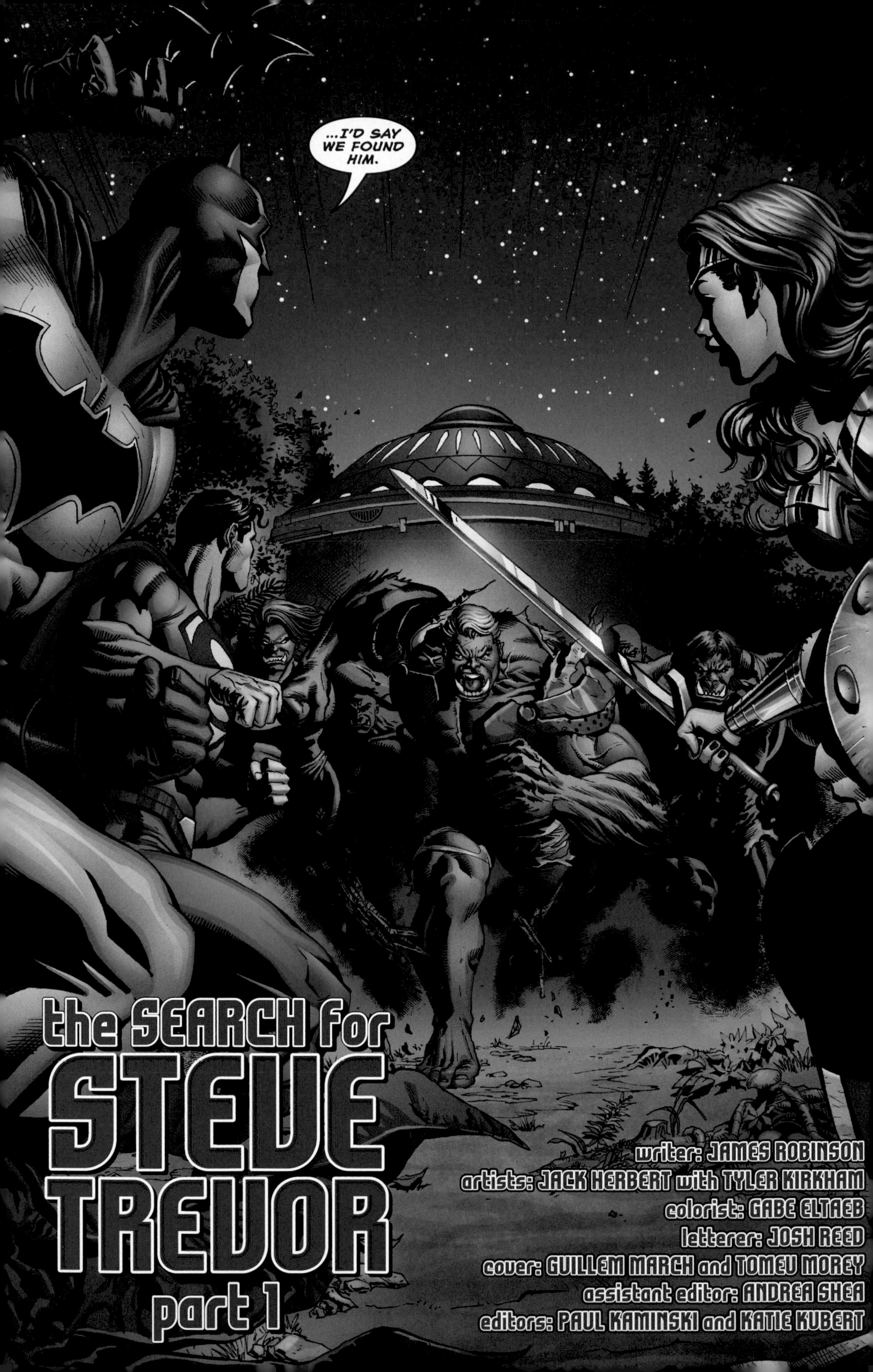
...I'D SAY WE FOUND HIM.
the SEARCH for STEVE TREVOR part 1
writer: JAMES ROBINSON
artists: JACK HERBERT with TYLER KIRKHAM
colorist: GABE ELTAEB
letterer: JOSH REED
cover: GUILLEM MARCH and TOMEU MOREY
assistant editor: ANDREA SHEA
editors: PAUL KAMINSKI and KATIE KUBERT

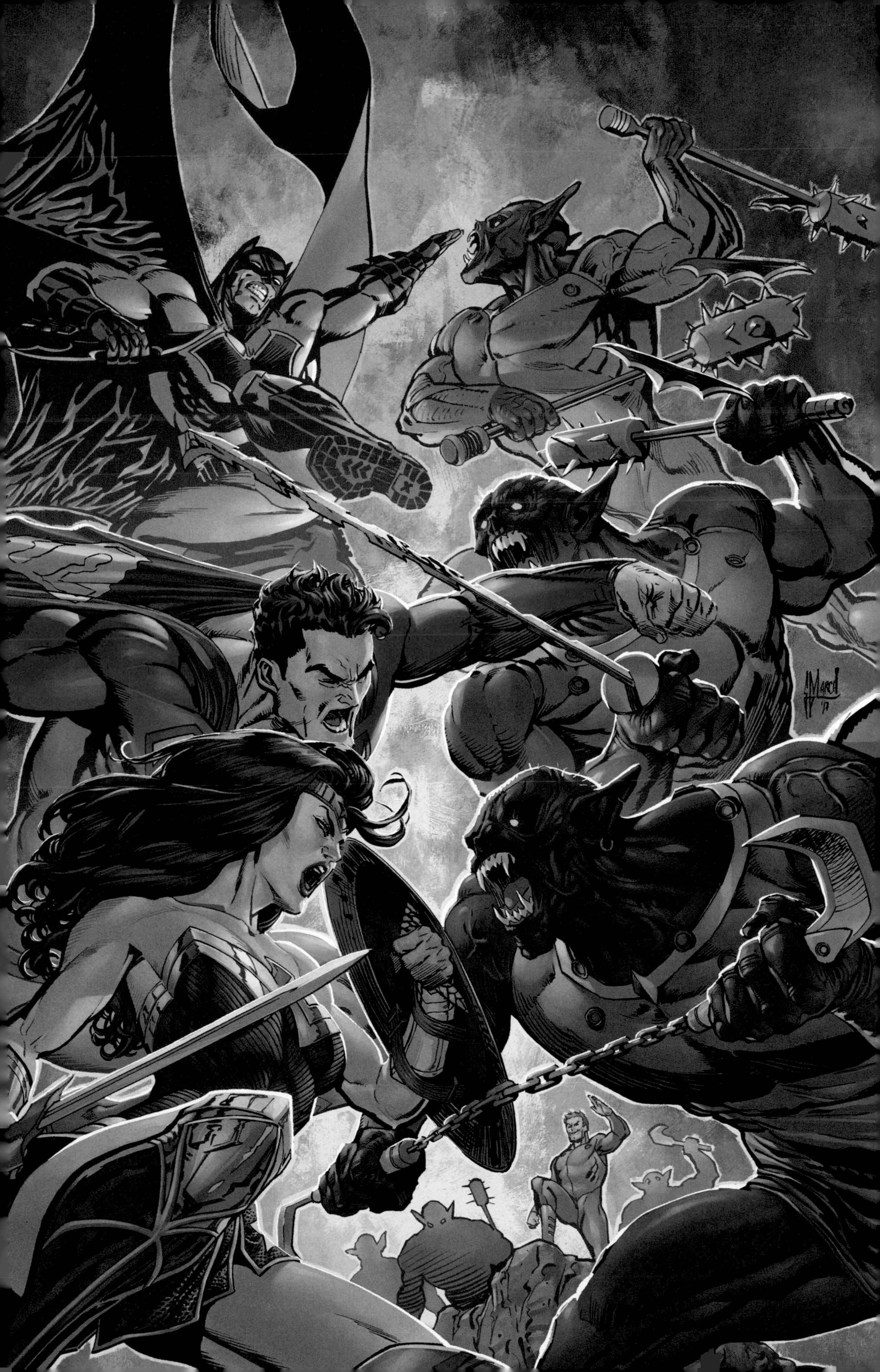

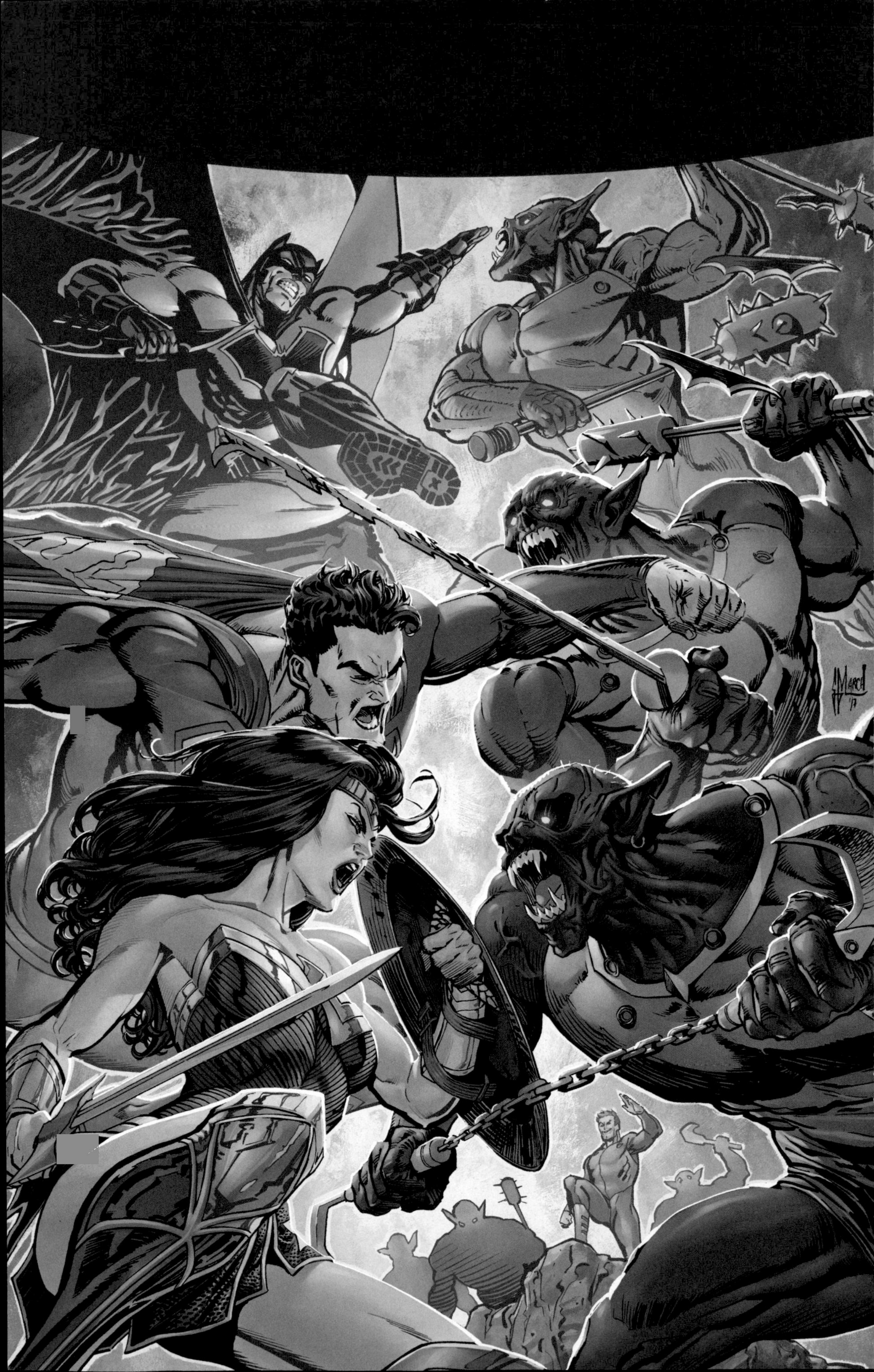

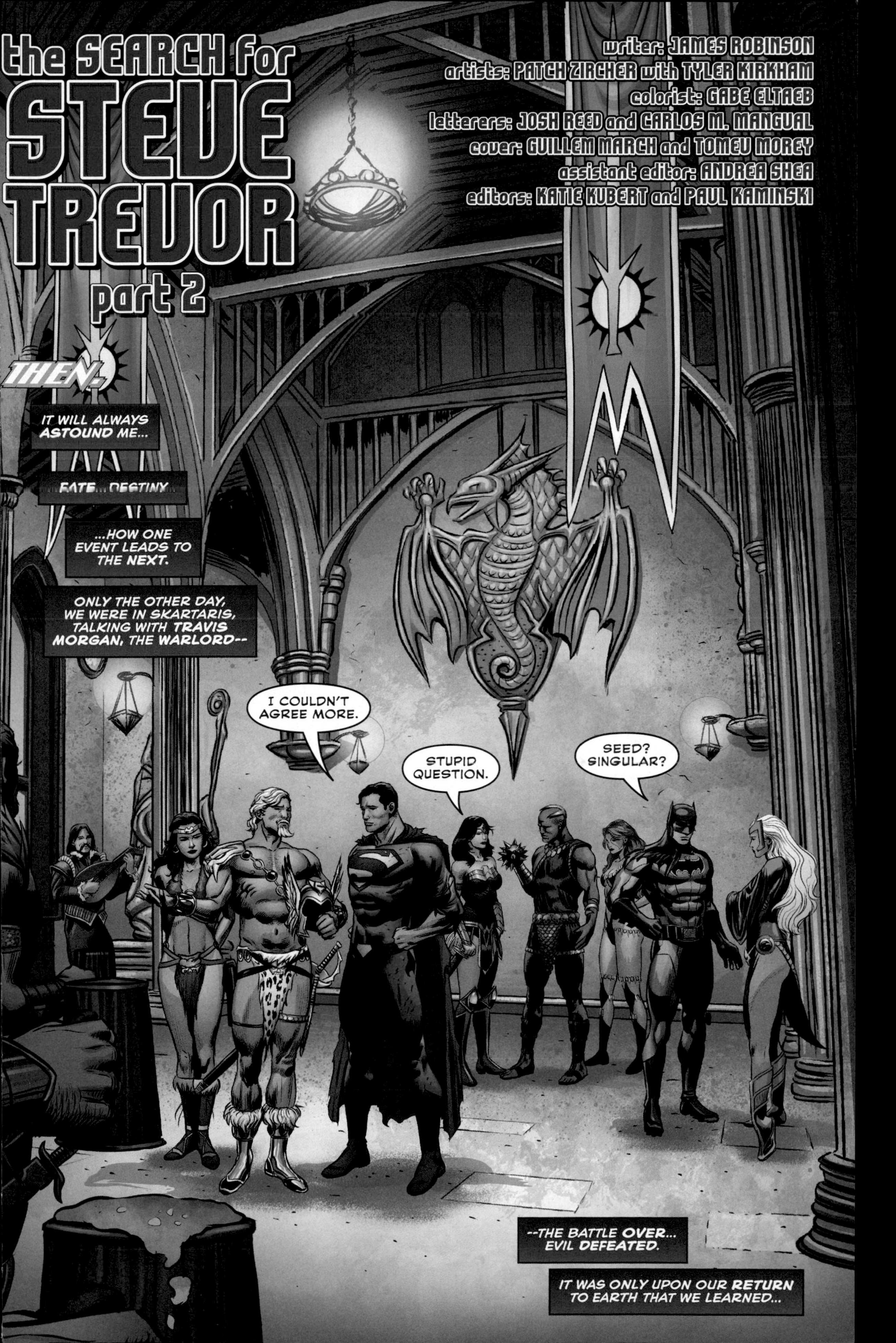
the SEARCH for STEVE TREVOR part 2
writer: JAMES ROBINSON
artists: PATCH ZIRCHER with TYLER KIRKHAM
colorist: GABE ELTAEB
letterers: JOSH REED and CARLOS M. MANGUAL
cover: GUILLEM MARCH and TOMEU MOREY
assistant editor: ANDREA SHEA
editors: KATIE KUBERT and PAUL KAMINSKI
THEN.
IT WILL ALWAYS ASTOUND ME...
FATE... DESTINY.
...HOW ONE EVENT LEADS TO THE NEXT.
ONLY THE OTHER DAY, WE WERE IN SKARTARIS, TALKING WITH TRAVIS MORGAN, THE WARLORD--
I COULDN'T AGREE MORE.
STUPID QUESTION.
SEED? SINGULAR?
--THE BATTLE OVER... EVIL DEFEATED.
IT WAS ONLY UPON OUR RETURN TO EARTH THAT WE LEARNED...

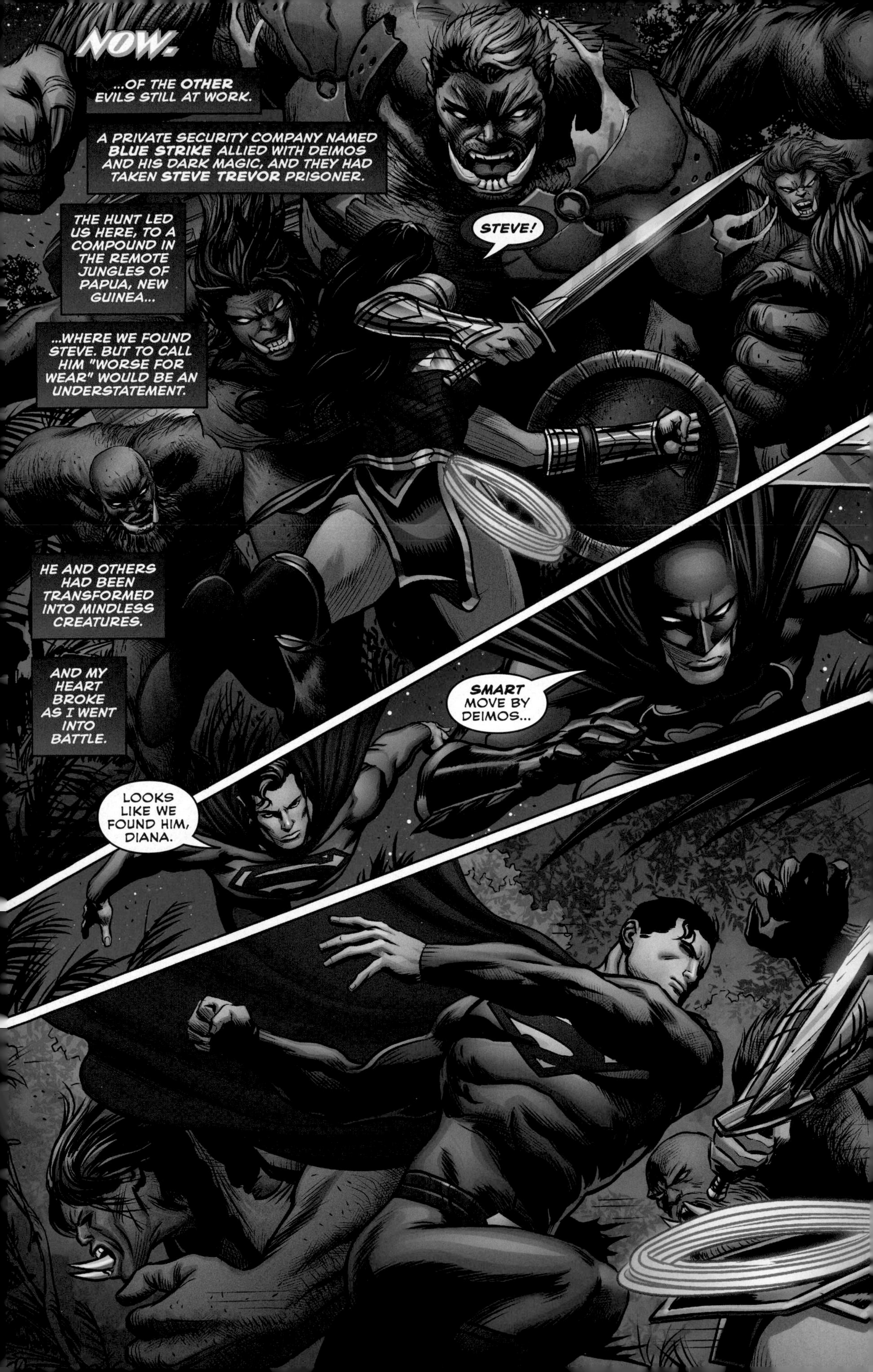
NOW.
...OF THE OTHER EVILS STILL AT WORK.
A PRIVATE SECURITY COMPANY NAMED BLUE STRIKE ALLIED WITH DEIMOS AND HIS DARK MAGIC, AND THEY HAD TAKEN STEVE TREVOR PRISONER.
THE HUNT LED US HERE, TO A COMPOUND IN THE REMOTE JUNGLES OF PAPUA, NEW GUINEA...
STEVE!
...WHERE WE FOUND STEVE. BUT TO CALL HIM "WORSE FOR WEAR" WOULD BE AN UNDERSTATEMENT.
HE AND OTHERS HAD BEEN TRANSFORMED INTO MINDLESS CREATURES.
AND MY HEART BROKE AS I WENT INTO BATTLE.
SMART MOVE BY DEIMOS...
LOOKS LIKE WE FOUND HIM, DIANA.

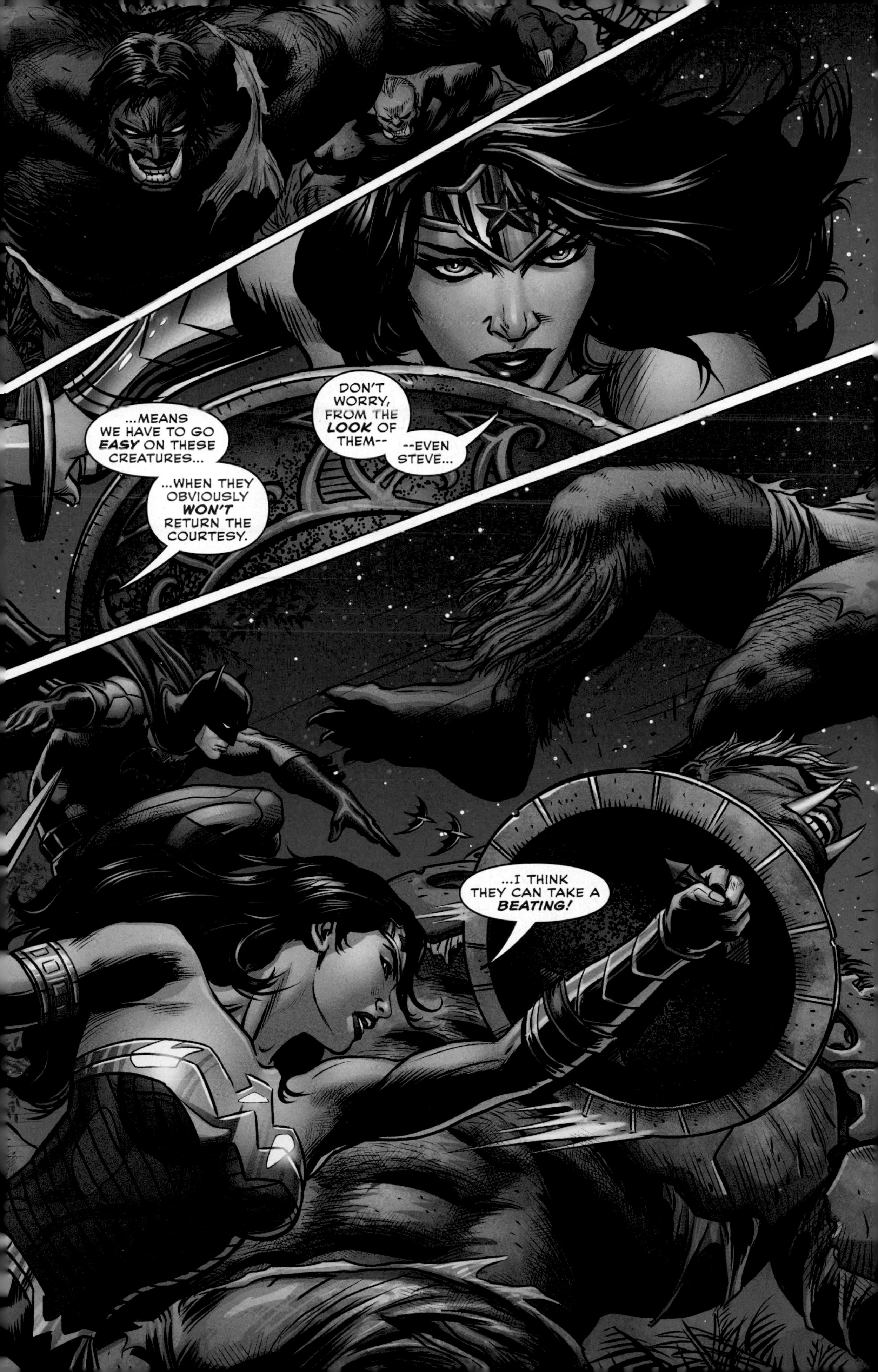
...MEANS WE HAVE TO GO EASY ON THESE CREATURES...
...WHEN THEY OBVIOUSLY WON'T RETURN THE COURTESY.
DON'T WORRY, FROM THE LOOK OF THEM--
--EVEN STEVE...
...I THINK THEY CAN TAKE A BEATING!

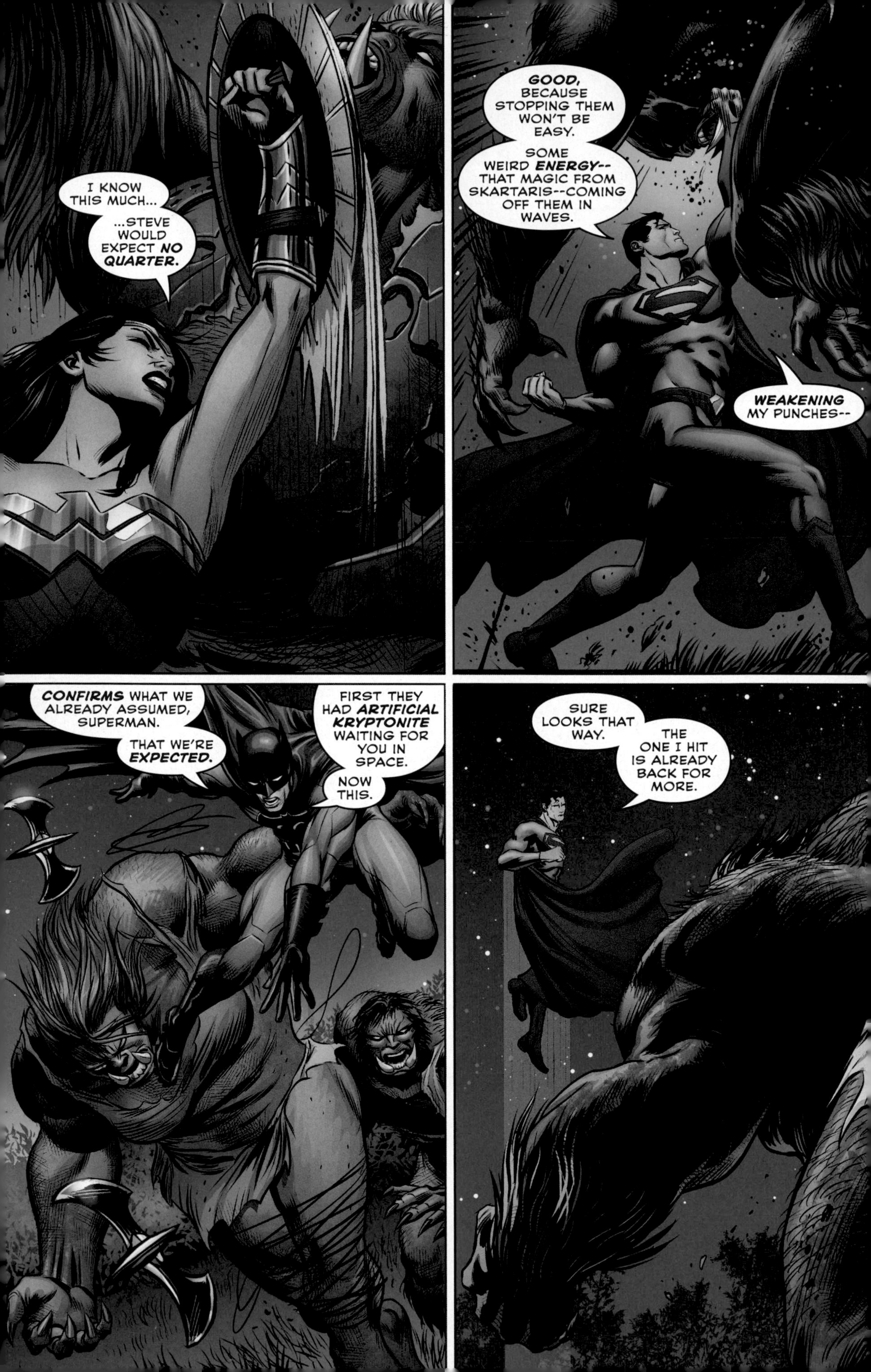
I KNOW THIS MUCH...
...STEVE WOULD EXPECT NO QUARTER.
GOOD, BECAUSE STOPPING THEM WON'T BE EASY.
SOME WEIRD ENERGY--THAT MAGIC FROM SKARTARIS--COMING OFF THEM IN WAVES.
WEAKENING MY PUNCHES--
CONFIRMS WHAT WE ALREADY ASSUMED, SUPERMAN.
THAT WE'RE EXPECTED.
FIRST THEY HAD ARTIFICIAL KRYPTONITE WAITING FOR YOU IN SPACE.
NOW THIS.
SURE LOOKS THAT WAY.
THE ONE I HIT IS ALREADY BACK FOR MORE.

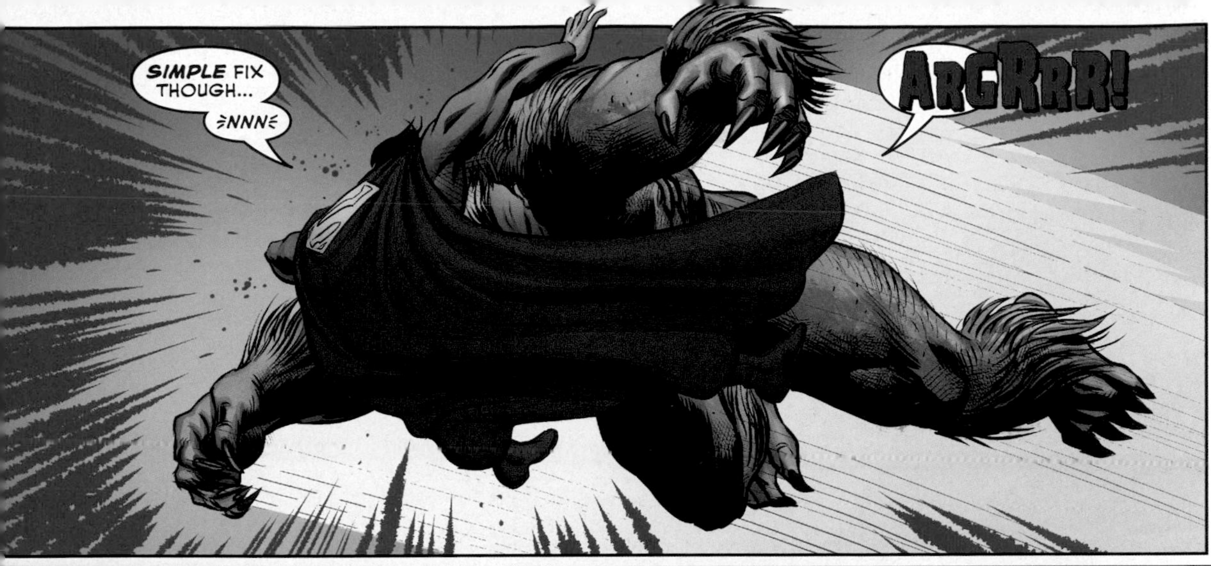
SIMPLE FIX THOUGH...
NNN
ARGRRR!
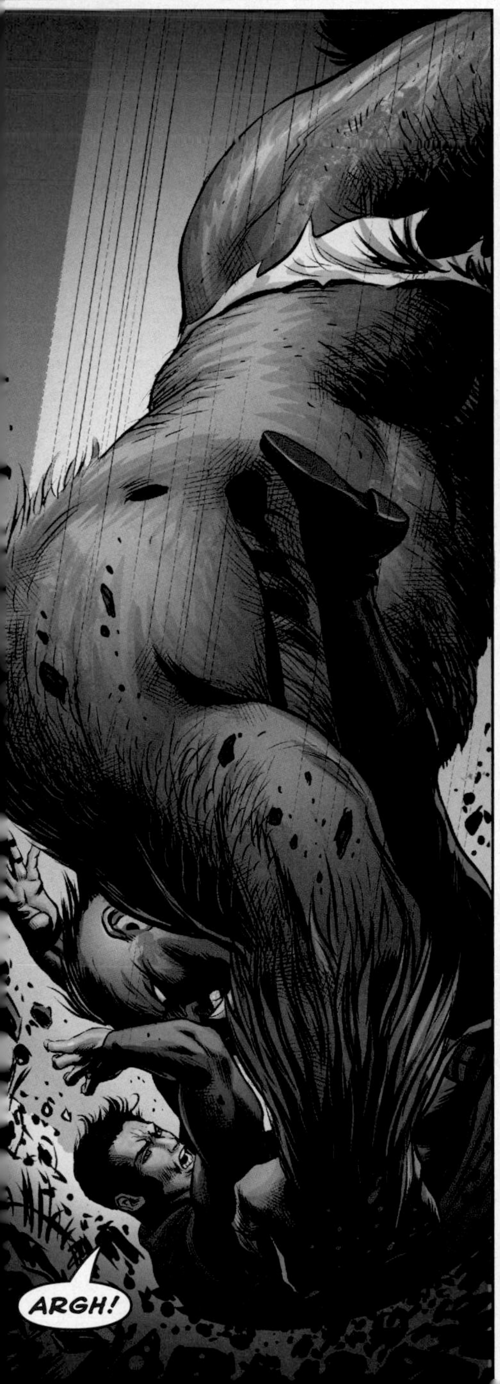
ARGH!
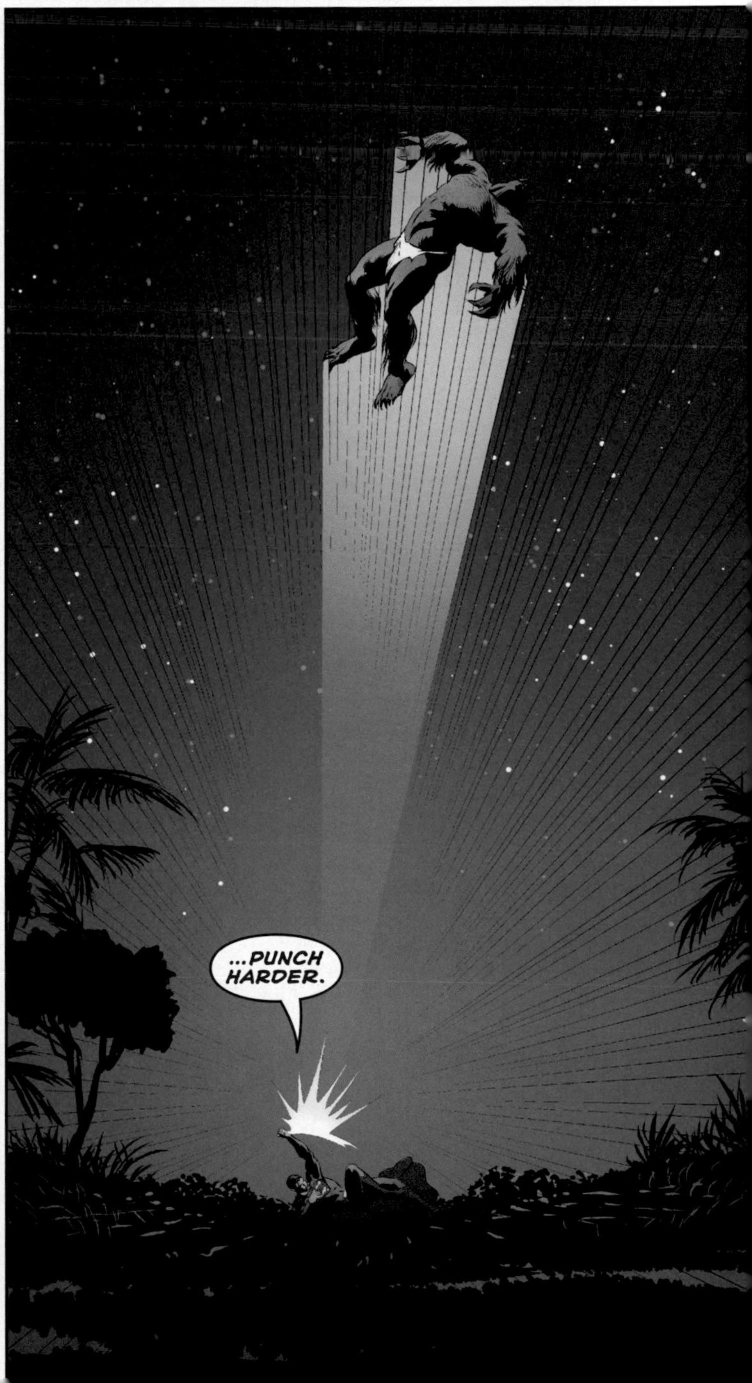
...PUNCH HARDER.

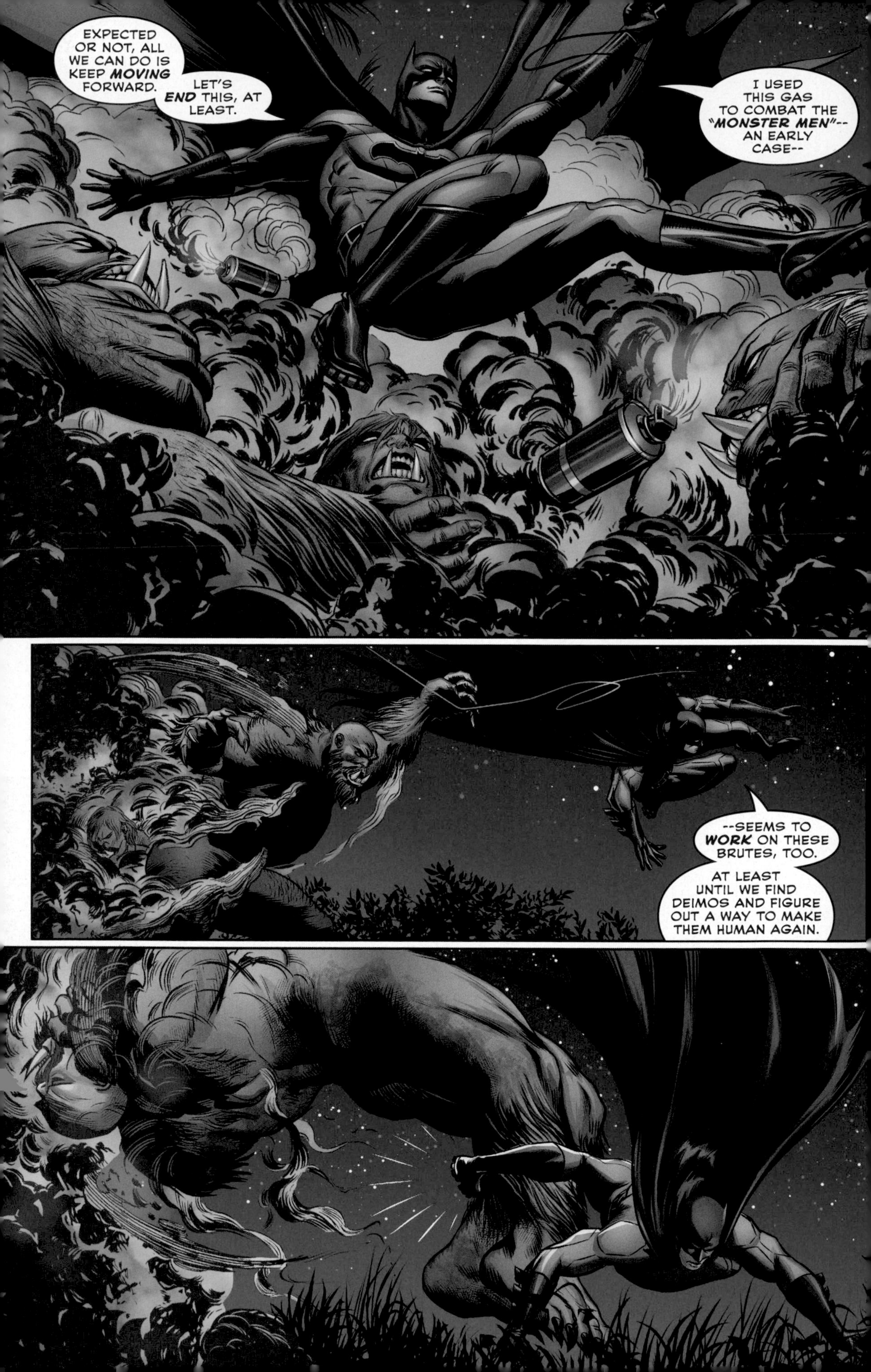
EXPECTED OR NOT, ALL WE CAN DO IS KEEP MOVING FORWARD.
LET'S END THIS, AT LEAST.
I USED THIS GAS TO COMBAT THE "MONSTER MEN"-- AN EARLY CASE--
--SEEMS TO WORK ON THESE BRUTES, TOO.
AT LEAST UNTIL WE FIND DEIMOS AND FIGURE OUT A WAY TO MAKE THEM HUMAN AGAIN.

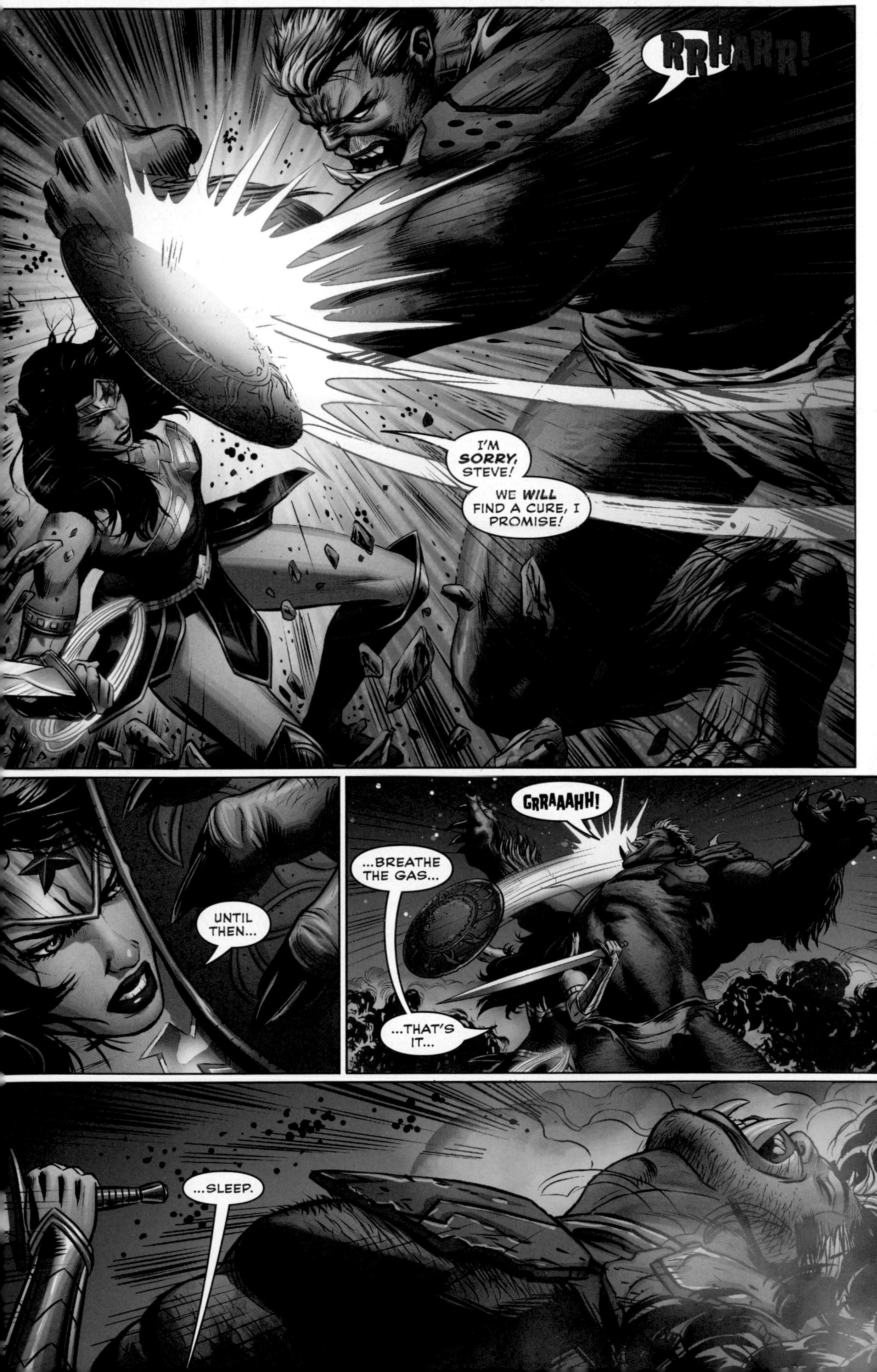
RRHARRR!
I'M SORRY, STEVE!
WE WILL FIND A CURE, I PROMISE!
UNTIL THEN...
GRRAAAHH!
...BREATHE THE GAS...
...THAT'S IT...
...SLEEP.

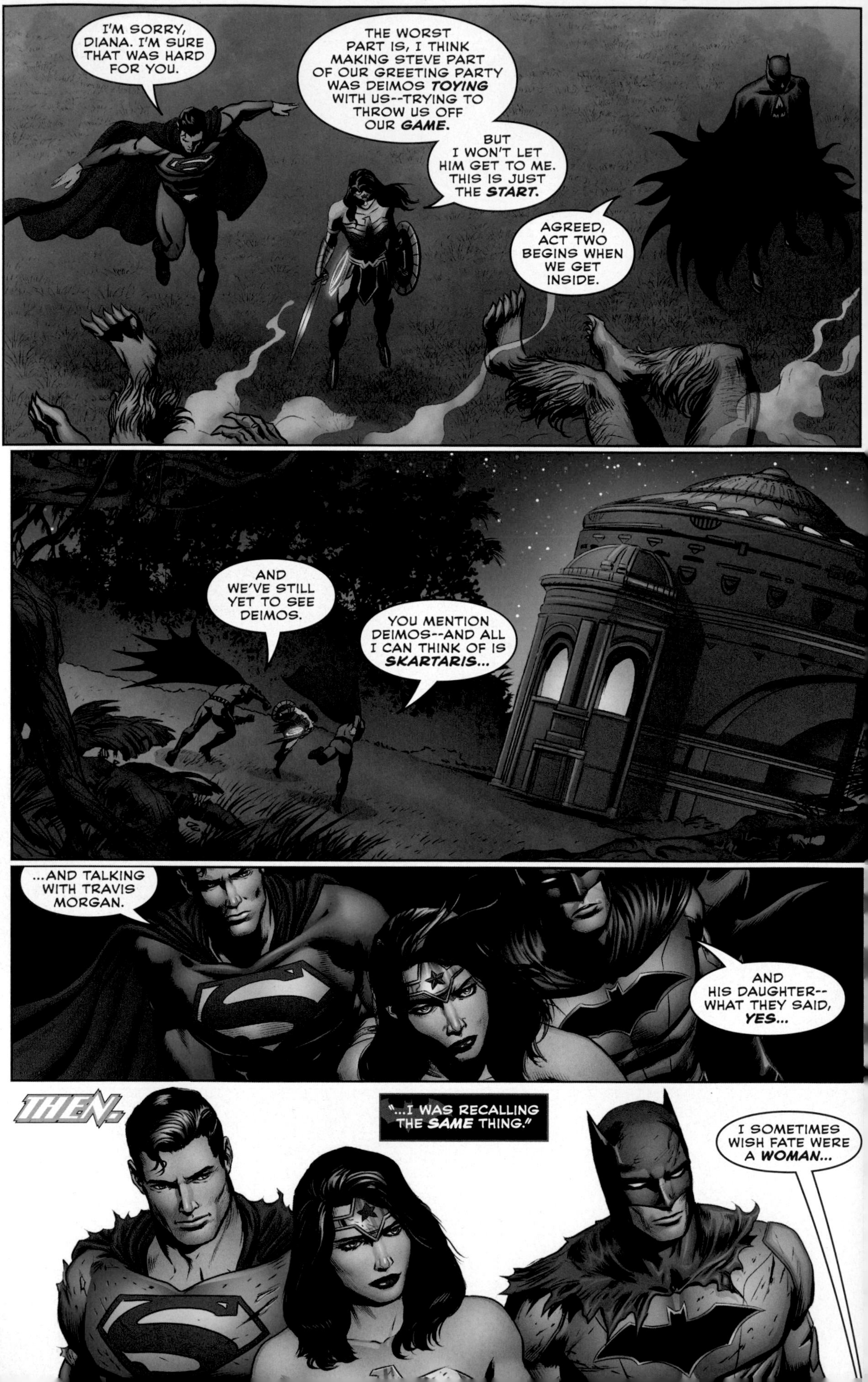
I'M SORRY, DIANA. I'M SURE THAT WAS HARD FOR YOU.
THE WORST PART IS, I THINK MAKING STEVE PART OF OUR GREETING PARTY WAS DEIMOS TOYING WITH US--TRYING TO THROW US OFF OUR GAME.
BUT I WON'T LET HIM GET TO ME. THIS IS JUST THE START.
AGREED, ACT TWO BEGINS WHEN WE GET INSIDE.
AND WE'VE STILL YET TO SEE DEIMOS.
YOU MENTION DEIMOS--AND ALL I CAN THINK OF IS SKARTARIS...
...AND TALKING WITH TRAVIS MORGAN.
AND HIS DAUGHTER--WHAT THEY SAID, YES...
THEN.
"...I WAS RECALLING THE SAME THING."
I SOMETIMES WISH FATE WERE A WOMAN...

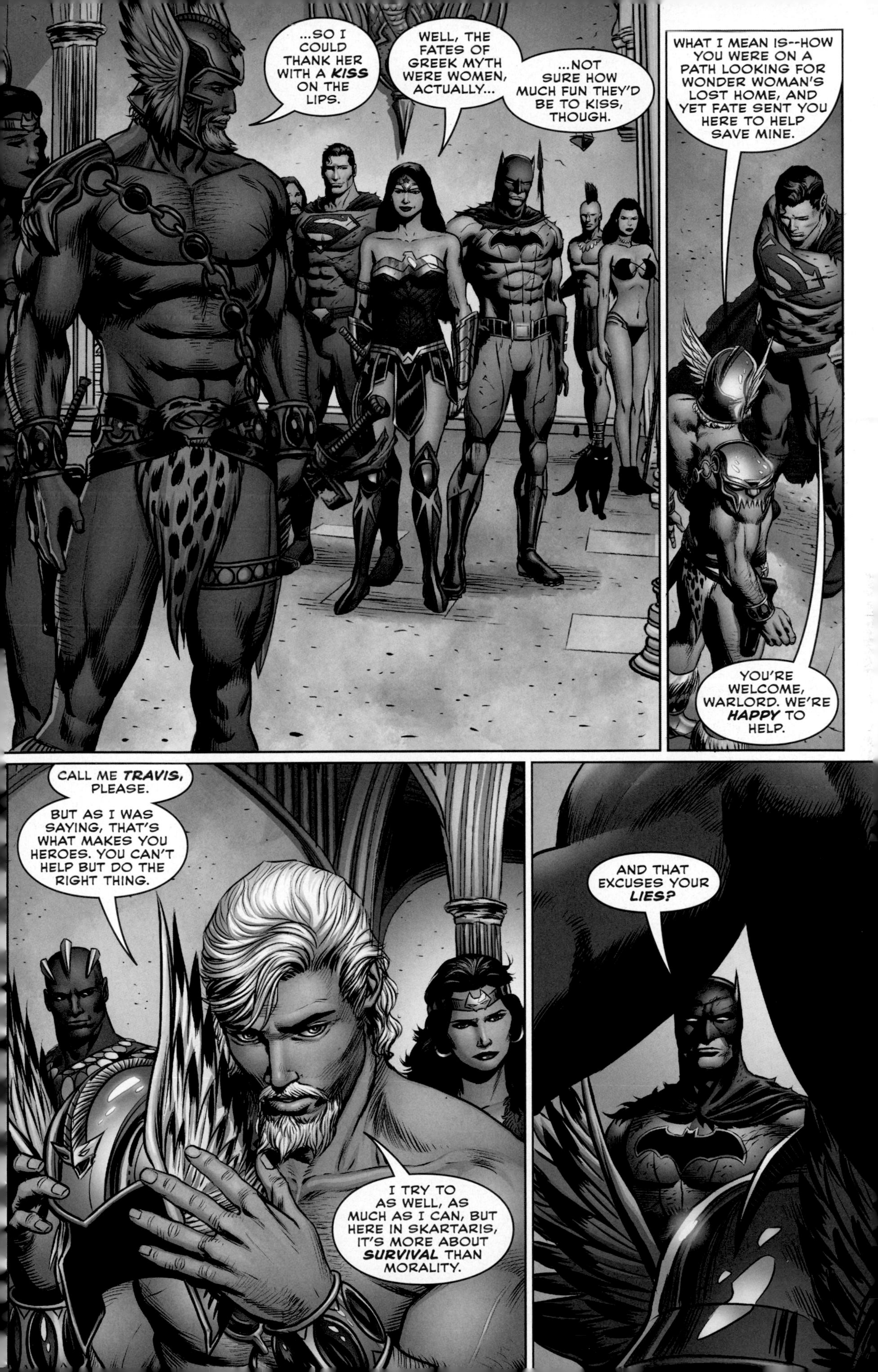
...SO I COULD THANK HER WITH A KISS ON THE LIPS.
WELL, THE FATES OF GREEK MYTH WERE WOMEN, ACTUALLY...
...NOT SURE HOW MUCH FUN THEY'D BE TO KISS, THOUGH.
WHAT I MEAN IS--HOW YOU WERE ON A PATH LOOKING FOR WONDER WOMAN'S LOST HOME, AND YET FATE SENT YOU HERE TO HELP SAVE MINE.
YOU'RE WELCOME, WARLORD. WE'RE HAPPY TO HELP.
CALL ME TRAVIS, PLEASE.
BUT AS I WAS SAYING, THAT'S WHAT MAKES YOU HEROES. YOU CAN'T HELP BUT DO THE RIGHT THING.
I TRY TO AS WELL, AS MUCH AS I CAN, BUT HERE IN SKARTARIS, IT'S MORE ABOUT SURVIVAL THAN MORALITY.
AND THAT EXCUSES YOUR LIES?

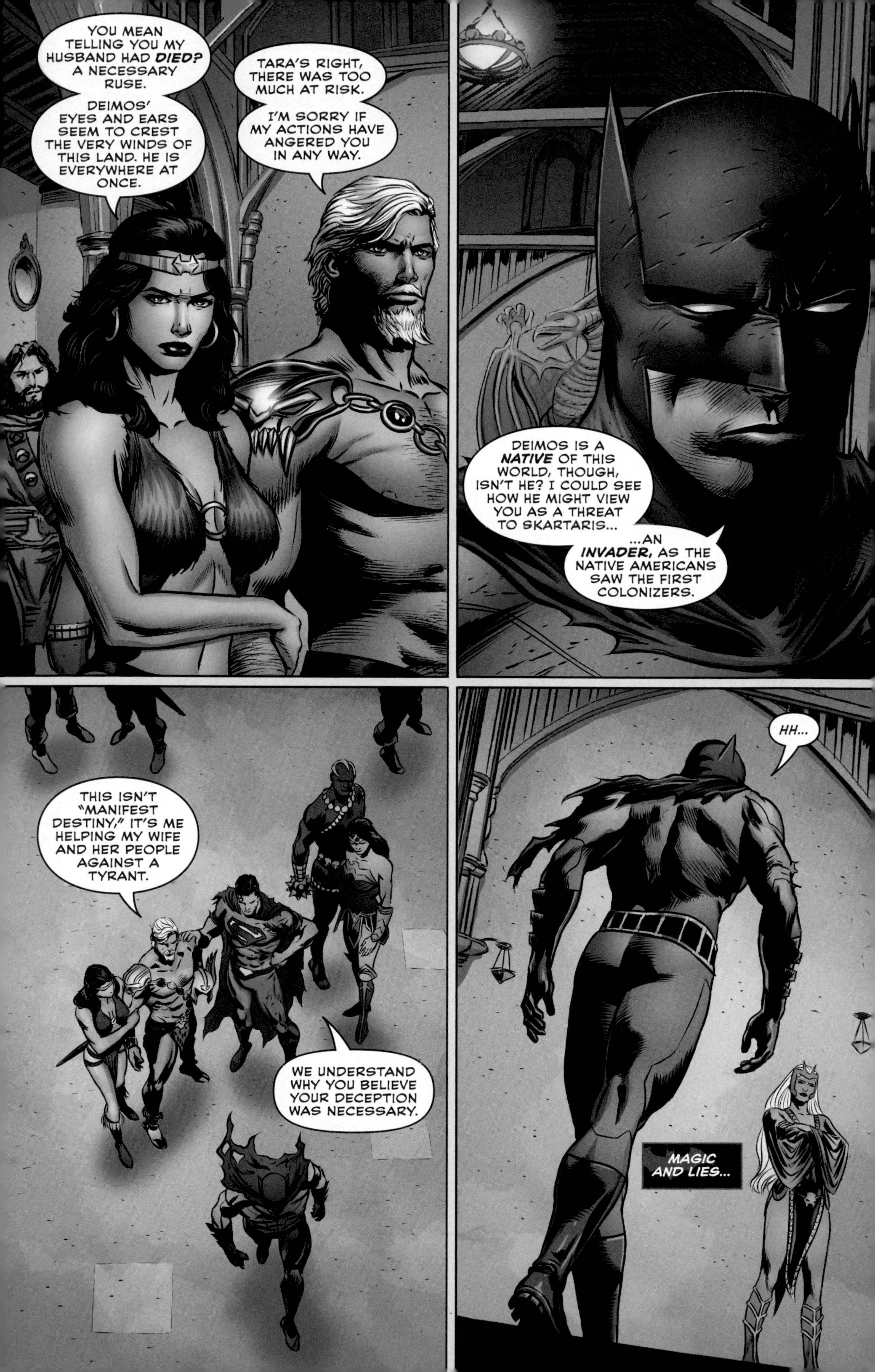
YOU MEAN TELLING YOU MY HUSBAND HAD DIED? A NECESSARY RUSE.
DEIMOS' EYES AND EARS SEEM TO CREST THE VERY WINDS OF THIS LAND. HE IS EVERYWHERE AT ONCE.
TARA'S RIGHT, THERE WAS TOO MUCH AT RISK.
I'M SORRY IF MY ACTIONS HAVE ANGERED YOU IN ANY WAY.
DEIMOS IS A NATIVE OF THIS WORLD, THOUGH, ISN'T HE? I COULD SEE HOW HE MIGHT VIEW YOU AS A THREAT TO SKARTARIS...
...AN INVADER, AS THE NATIVE AMERICANS SAW THE FIRST COLONIZERS.
THIS ISN'T "MANIFEST DESTINY," IT'S ME HELPING MY WIFE AND HER PEOPLE AGAINST A TYRANT.
WE UNDERSTAND WHY YOU BELIEVE YOUR DECEPTION WAS NECESSARY.
HH...
MAGIC AND LIES...

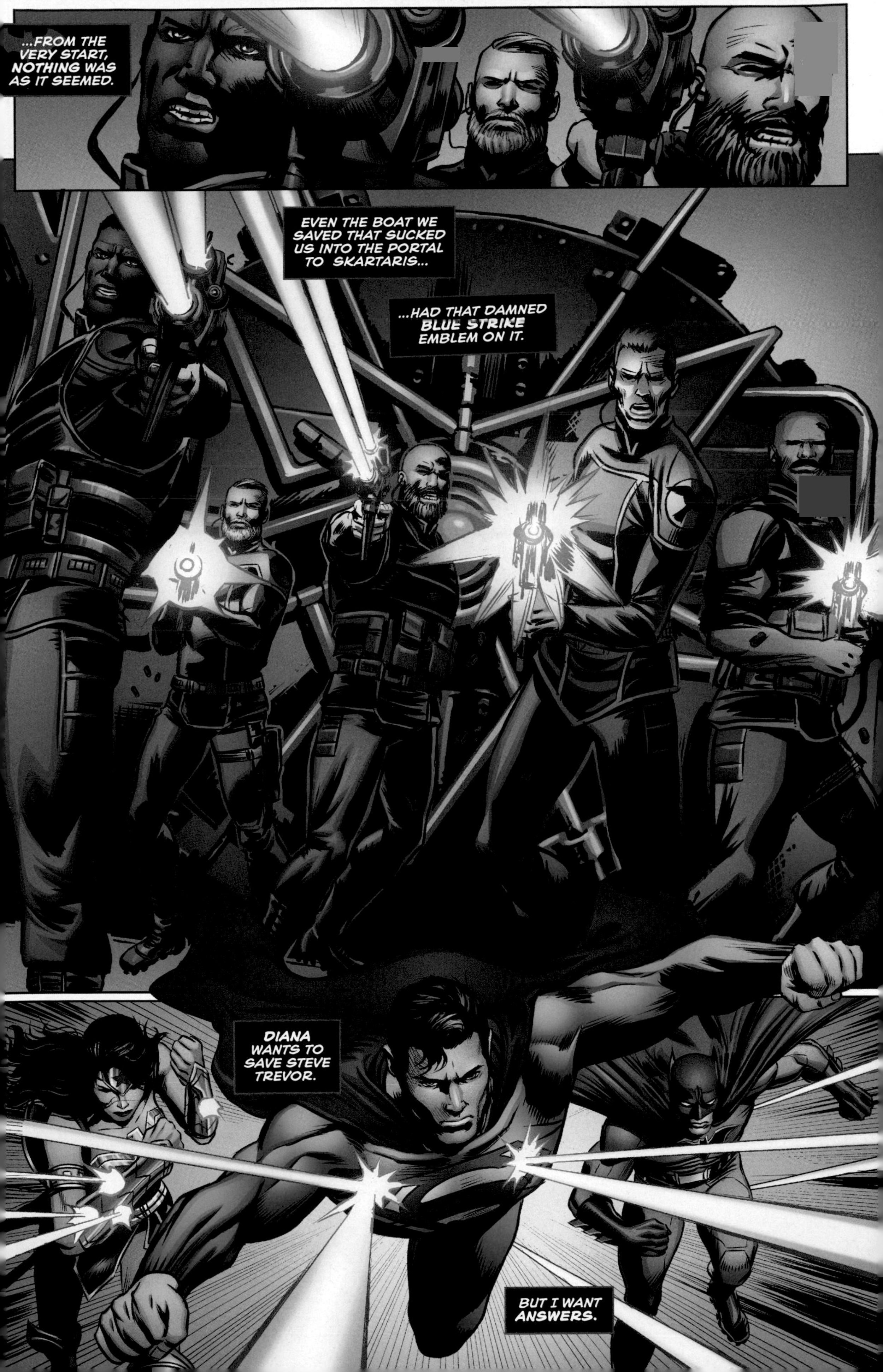
...FROM THE VERY START, NOTHING WAS AS IT SEEMED.
EVEN THE BOAT WE SAVED THAT SUCKED US INTO THE PORTAL TO SKARTARIS...
...HAD THAT DAMNED BLUE STRIKE EMBLEM ON IT.
DIANA WANTS TO SAVE STEVE TREVOR.
BUT I WANT ANSWERS.

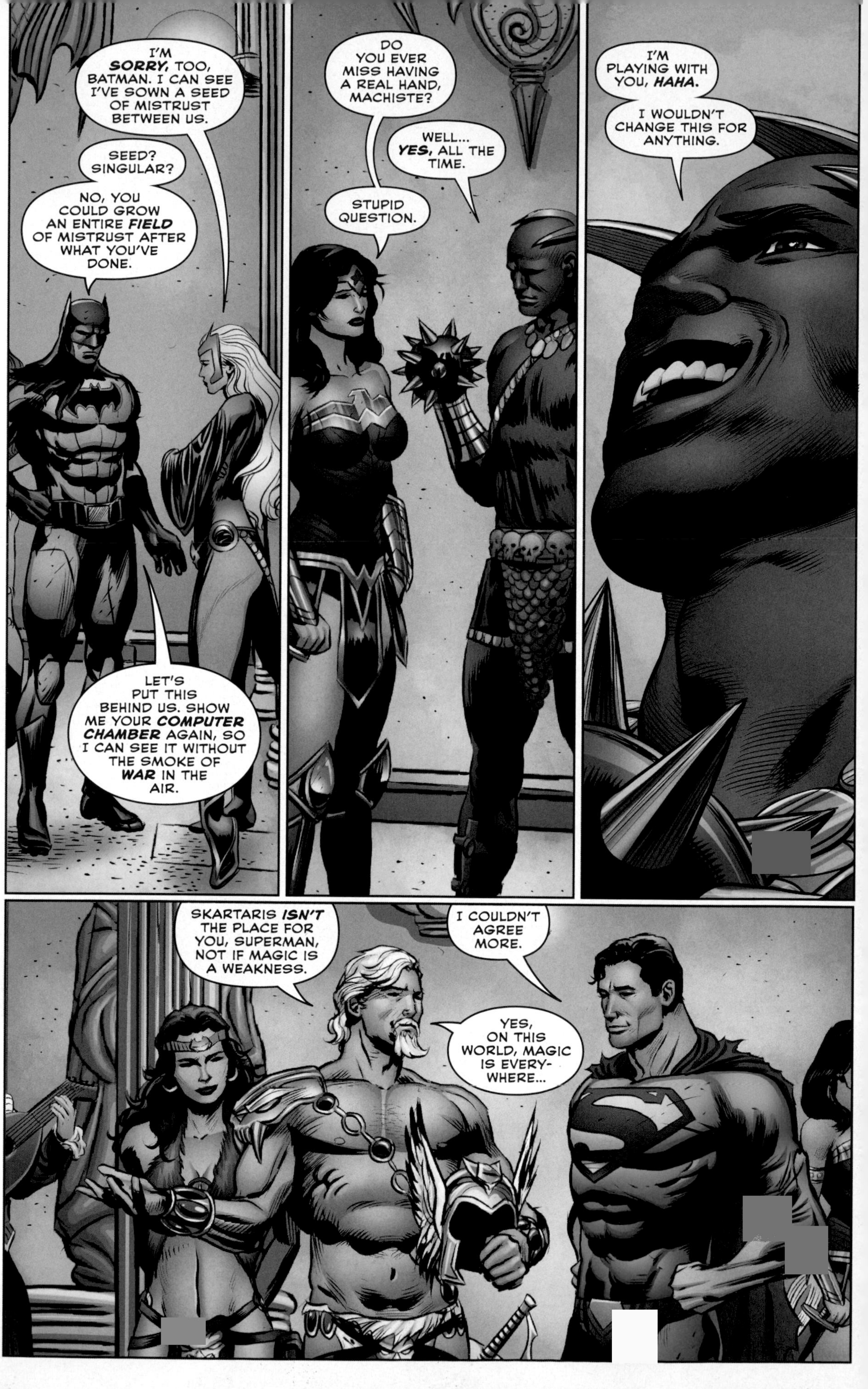

I'M SORRY, TOO, BATMAN. I CAN SEE I'VE SOWN A SEED OF MISTRUST BETWEEN US.
SEED? SINGULAR?
NO, YOU COULD GROW AN ENTIRE FIELD OF MISTRUST AFTER WHAT YOU'VE DONE.
LET'S PUT THIS BEHIND US. SHOW ME YOUR COMPUTER CHAMBER AGAIN, SO I CAN SEE IT WITHOUT THE SMOKE OF WAR IN THE AIR.
DO YOU EVER MISS HAVING A REAL HAND, MACHISTE?
WELL... YES, ALL THE TIME.
STUPID QUESTION.
I'M PLAYING WITH YOU, HAHA.
I WOULDN'T CHANGE THIS FOR ANYTHING.
SKARTARIS ISN'T THE PLACE FOR YOU, SUPERMAN, NOT IF MAGIC IS A WEAKNESS.
I COULDN'T AGREE MORE.
YES, ON THIS WORLD, MAGIC IS EVERY-WHERE...

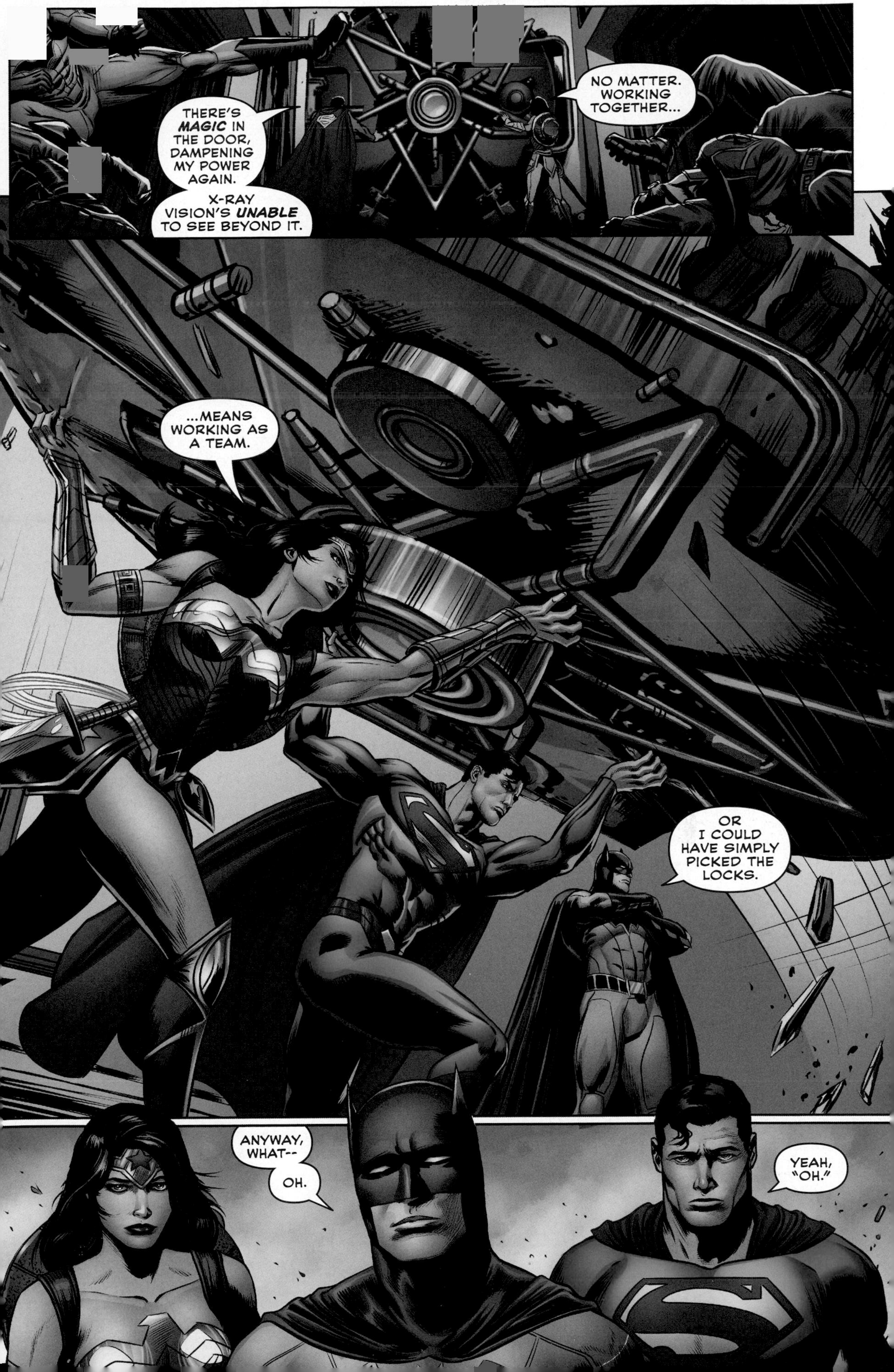
THERE'S ***MAGIC*** IN THE DOOR, DAMPENING MY POWER AGAIN.
X-RAY VISION'S ***UNABLE*** TO SEE BEYOND IT.
NO MATTER. WORKING TOGETHER...
...MEANS WORKING AS A TEAM.
OR I COULD HAVE SIMPLY PICKED THE LOCKS.
ANYWAY, WHAT--
OH.
YEAH, "OH."

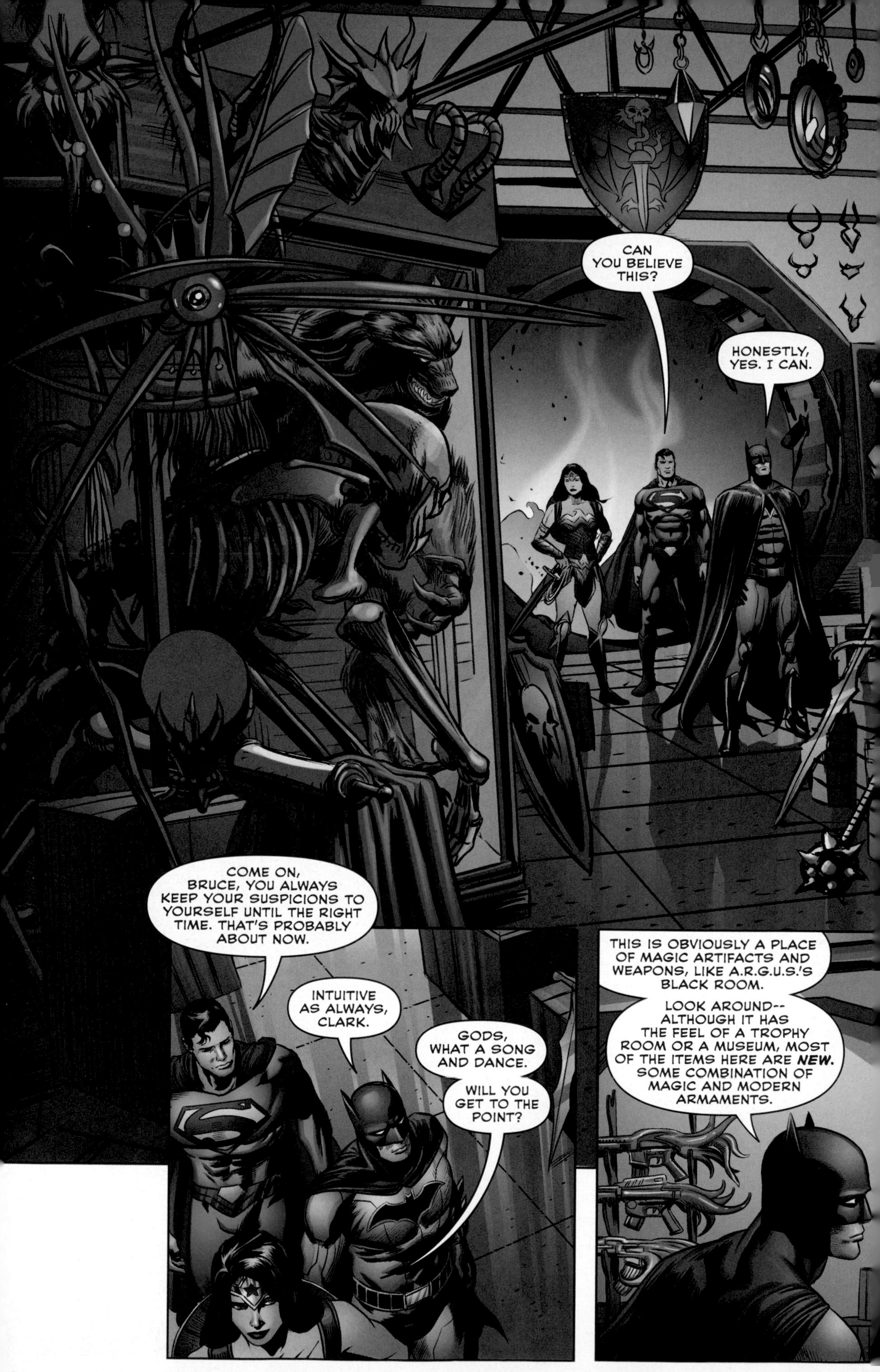
CAN YOU BELIEVE THIS?
HONESTLY, YES. I CAN.
COME ON, BRUCE, YOU ALWAYS KEEP YOUR SUSPICIONS TO YOURSELF UNTIL THE RIGHT TIME. THAT'S PROBABLY ABOUT NOW.
INTUITIVE AS ALWAYS, CLARK.
GODS, WHAT A SONG AND DANCE.
WILL YOU GET TO THE POINT?
THIS IS OBVIOUSLY A PLACE OF MAGIC ARTIFACTS AND WEAPONS, LIKE A.R.G.U.S.'s BLACK ROOM.
LOOK AROUND-- ALTHOUGH IT HAS THE FEEL OF A TROPHY ROOM OR A MUSEUM, MOST OF THE ITEMS HERE ARE ***NEW***. SOME COMBINATION OF MAGIC AND MODERN ARMAMENTS.

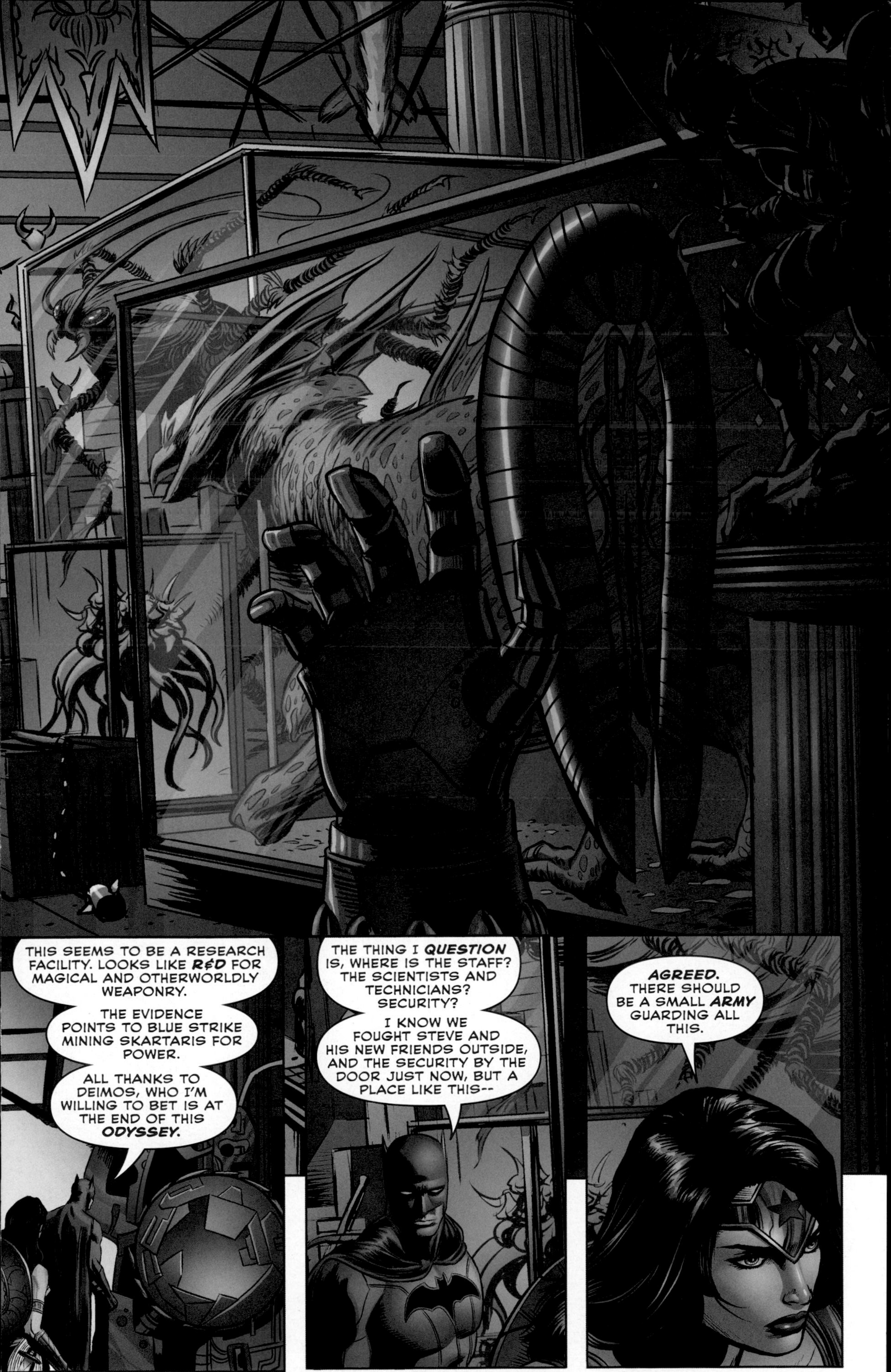
THIS SEEMS TO BE A RESEARCH FACILITY. LOOKS LIKE R&D FOR MAGICAL AND OTHERWORLDLY WEAPONRY.
THE EVIDENCE POINTS TO BLUE STRIKE MINING SKARTARIS FOR POWER.
ALL THANKS TO DEIMOS, WHO I'M WILLING TO BET IS AT THE END OF THIS ODYSSEY.
THE THING I QUESTION IS, WHERE IS THE STAFF? THE SCIENTISTS AND TECHNICIANS? SECURITY?
I KNOW WE FOUGHT STEVE AND HIS NEW FRIENDS OUTSIDE, AND THE SECURITY BY THE DOOR JUST NOW, BUT A PLACE LIKE THIS--
AGREED. THERE SHOULD BE A SMALL ARMY GUARDING ALL THIS.

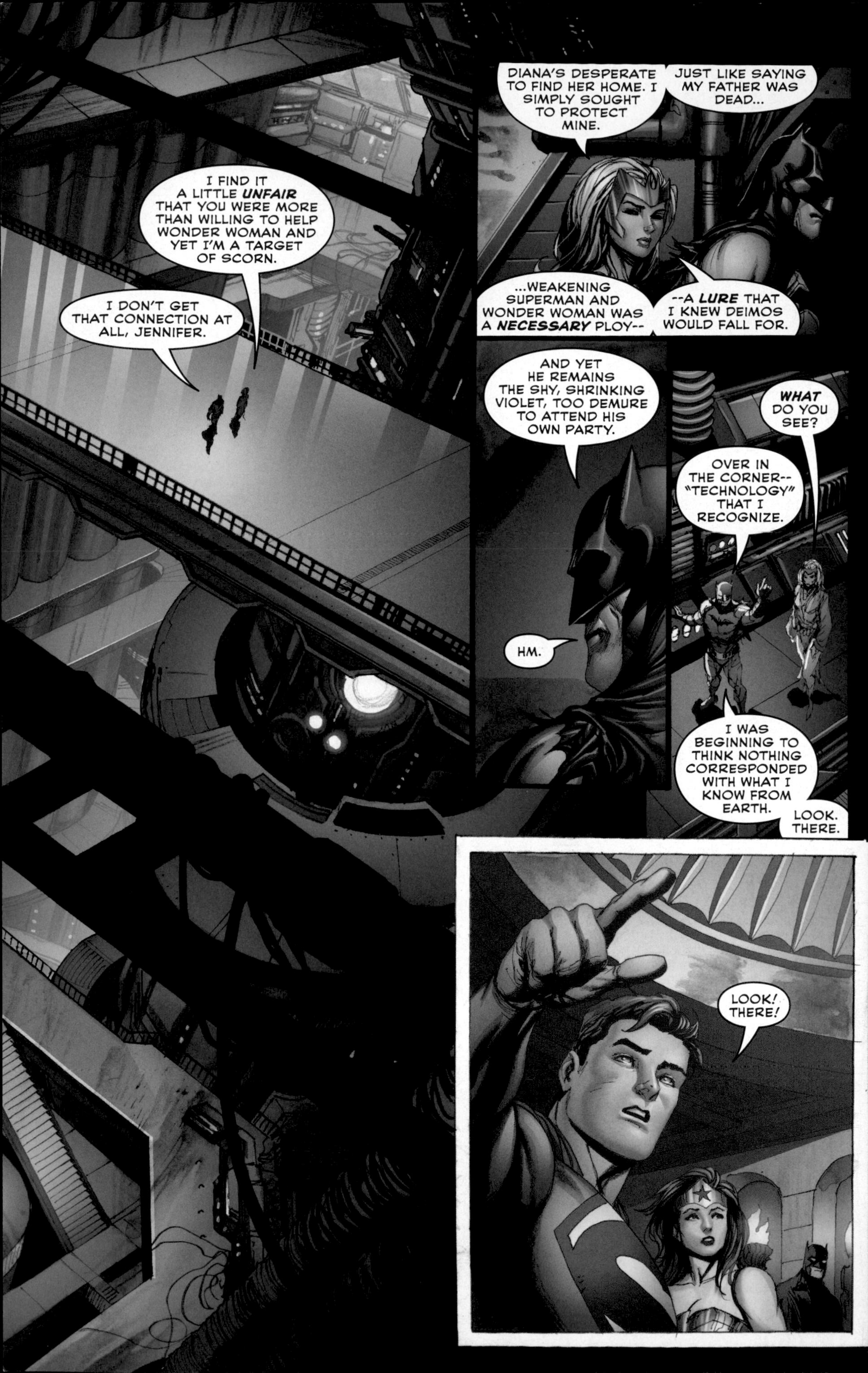
I FIND IT A LITTLE UNFAIR THAT YOU WERE MORE THAN WILLING TO HELP WONDER WOMAN AND YET I'M A TARGET OF SCORN.
I DON'T GET THAT CONNECTION AT ALL, JENNIFER.
DIANA'S DESPERATE TO FIND HER HOME. I SIMPLY SOUGHT TO PROTECT MINE.
JUST LIKE SAYING MY FATHER WAS DEAD...
...WEAKENING SUPERMAN AND WONDER WOMAN WAS A NECESSARY PLOY--
--A LURE THAT I KNEW DEIMOS WOULD FALL FOR.
AND YET HE REMAINS THE SHY, SHRINKING VIOLET, TOO DEMURE TO ATTEND HIS OWN PARTY.
HM.
WHAT DO YOU SEE?
OVER IN THE CORNER-- "TECHNOLOGY" THAT I RECOGNIZE.
I WAS BEGINNING TO THINK NOTHING CORRESPONDED WITH WHAT I KNOW FROM EARTH.
LOOK. THERE.
LOOK! THERE!

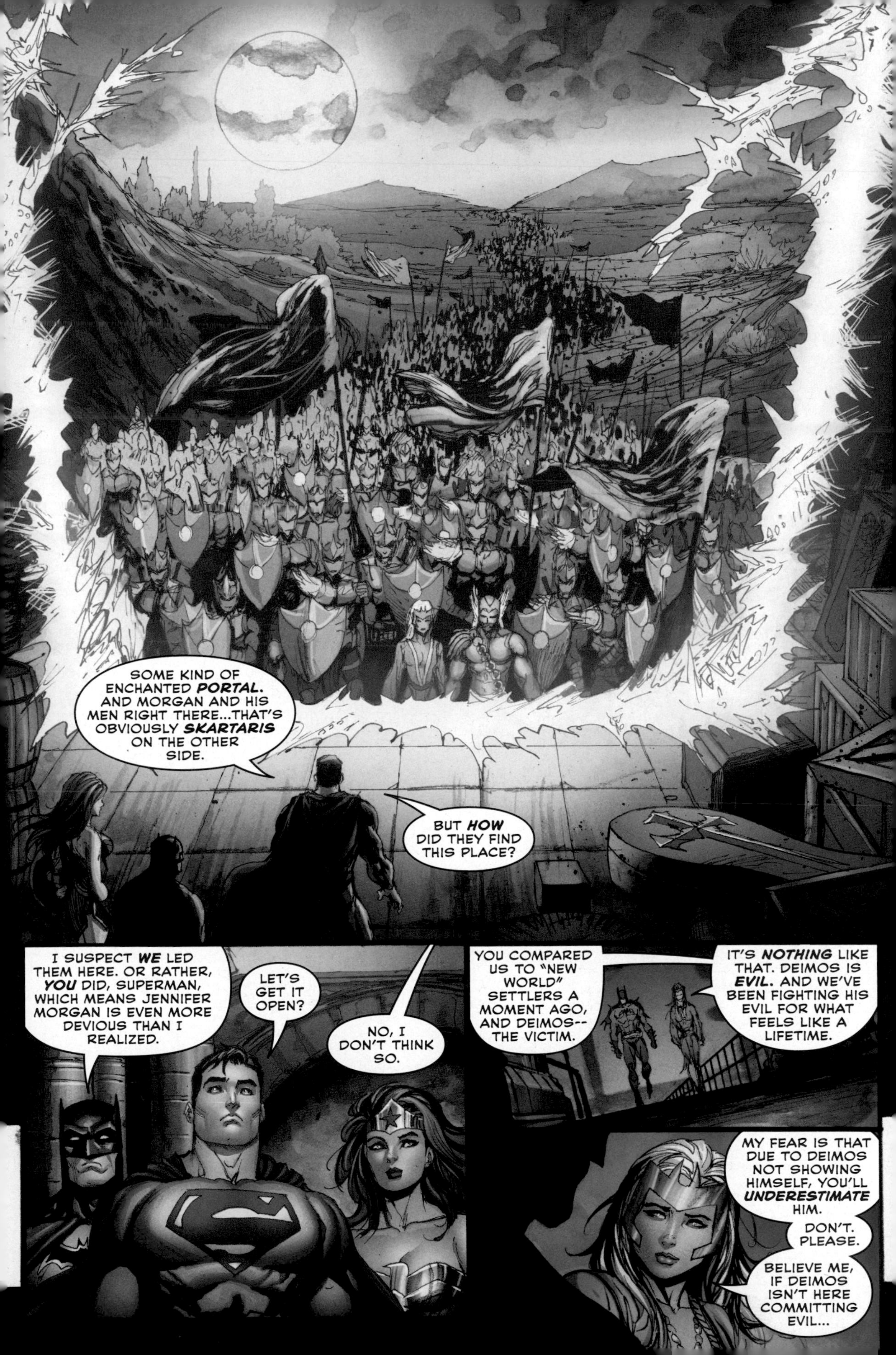
SOME KIND OF ENCHANTED PORTAL. AND MORGAN AND HIS MEN RIGHT THERE...THAT'S OBVIOUSLY SKARTARIS ON THE OTHER SIDE.
BUT HOW DID THEY FIND THIS PLACE?
I SUSPECT WE LED THEM HERE. OR RATHER, YOU DID, SUPERMAN, WHICH MEANS JENNIFER MORGAN IS EVEN MORE DEVIOUS THAN I REALIZED.
LET'S GET IT OPEN?
NO, I DON'T THINK SO.
YOU COMPARED US TO "NEW WORLD" SETTLERS A MOMENT AGO, AND DEIMOS-- THE VICTIM.
IT'S NOTHING LIKE THAT. DEIMOS IS EVIL. AND WE'VE BEEN FIGHTING HIS EVIL FOR WHAT FEELS LIKE A LIFETIME.
MY FEAR IS THAT DUE TO DEIMOS NOT SHOWING HIMSELF, YOU'LL UNDERESTIMATE HIM.
DON'T. PLEASE.
BELIEVE ME, IF DEIMOS ISN'T HERE COMMITTING EVIL...

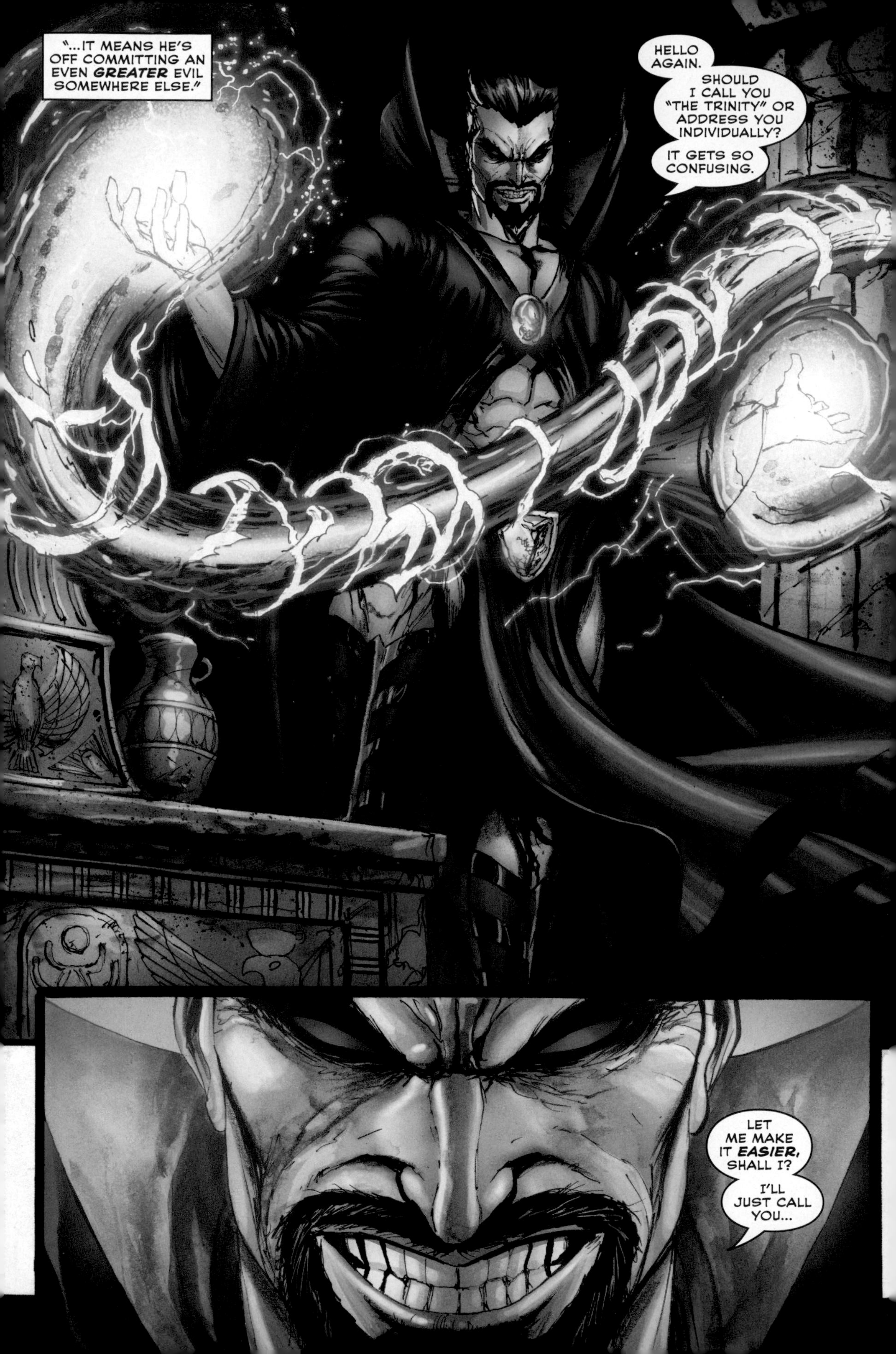
"...IT MEANS HE'S OFF COMMITTING AN EVEN **GREATER** EVIL SOMEWHERE ELSE."
HELLO AGAIN.
SHOULD I CALL YOU "THE TRINITY" OR ADDRESS YOU INDIVIDUALLY?
IT GETS SO CONFUSING.
LET ME MAKE IT **EASIER,** SHALL I?
I'LL JUST CALL YOU...

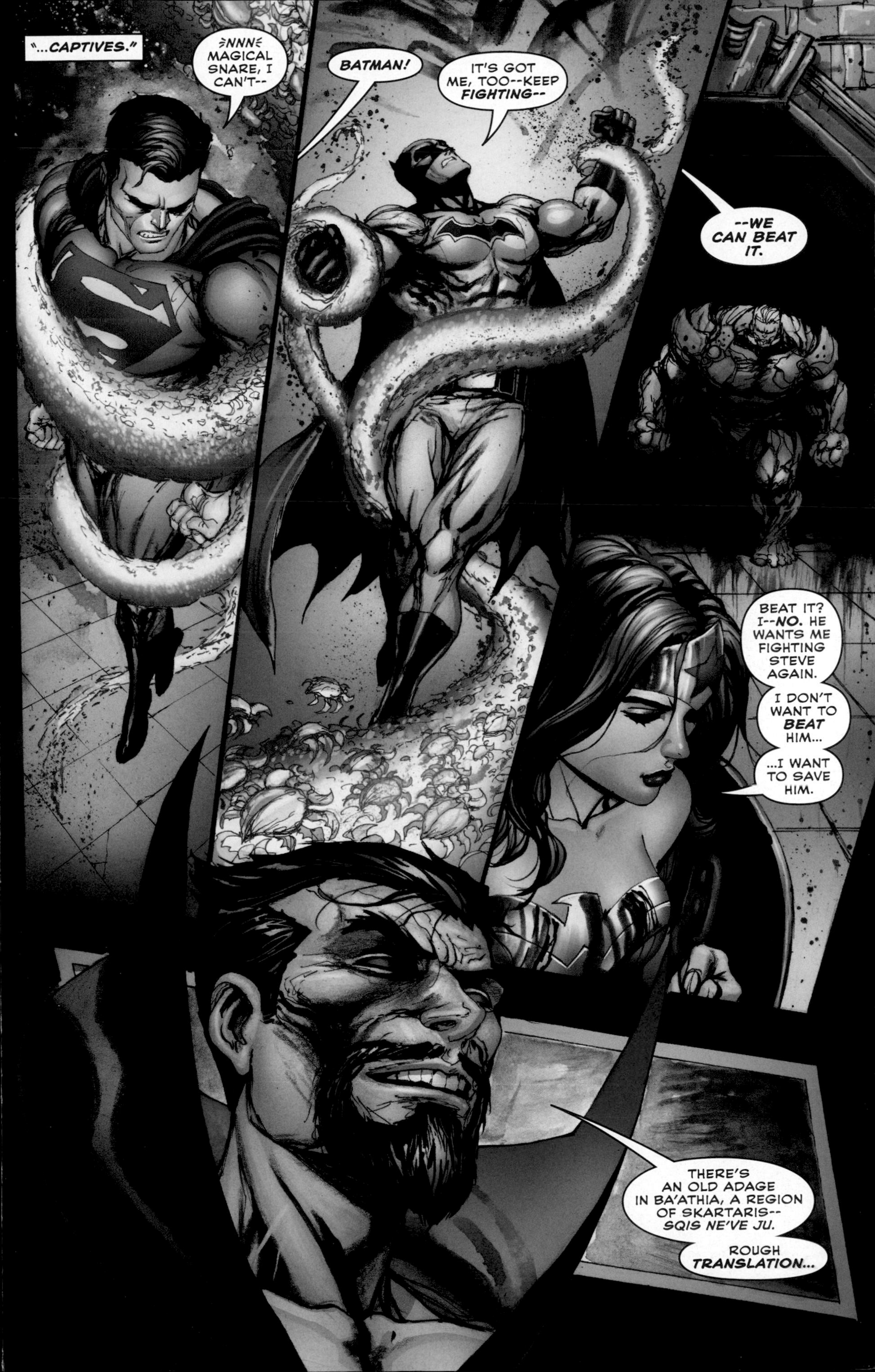
"...CAPTIVES."
NNN MAGICAL SNARE, I CAN'T--
BATMAN!
IT'S GOT ME, TOO--KEEP FIGHTING--
--WE CAN BEAT IT.
BEAT IT? I--NO. HE WANTS ME FIGHTING STEVE AGAIN.
I DON'T WANT TO BEAT HIM...
...I WANT TO SAVE HIM.
THERE'S AN OLD ADAGE IN BA'ATHIA, A REGION OF SKARTARIS-- SQIS NE'VE JU.
ROUGH TRANSLATION...

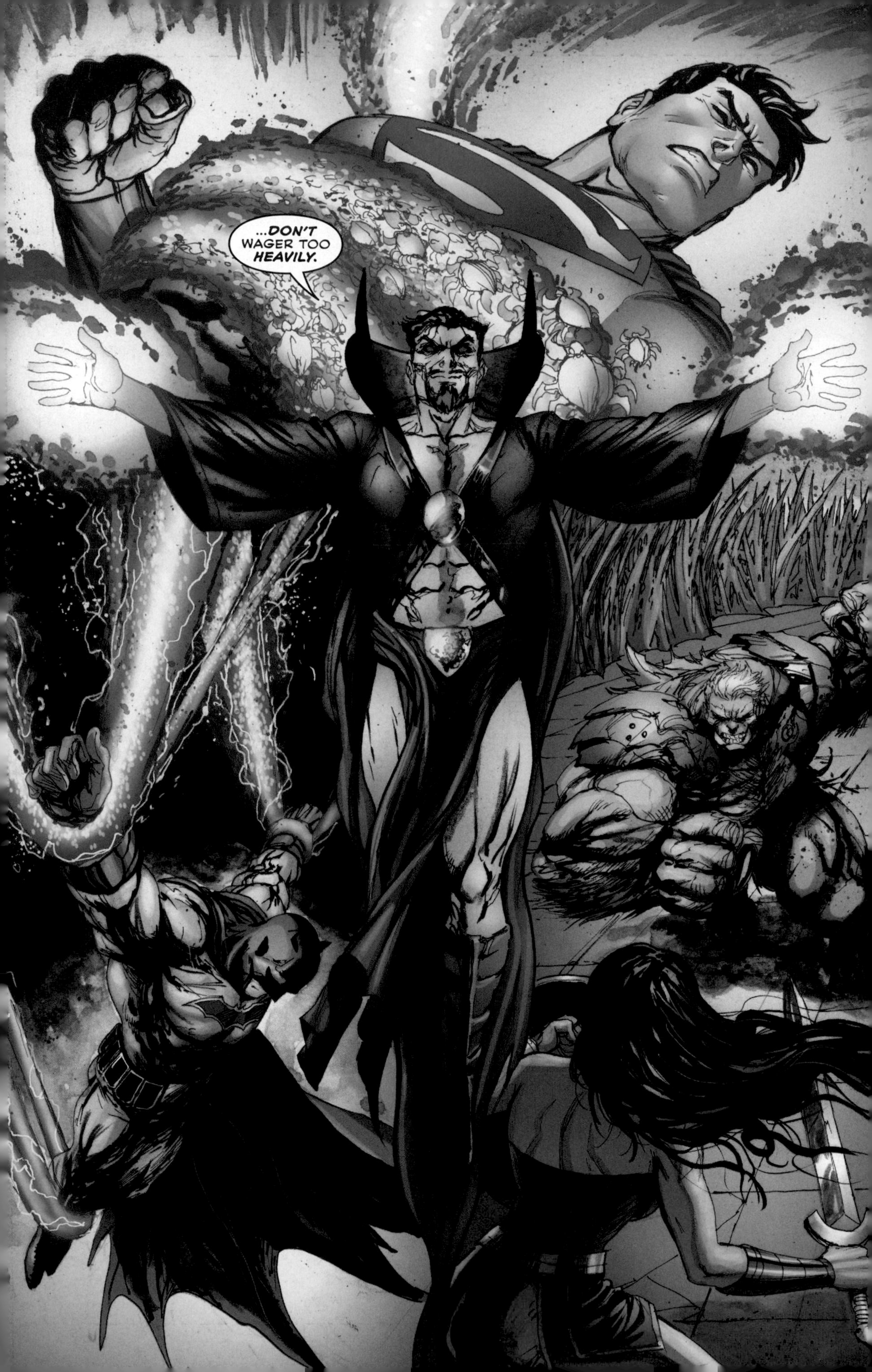
...DON'T WAGER TOO HEAVILY.

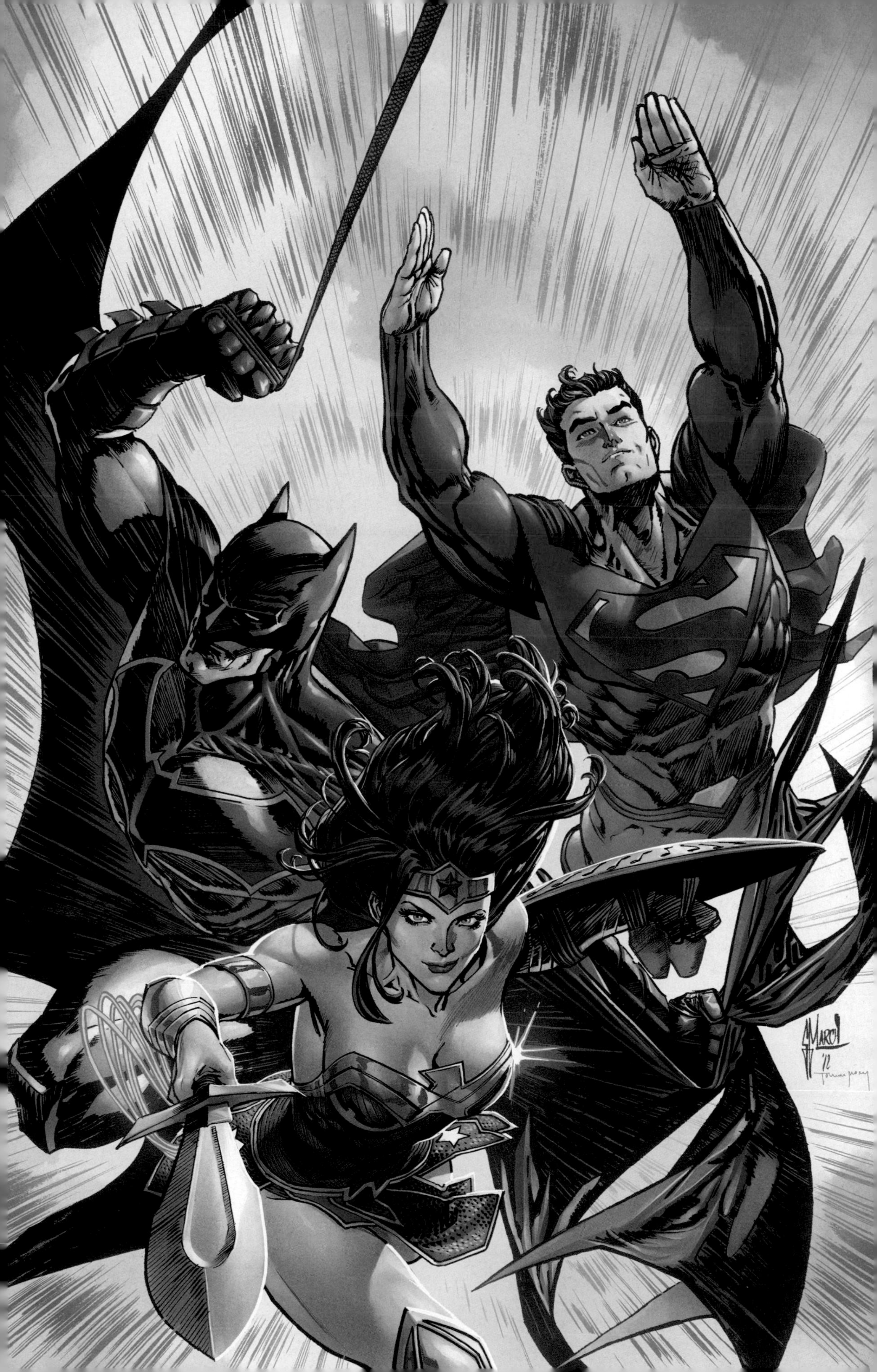

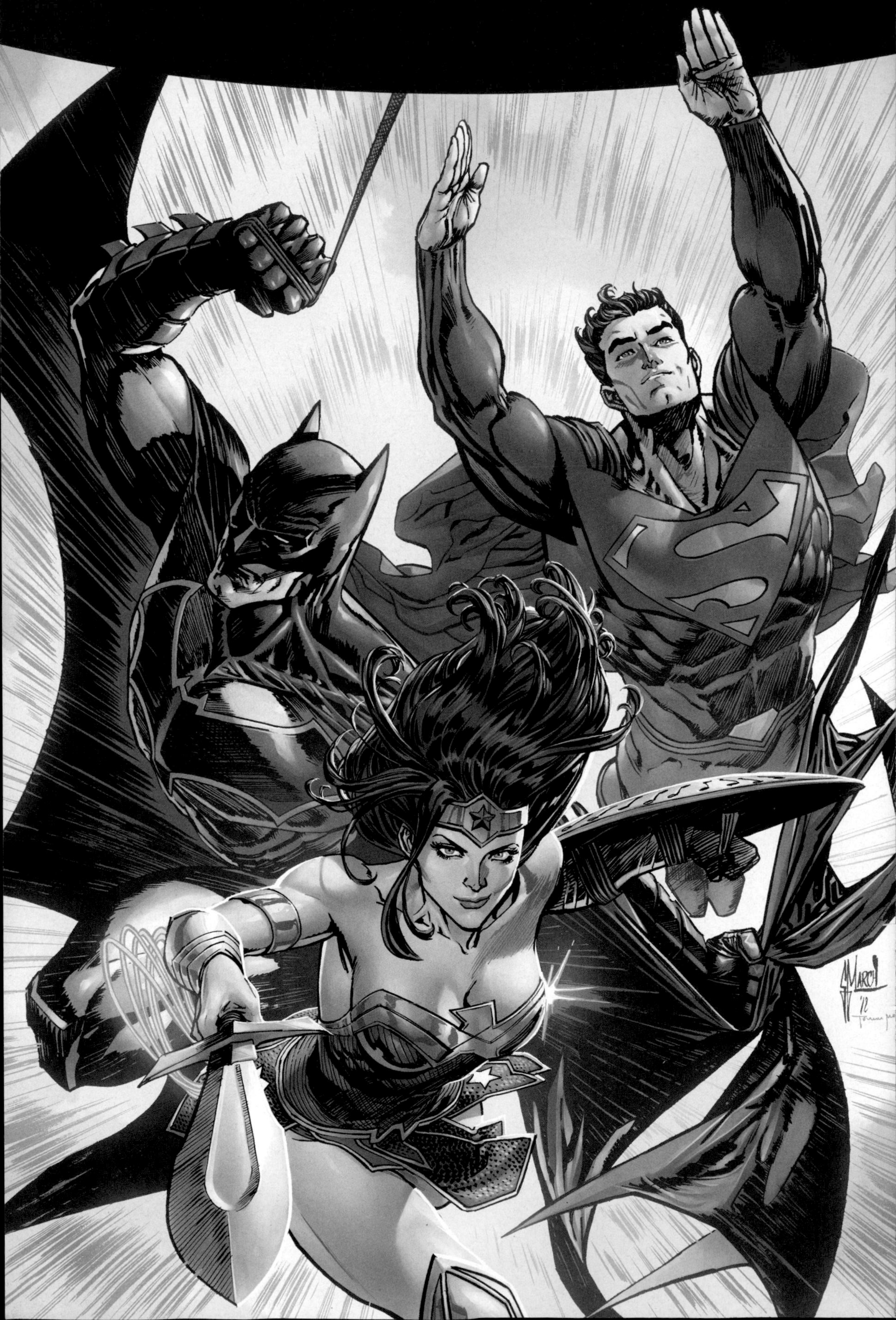

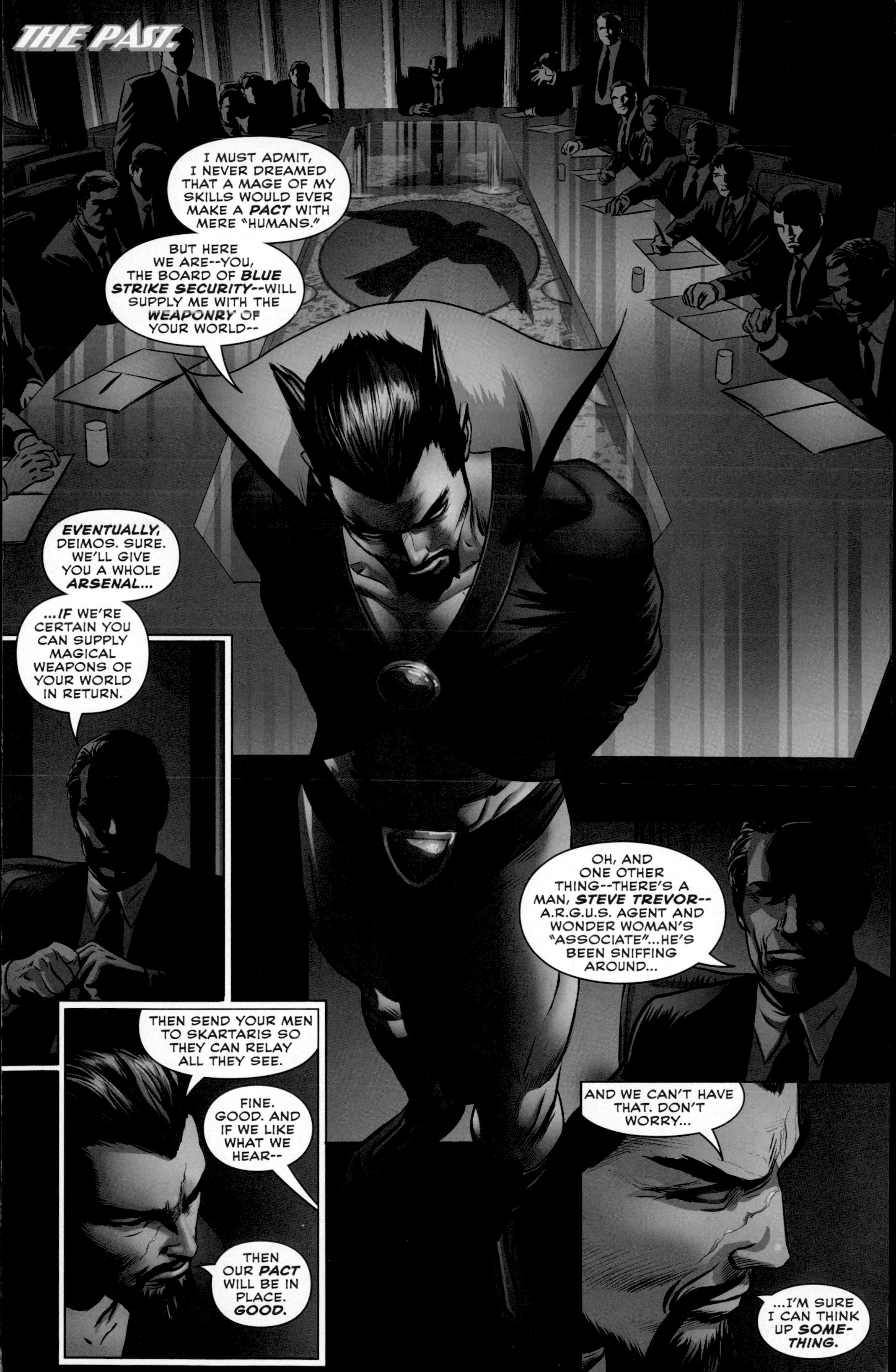
THE PAST.
I MUST ADMIT, I NEVER DREAMED THAT A MAGE OF MY SKILLS WOULD EVER MAKE A *PACT* WITH MERE "HUMANS."
BUT HERE WE ARE--YOU, THE BOARD OF *BLUE STRIKE SECURITY*--WILL SUPPLY ME WITH THE *WEAPONRY* OF YOUR WORLD--
EVENTUALLY, DEIMOS. SURE. WE'LL GIVE YOU A WHOLE *ARSENAL*...
...*IF* WE'RE CERTAIN YOU CAN SUPPLY MAGICAL WEAPONS OF YOUR WORLD IN RETURN.
OH, AND ONE OTHER THING--THERE'S A MAN, *STEVE TREVOR*--A.R.G.U.S. AGENT AND WONDER WOMAN'S "ASSOCIATE"...HE'S BEEN SNIFFING AROUND...
THEN SEND YOUR MEN TO SKARTARIS SO THEY CAN RELAY ALL THEY SEE.
FINE. GOOD. AND IF WE LIKE WHAT WE HEAR--
THEN OUR *PACT* WILL BE IN PLACE. *GOOD.*
AND WE CAN'T HAVE THAT. DON'T WORRY...
...I'M SURE I CAN THINK UP *SOME-THING.*

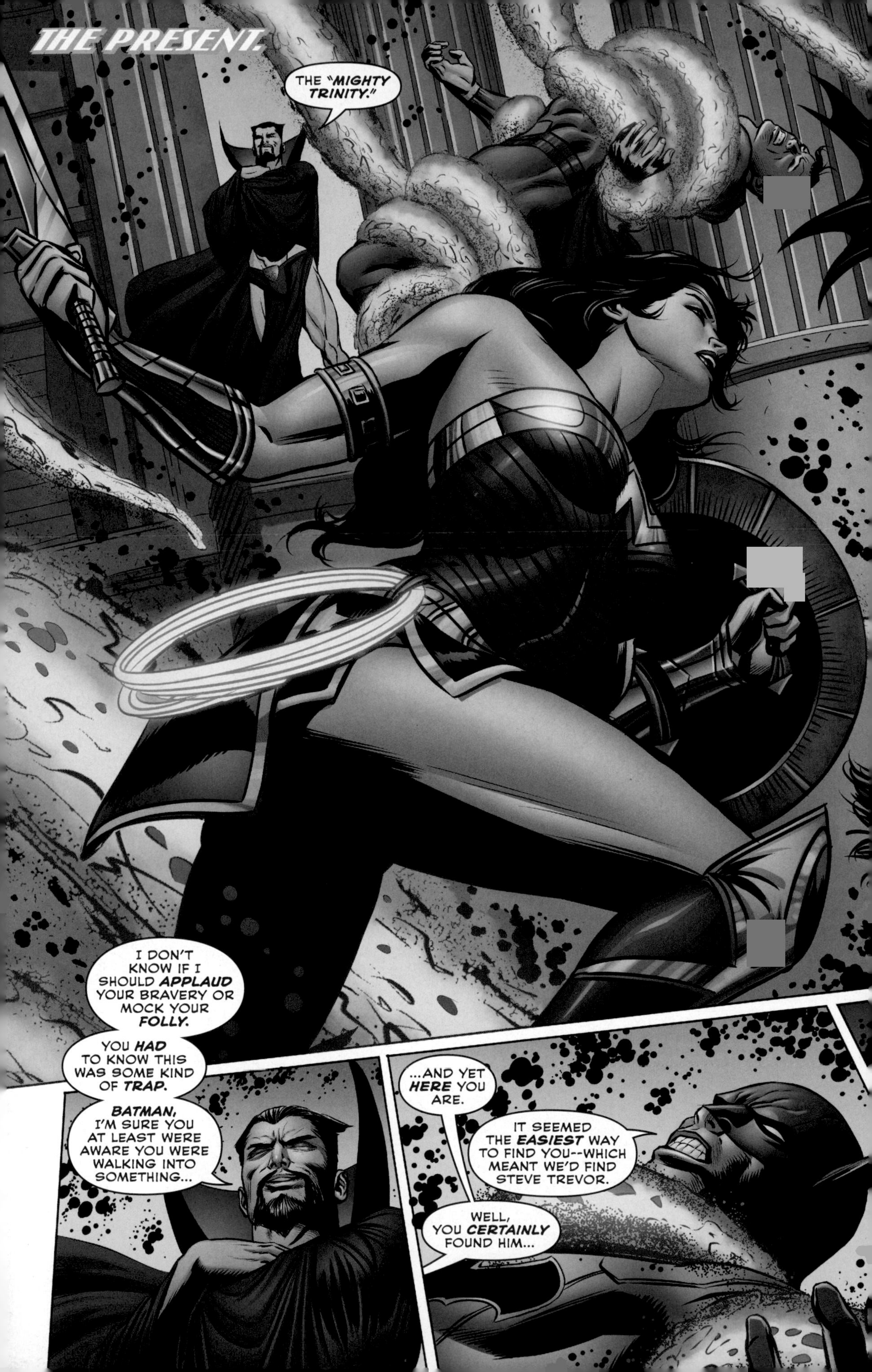
THE PRESENT.
THE "MIGHTY TRINITY."
I DON'T KNOW IF I SHOULD APPLAUD YOUR BRAVERY OR MOCK YOUR FOLLY.
YOU HAD TO KNOW THIS WAS SOME KIND OF TRAP.
BATMAN, I'M SURE YOU AT LEAST WERE AWARE YOU WERE WALKING INTO SOMETHING...
...AND YET HERE YOU ARE.
IT SEEMED THE EASIEST WAY TO FIND YOU--WHICH MEANT WE'D FIND STEVE TREVOR.
WELL, YOU CERTAINLY FOUND HIM...

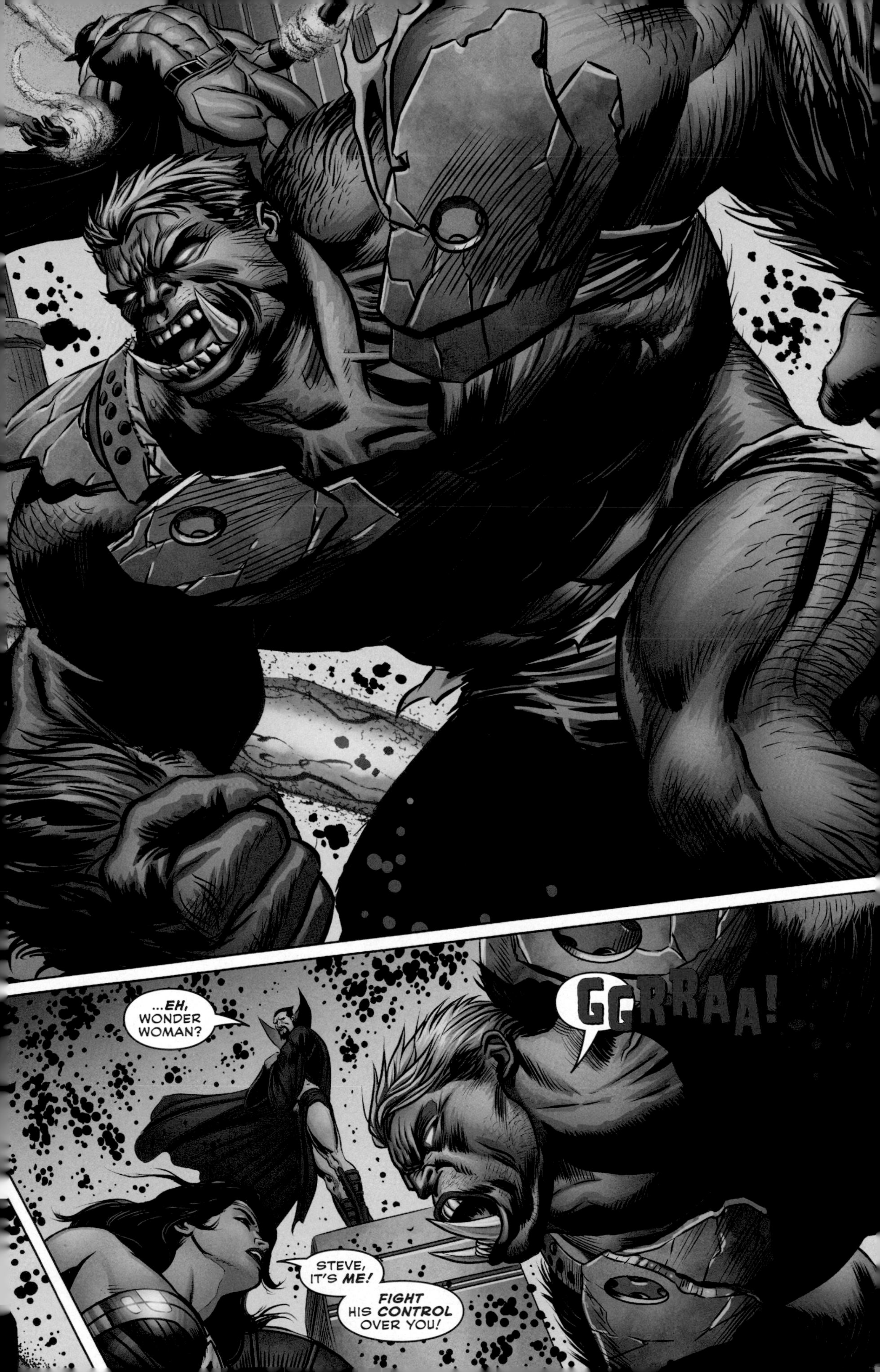
...EH, WONDER WOMAN?
GGRRAA!
STEVE, IT'S ME!
FIGHT HIS CONTROL OVER YOU!

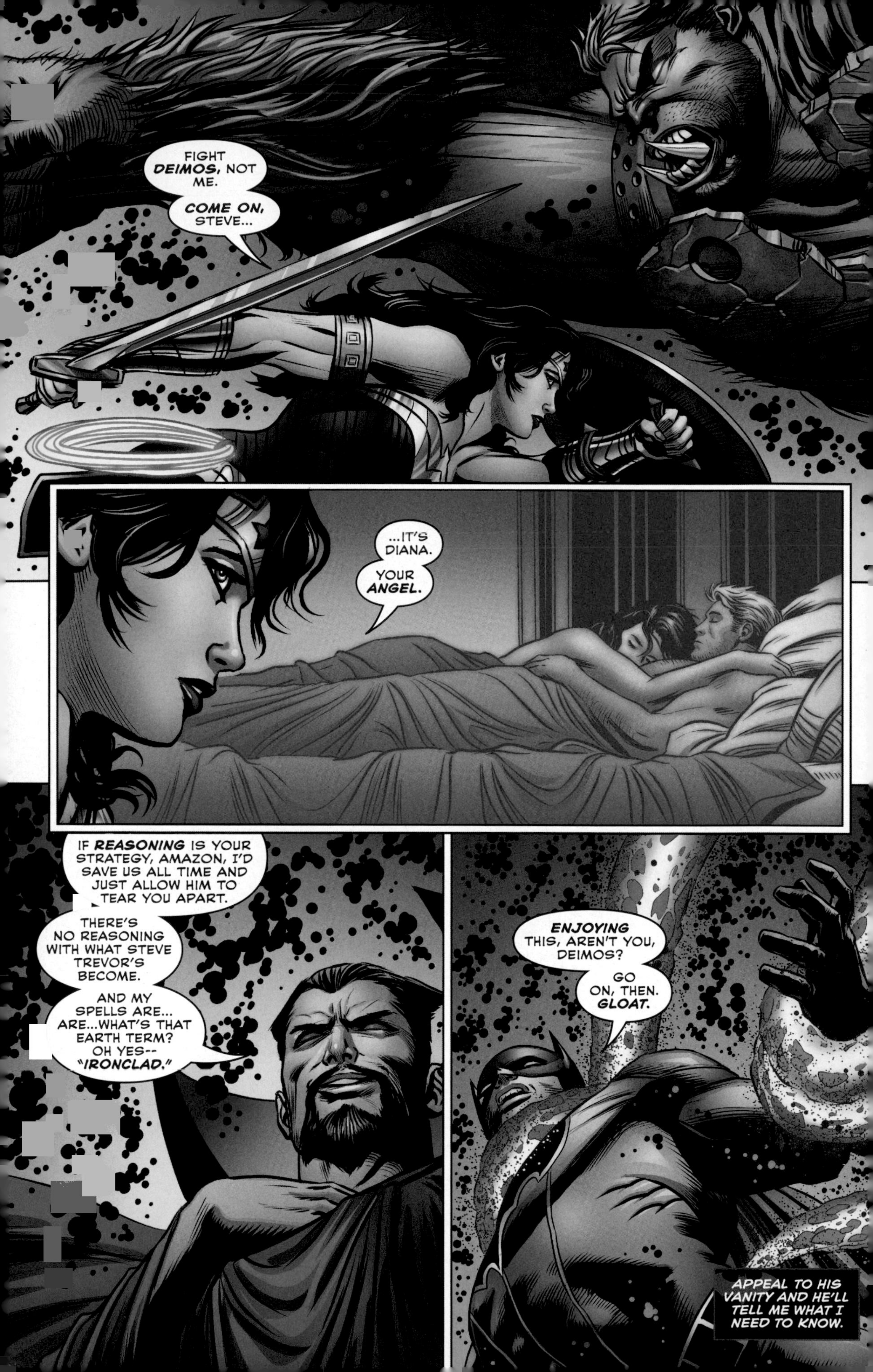
FIGHT DEIMOS, NOT ME.
COME ON, STEVE...
...IT'S DIANA.
YOUR ANGEL.
IF REASONING IS YOUR STRATEGY, AMAZON, I'D SAVE US ALL TIME AND JUST ALLOW HIM TO TEAR YOU APART.
THERE'S NO REASONING WITH WHAT STEVE TREVOR'S BECOME.
AND MY SPELLS ARE... ARE...WHAT'S THAT EARTH TERM? OH YES-- "IRONCLAD."
ENJOYING THIS, AREN'T YOU, DEIMOS?
GO ON, THEN. GLOAT.
APPEAL TO HIS VANITY AND HE'LL TELL ME WHAT I NEED TO KNOW.

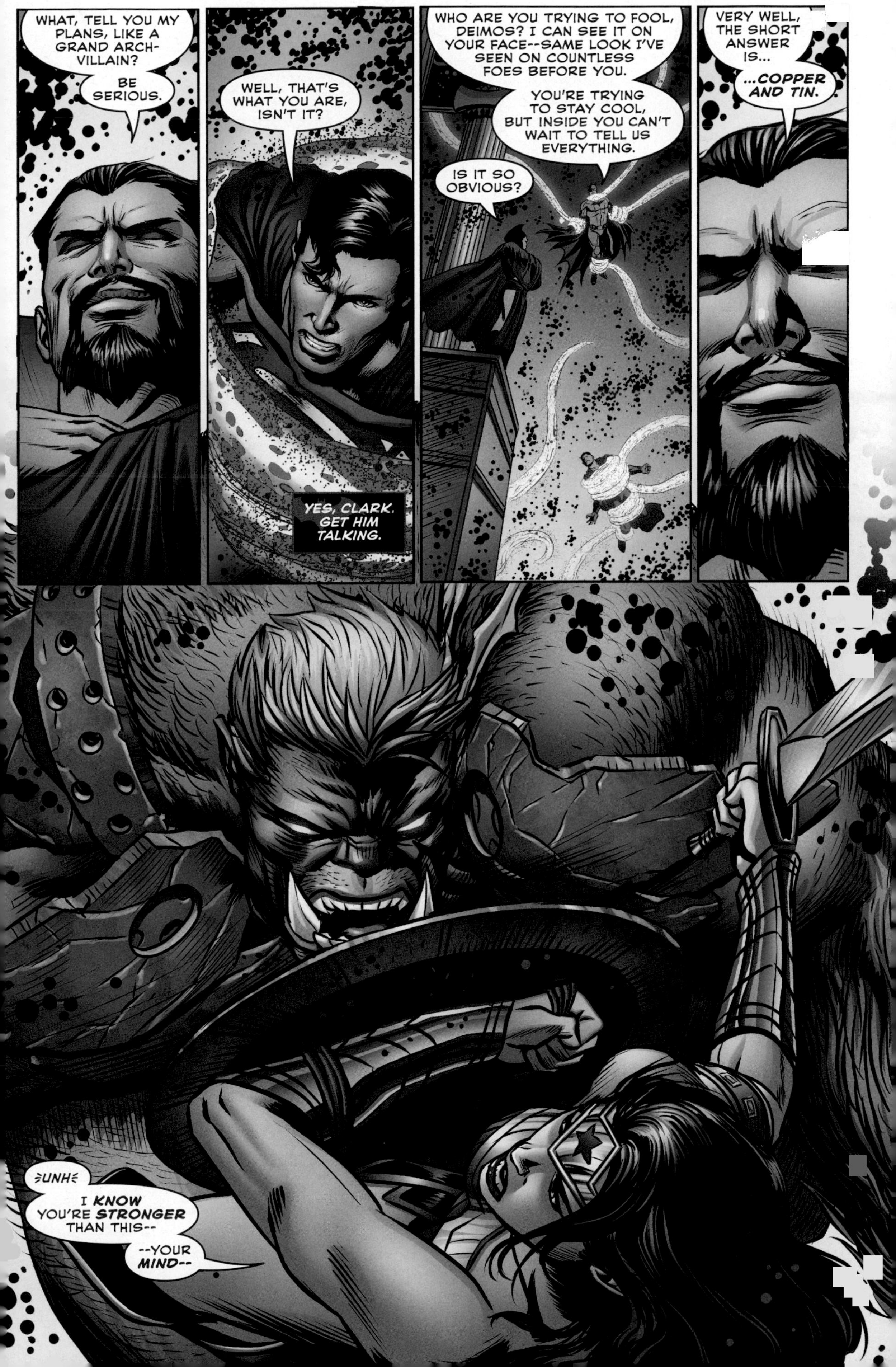

WHAT, TELL YOU MY PLANS, LIKE A GRAND ARCH-VILLAIN?
BE SERIOUS.
WELL, THAT'S WHAT YOU ARE, ISN'T IT?
YES, CLARK. GET HIM TALKING.
WHO ARE YOU TRYING TO FOOL, DEIMOS? I CAN SEE IT ON YOUR FACE--SAME LOOK I'VE SEEN ON COUNTLESS FOES BEFORE YOU.
YOU'RE TRYING TO STAY COOL, BUT INSIDE YOU CAN'T WAIT TO TELL US EVERYTHING.
IS IT SO OBVIOUS?
VERY WELL, THE SHORT ANSWER IS...
...COPPER AND TIN.
UNH
I KNOW YOU'RE STRONGER THAN THIS--
--YOUR MIND--

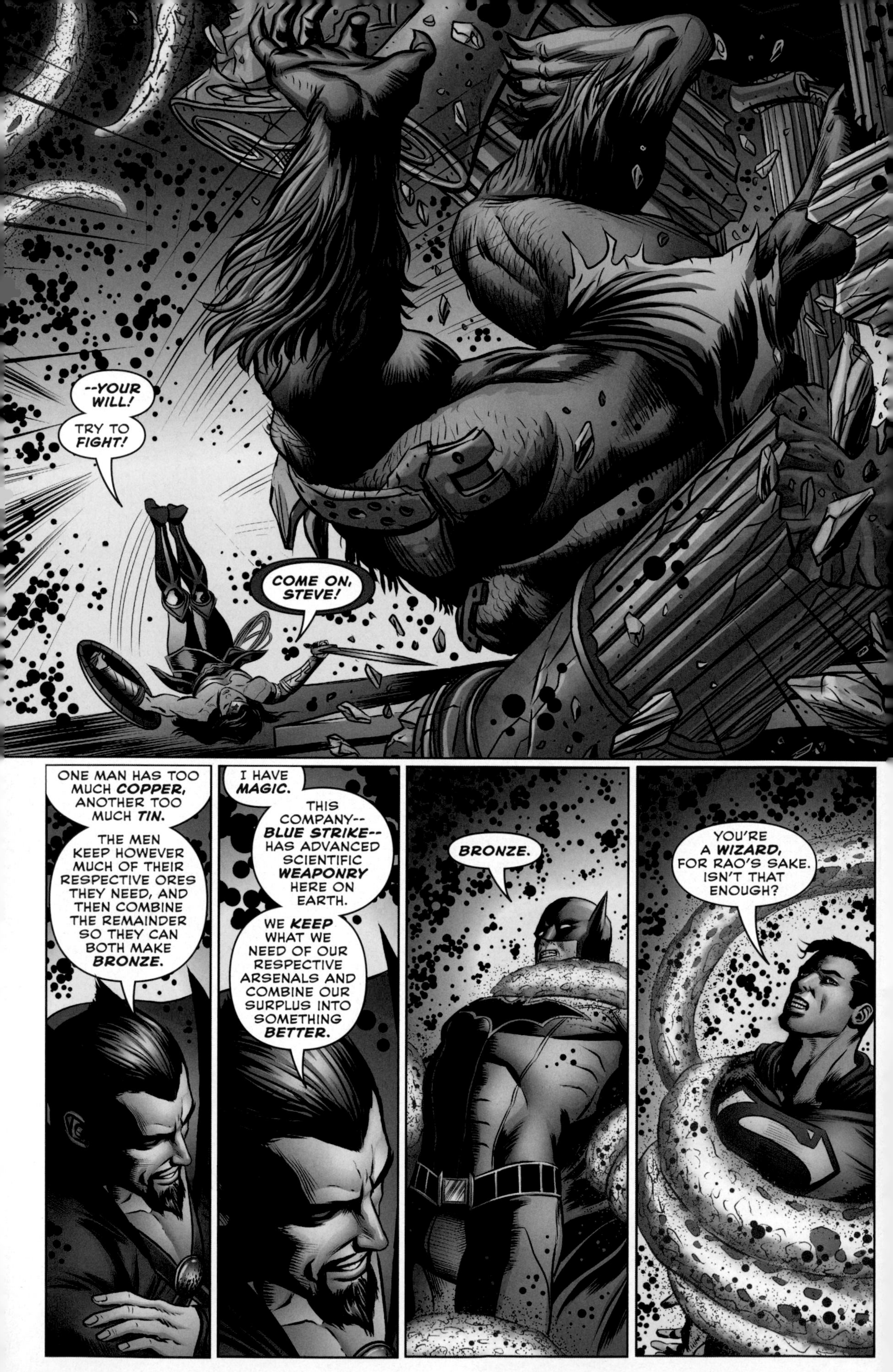
--YOUR WILL!
TRY TO FIGHT!
COME ON, STEVE!
ONE MAN HAS TOO MUCH COPPER, ANOTHER TOO MUCH TIN.
THE MEN KEEP HOWEVER MUCH OF THEIR RESPECTIVE ORES THEY NEED, AND THEN COMBINE THE REMAINDER SO THEY CAN BOTH MAKE BRONZE.
I HAVE MAGIC.
THIS COMPANY-- BLUE STRIKE-- HAS ADVANCED SCIENTIFIC WEAPONRY HERE ON EARTH.
WE KEEP WHAT WE NEED OF OUR RESPECTIVE ARSENALS AND COMBINE OUR SURPLUS INTO SOMETHING BETTER.
BRONZE.
YOU'RE A WIZARD, FOR RAO'S SAKE. ISN'T THAT ENOUGH?

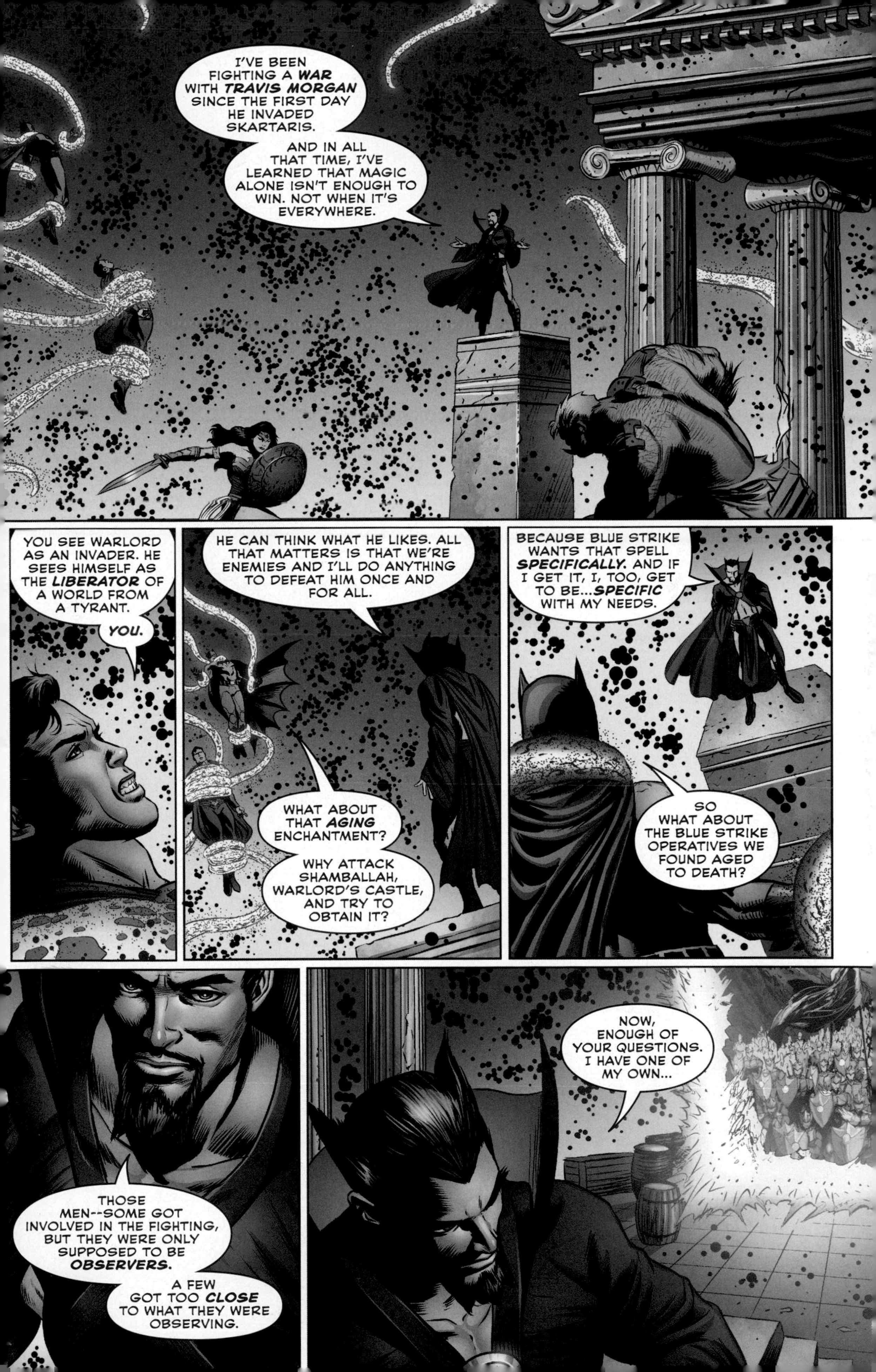
I'VE BEEN FIGHTING A WAR WITH TRAVIS MORGAN SINCE THE FIRST DAY HE INVADED SKARTARIS.
AND IN ALL THAT TIME, I'VE LEARNED THAT MAGIC ALONE ISN'T ENOUGH TO WIN. NOT WHEN IT'S EVERYWHERE.
YOU SEE WARLORD AS AN INVADER. HE SEES HIMSELF AS THE LIBERATOR OF A WORLD FROM A TYRANT.
YOU.
HE CAN THINK WHAT HE LIKES. ALL THAT MATTERS IS THAT WE'RE ENEMIES AND I'LL DO ANYTHING TO DEFEAT HIM ONCE AND FOR ALL.
WHAT ABOUT THAT AGING ENCHANTMENT?
WHY ATTACK SHAMBALLAH, WARLORD'S CASTLE, AND TRY TO OBTAIN IT?
BECAUSE BLUE STRIKE WANTS THAT SPELL SPECIFICALLY. AND IF I GET IT, I, TOO, GET TO BE...SPECIFIC WITH MY NEEDS.
SO WHAT ABOUT THE BLUE STRIKE OPERATIVES WE FOUND AGED TO DEATH?
THOSE MEN--SOME GOT INVOLVED IN THE FIGHTING, BUT THEY WERE ONLY SUPPOSED TO BE OBSERVERS.
A FEW GOT TOO CLOSE TO WHAT THEY WERE OBSERVING.
NOW, ENOUGH OF YOUR QUESTIONS. I HAVE ONE OF MY OWN...

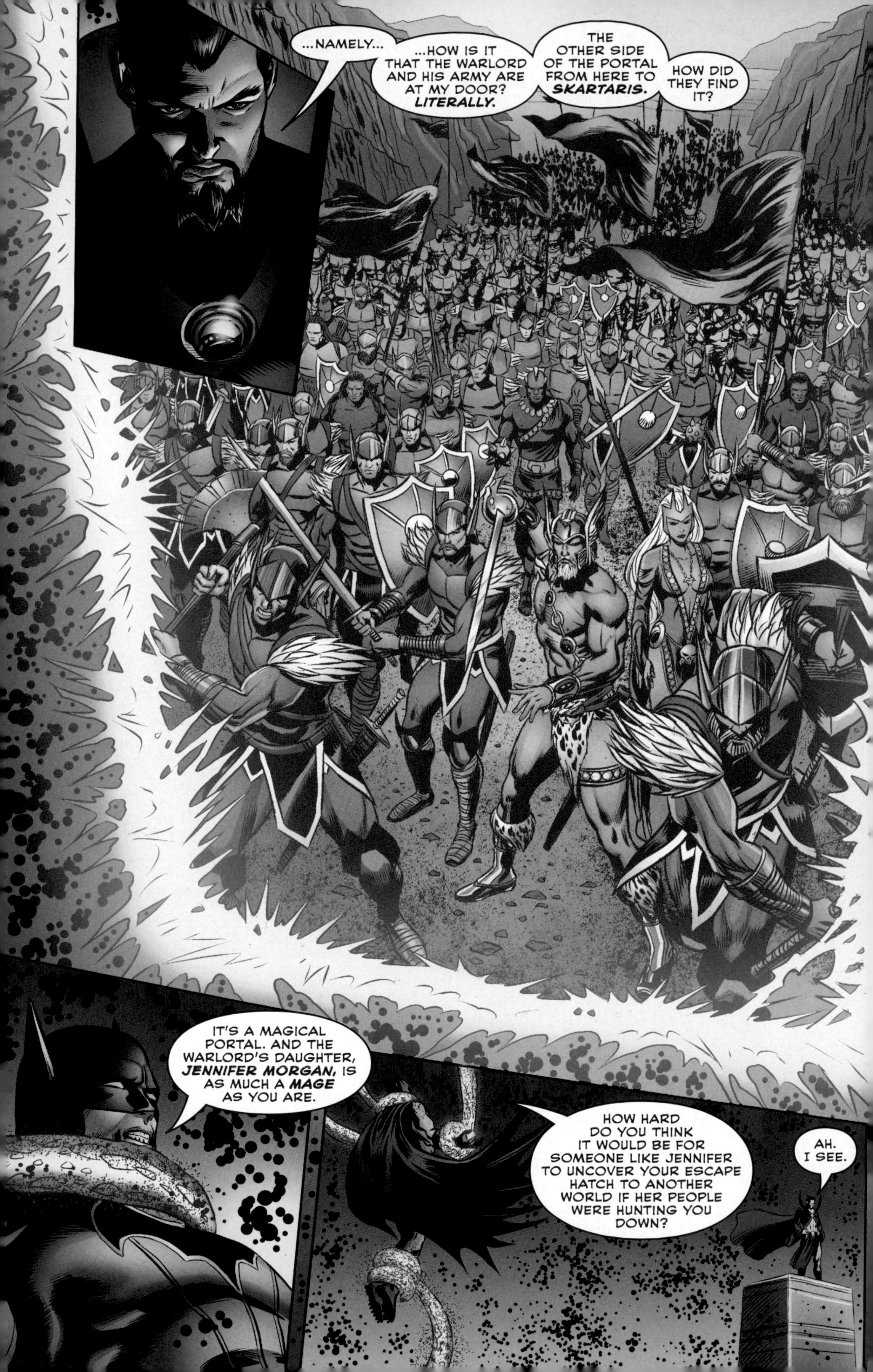
...NAMELY...
...HOW IS IT THAT THE WARLORD AND HIS ARMY ARE AT MY DOOR? LITERALLY.
THE OTHER SIDE OF THE PORTAL FROM HERE TO SKARTARIS.
HOW DID THEY FIND IT?
IT'S A MAGICAL PORTAL. AND THE WARLORD'S DAUGHTER, JENNIFER MORGAN, IS AS MUCH A MAGE AS YOU ARE.
HOW HARD DO YOU THINK IT WOULD BE FOR SOMEONE LIKE JENNIFER TO UNCOVER YOUR ESCAPE HATCH TO ANOTHER WORLD IF HER PEOPLE WERE HUNTING YOU DOWN?
AH. I SEE.

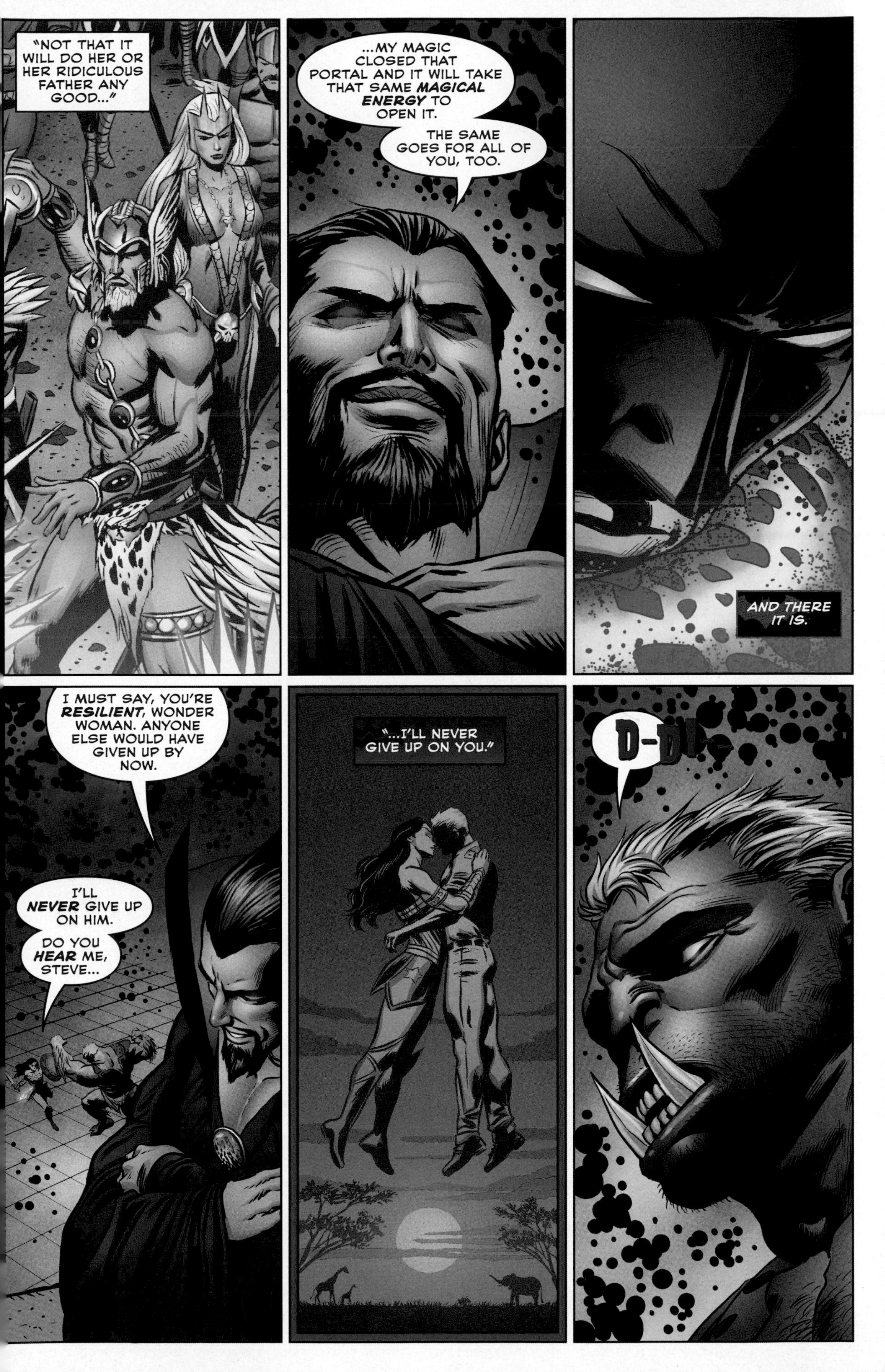
"NOT THAT IT WILL DO HER OR HER RIDICULOUS FATHER ANY GOOD..."
...MY MAGIC CLOSED THAT PORTAL AND IT WILL TAKE THAT SAME MAGICAL ENERGY TO OPEN IT.
THE SAME GOES FOR ALL OF YOU, TOO.
AND THERE IT IS.
I MUST SAY, YOU'RE RESILIENT, WONDER WOMAN. ANYONE ELSE WOULD HAVE GIVEN UP BY NOW.
I'LL NEVER GIVE UP ON HIM.
DO YOU HEAR ME, STEVE...
"...I'LL NEVER GIVE UP ON YOU."
D-DI-

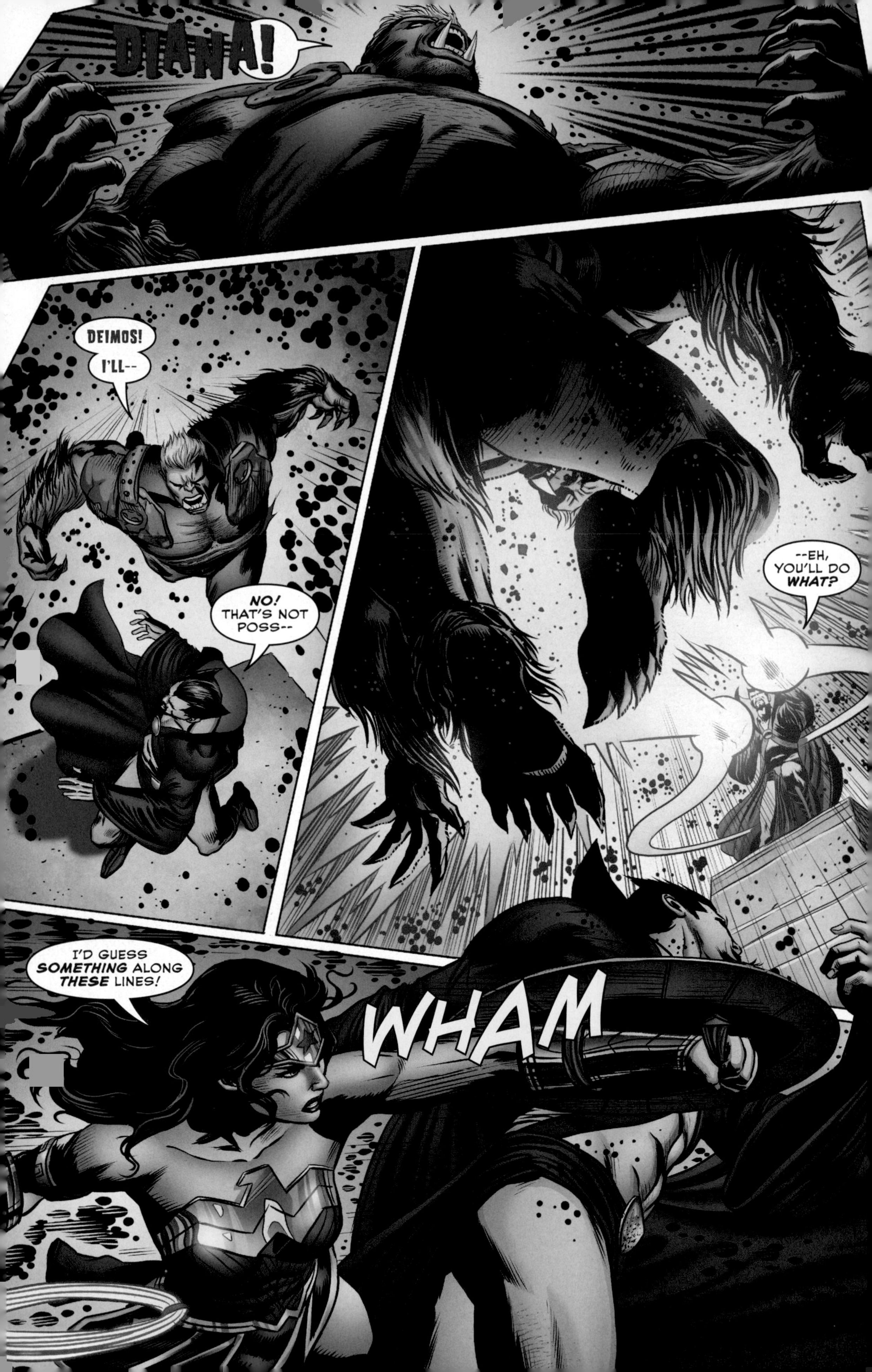
DIANA!
DEIMOS!
I'LL--
NO! THAT'S NOT POSS--
--EH, YOU'LL DO WHAT?
I'D GUESS SOMETHING ALONG THESE LINES!
WHAM

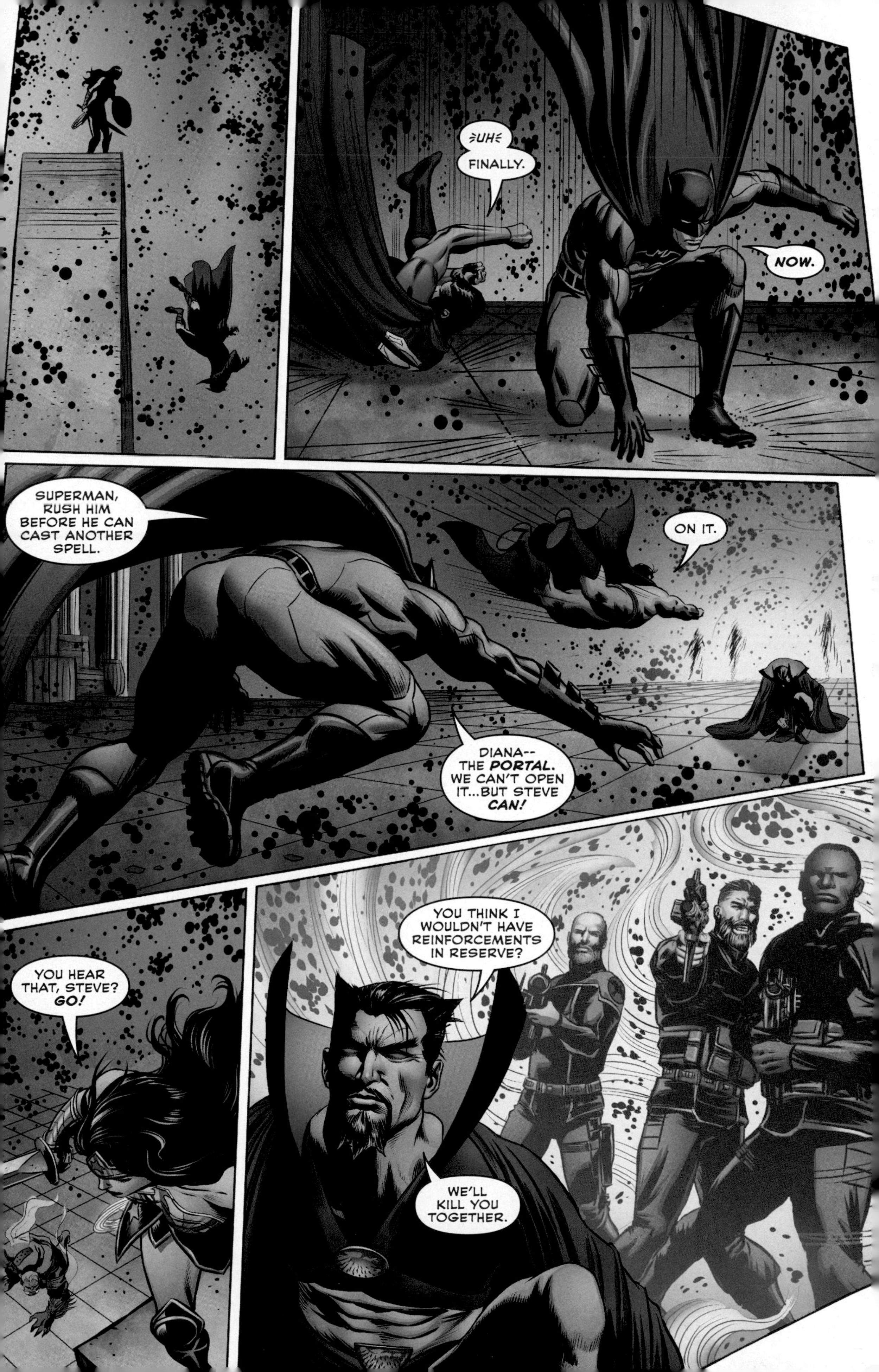
UH
FINALLY.
NOW.
SUPERMAN, RUSH HIM BEFORE HE CAN CAST ANOTHER SPELL.
ON IT.
DIANA-- THE PORTAL. WE CAN'T OPEN IT...BUT STEVE CAN!
YOU HEAR THAT, STEVE? GO!
YOU THINK I WOULDN'T HAVE REINFORCEMENTS IN RESERVE?
WE'LL KILL YOU TOGETHER.

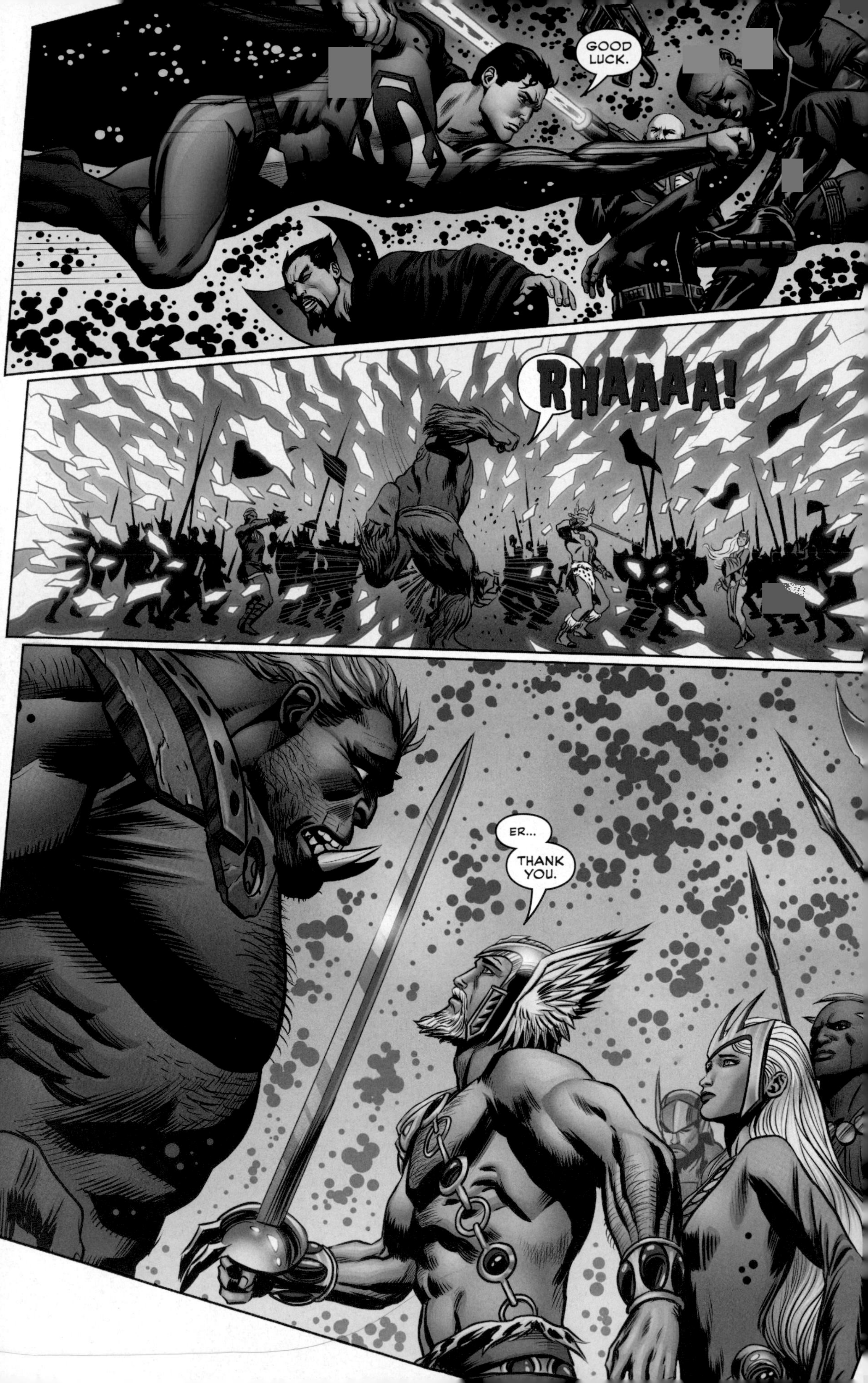
GOOD LUCK.
RHAAAA!
ER...
THANK YOU.

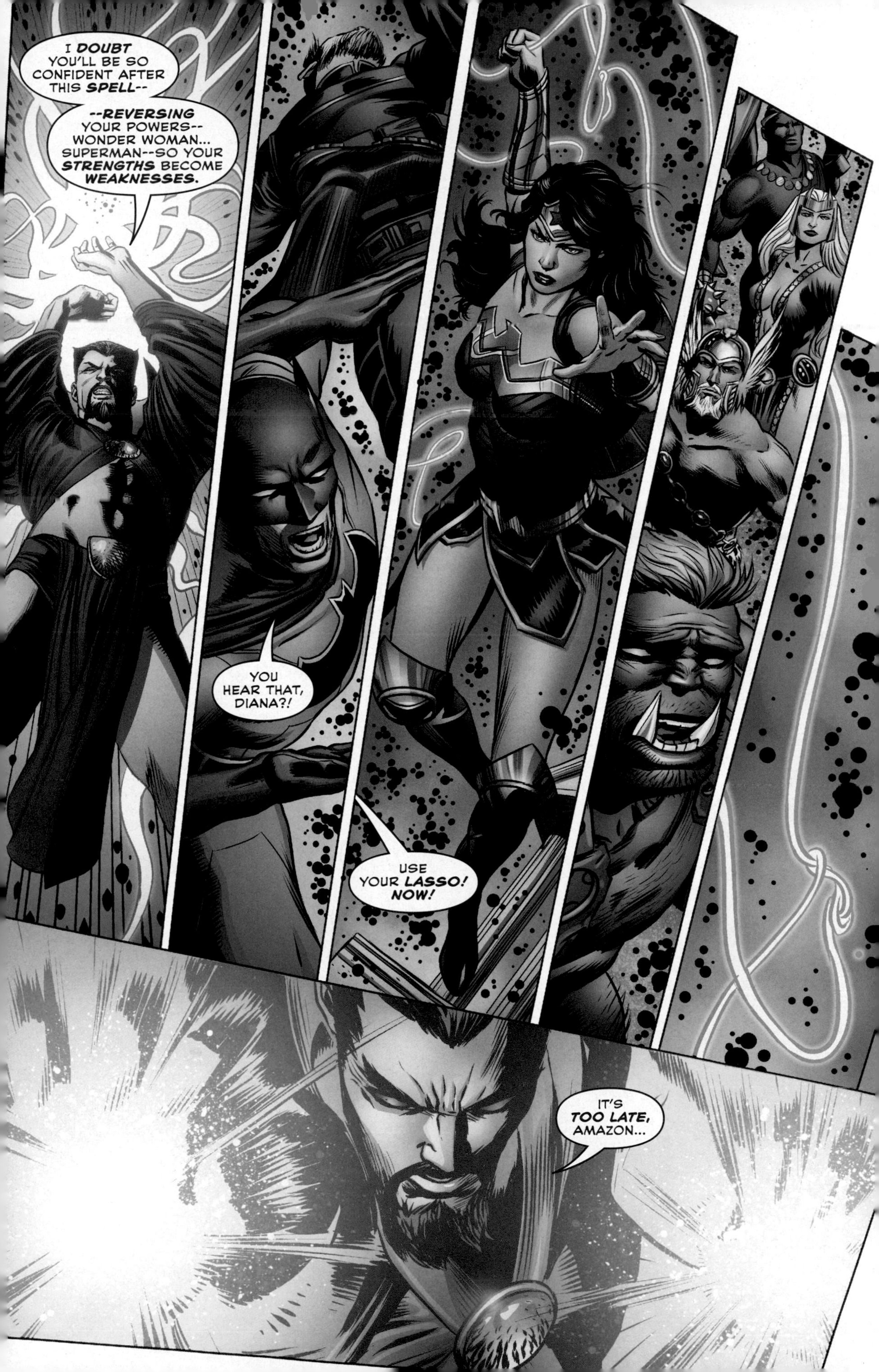
I DOUBT YOU'LL BE SO CONFIDENT AFTER THIS SPELL--
--REVERSING YOUR POWERS-- WONDER WOMAN... SUPERMAN--SO YOUR STRENGTHS BECOME WEAKNESSES.
YOU HEAR THAT, DIANA?!
USE YOUR LASSO! NOW!
IT'S TOO LATE, AMAZON...

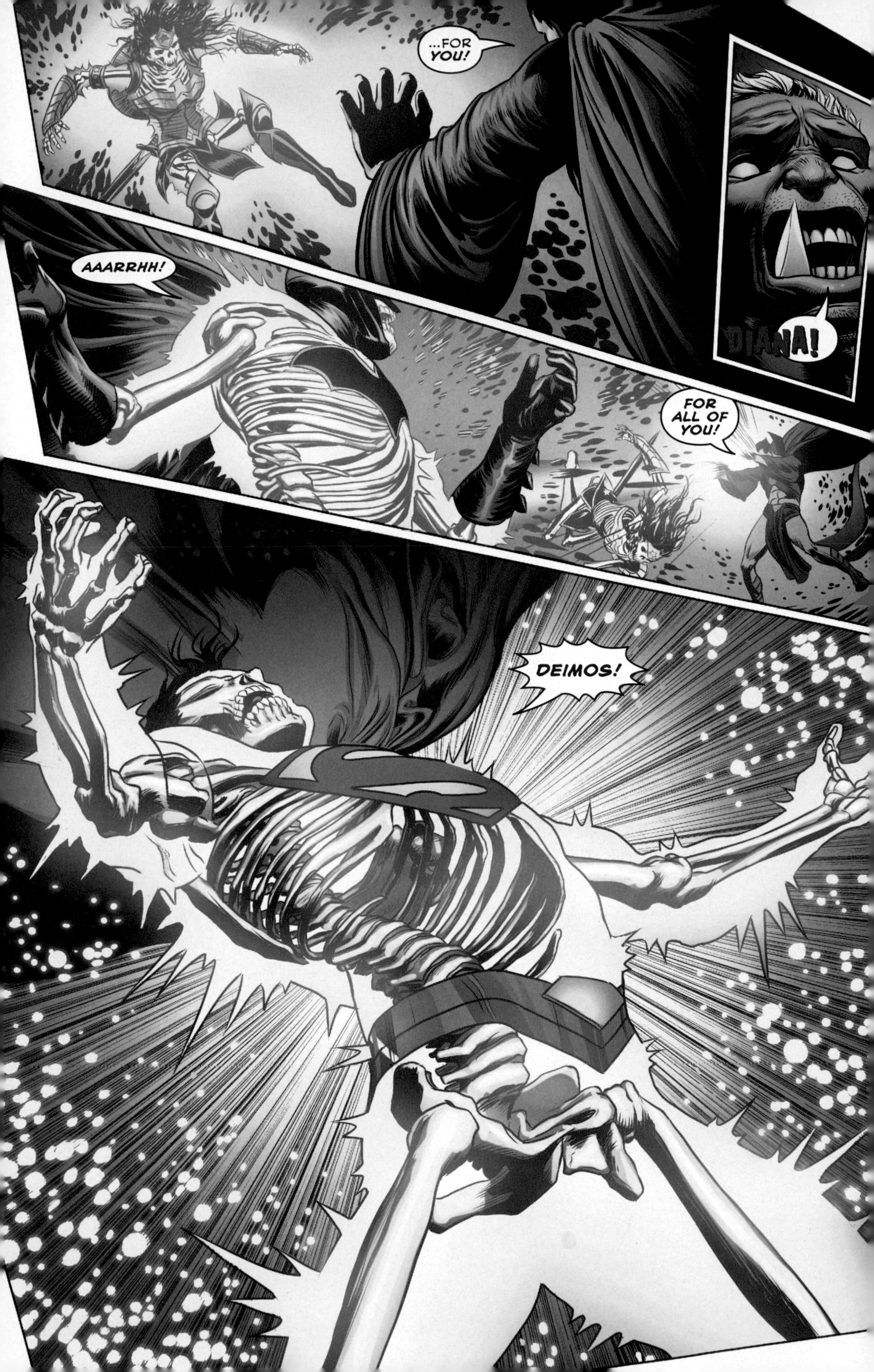
...FOR YOU!
DIANA!
AAARRHH!
FOR ALL OF YOU!
DEIMOS!

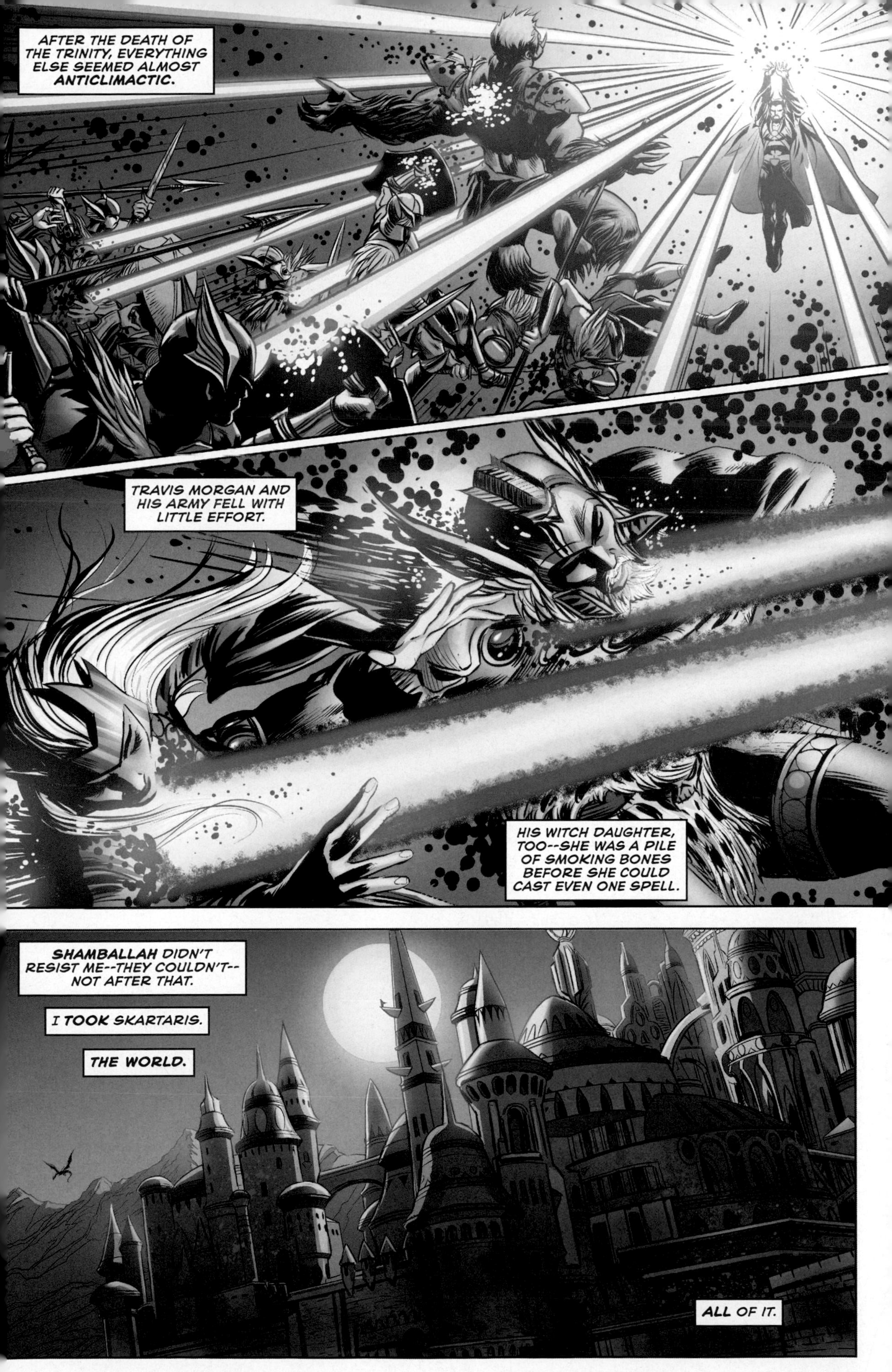
AFTER THE DEATH OF THE TRINITY, EVERYTHING ELSE SEEMED ALMOST ANTICLIMACTIC.
TRAVIS MORGAN AND HIS ARMY FELL WITH LITTLE EFFORT.
HIS WITCH DAUGHTER, TOO--SHE WAS A PILE OF SMOKING BONES BEFORE SHE COULD CAST EVEN ONE SPELL.
SHAMBALLAH DIDN'T RESIST ME--THEY COULDN'T--NOT AFTER THAT.
I TOOK SKARTARIS.
THE WORLD.
ALL OF IT.

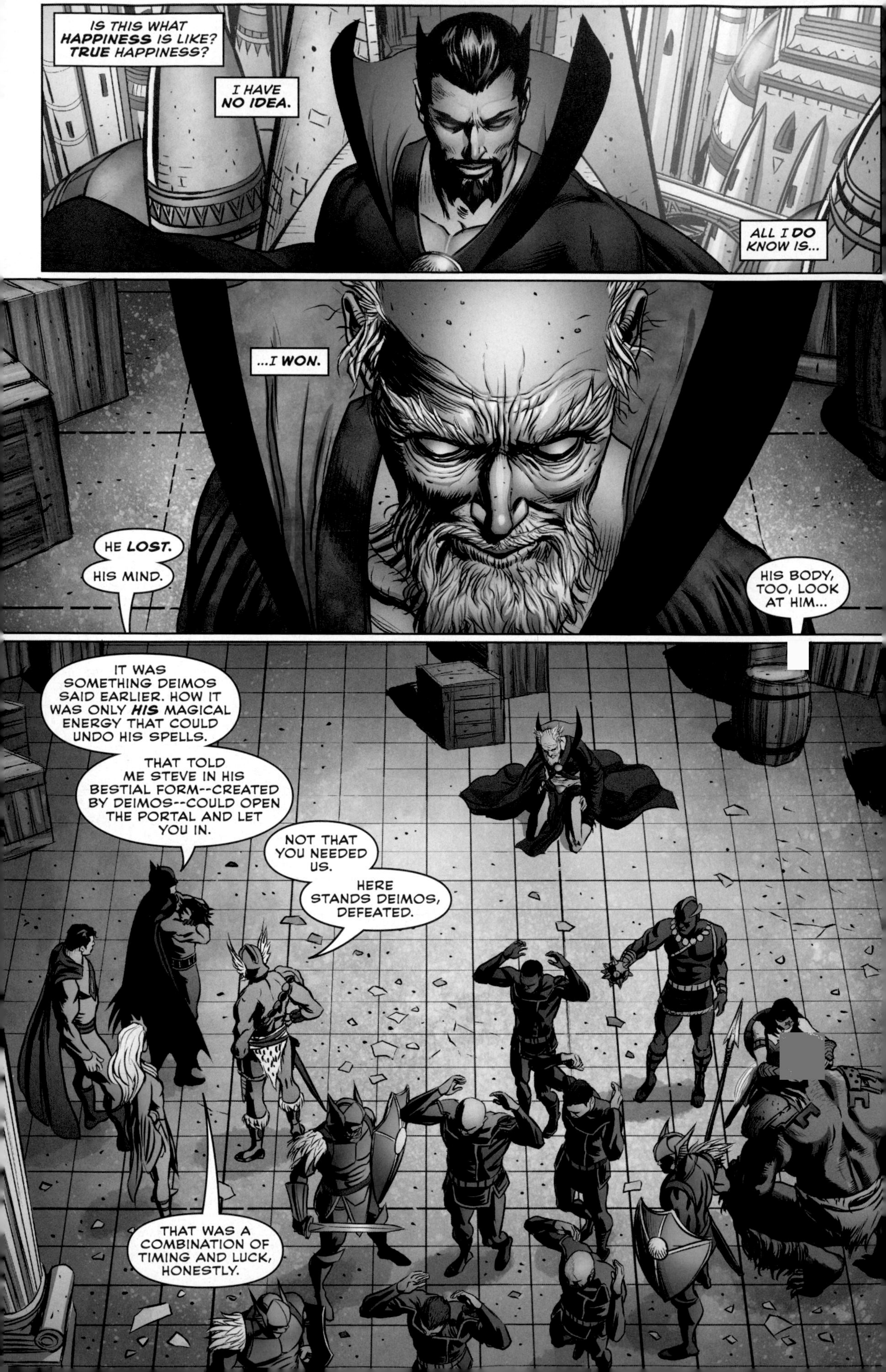
IS THIS WHAT HAPPINESS IS LIKE? TRUE HAPPINESS?
I HAVE NO IDEA.
ALL I DO KNOW IS...
...I WON.
HE LOST.
HIS MIND.
HIS BODY, TOO, LOOK AT HIM...
IT WAS SOMETHING DEIMOS SAID EARLIER. HOW IT WAS ONLY HIS MAGICAL ENERGY THAT COULD UNDO HIS SPELLS.
THAT TOLD ME STEVE IN HIS BESTIAL FORM--CREATED BY DEIMOS--COULD OPEN THE PORTAL AND LET YOU IN.
NOT THAT YOU NEEDED US.
HERE STANDS DEIMOS, DEFEATED.
THAT WAS A COMBINATION OF TIMING AND LUCK, HONESTLY.

WHEN DEIMOS CAST THE SPELL REVERSING OUR POWERS-- WHICH WORKED, MOMENTARILY--

--IT OCCURRED TO ME IN THAT INSTANT, IF DIANA'S POWERS WERE REVERSED--ALL OF THEM...

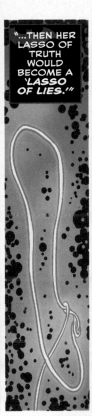

"...THEN HER LASSO OF TRUTH WOULD BECOME A 'LASSO OF LIES.'"

AS SUCH, ONCE DEIMOS WAS ROPED, ALL WE NEEDED TO DO WAS LET HIS OWN IMAGINATION DEFEAT HIM.

THAT REMINDS ME, BATMAN, HAND IT OVER.

I HAVE NO IDEA WHAT YOU'RE TALKING ABOUT.

OH? YOU'RE TELLING ME DEIMOS AGED HIMSELF?

"BECAUSE I'M PRETTY SURE IT WAS THE AGING DEVICE THAT YOU STOLE FROM ME IN SHAMBALLAH."

HM.

WHAT DO YOU SEE?

OVER IN THE CORNER-- "TECHNOLOGY" THAT I RECOGNIZE.

I WAS BEGINNING TO THINK NOTHING CORRESPONDED WITH WHAT I KNOW FROM EARTH.

LOOK. THERE.

COULD YOU HAVE BEEN MORE OBVIOUS?

I LET YOU HAVE IT, BECAUSE I SENSED WE WEREN'T DONE WITH DEIMOS. I TOOK A CHANCE ON YOU.

YES, THE THING DEIMOS WANTED WAS IN MY BELT THE WHOLE TIME. ALMOST FUNNY...

...YOU'RE A STRANGE, DUPLICITOUS WOMAN, JENNIFER MORGAN.

I DON'T TRUST YOU. BUT I LIKE YOU.

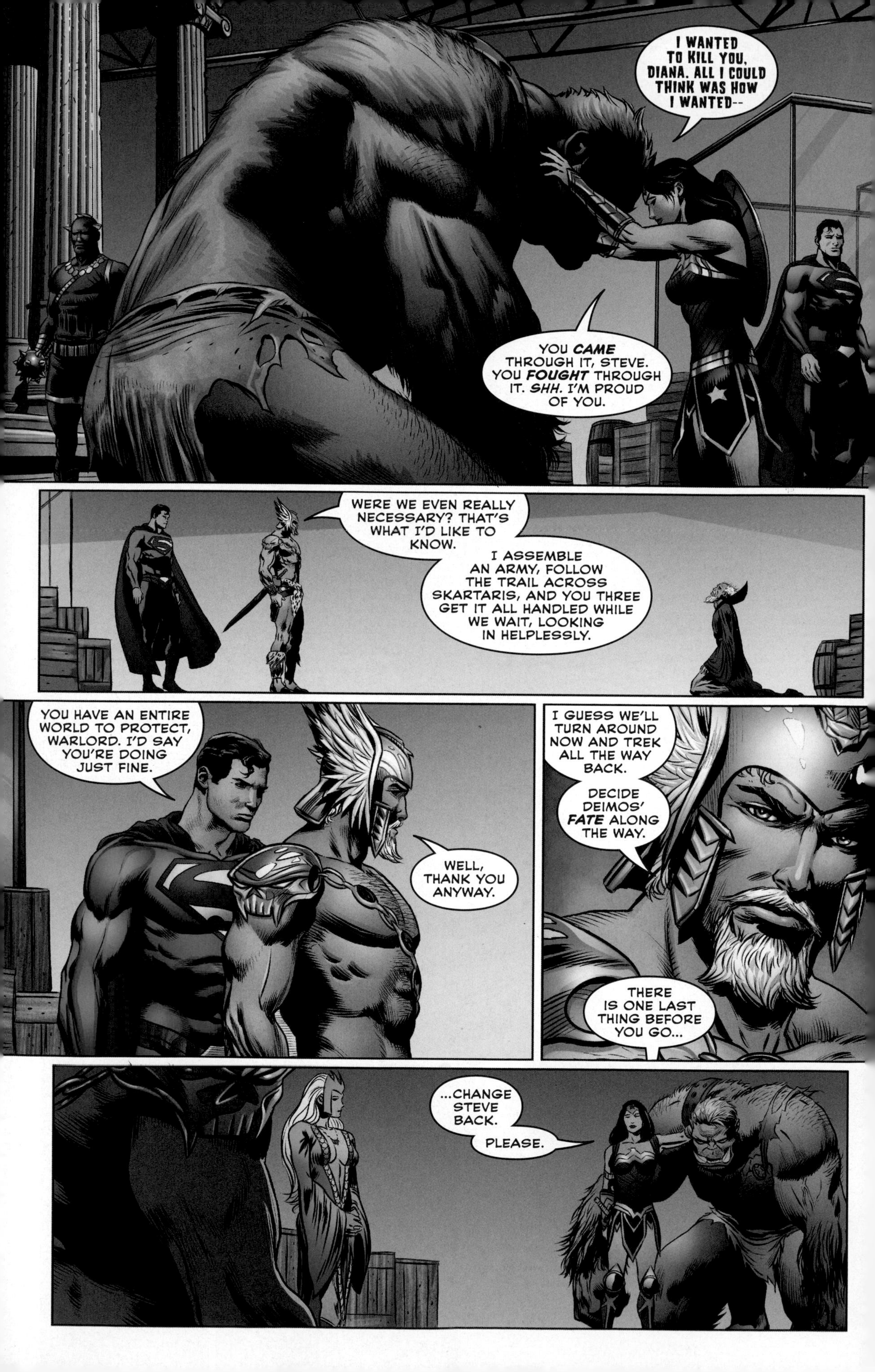
I WANTED TO KILL YOU, DIANA. ALL I COULD THINK WAS HOW I WANTED--
YOU *CAME* THROUGH IT, STEVE. YOU *FOUGHT* THROUGH IT. *SHH.* I'M PROUD OF YOU.
WERE WE EVEN REALLY NECESSARY? THAT'S WHAT I'D LIKE TO KNOW.
I ASSEMBLE AN ARMY, FOLLOW THE TRAIL ACROSS SKARTARIS, AND YOU THREE GET IT ALL HANDLED WHILE WE WAIT, LOOKING IN HELPLESSLY.
YOU HAVE AN ENTIRE WORLD TO PROTECT, WARLORD. I'D SAY YOU'RE DOING JUST FINE.
WELL, THANK YOU ANYWAY.
I GUESS WE'LL TURN AROUND NOW AND TREK ALL THE WAY BACK.
DECIDE DEIMOS' *FATE* ALONG THE WAY.
THERE IS ONE LAST THING BEFORE YOU GO...
...CHANGE STEVE BACK.
PLEASE.

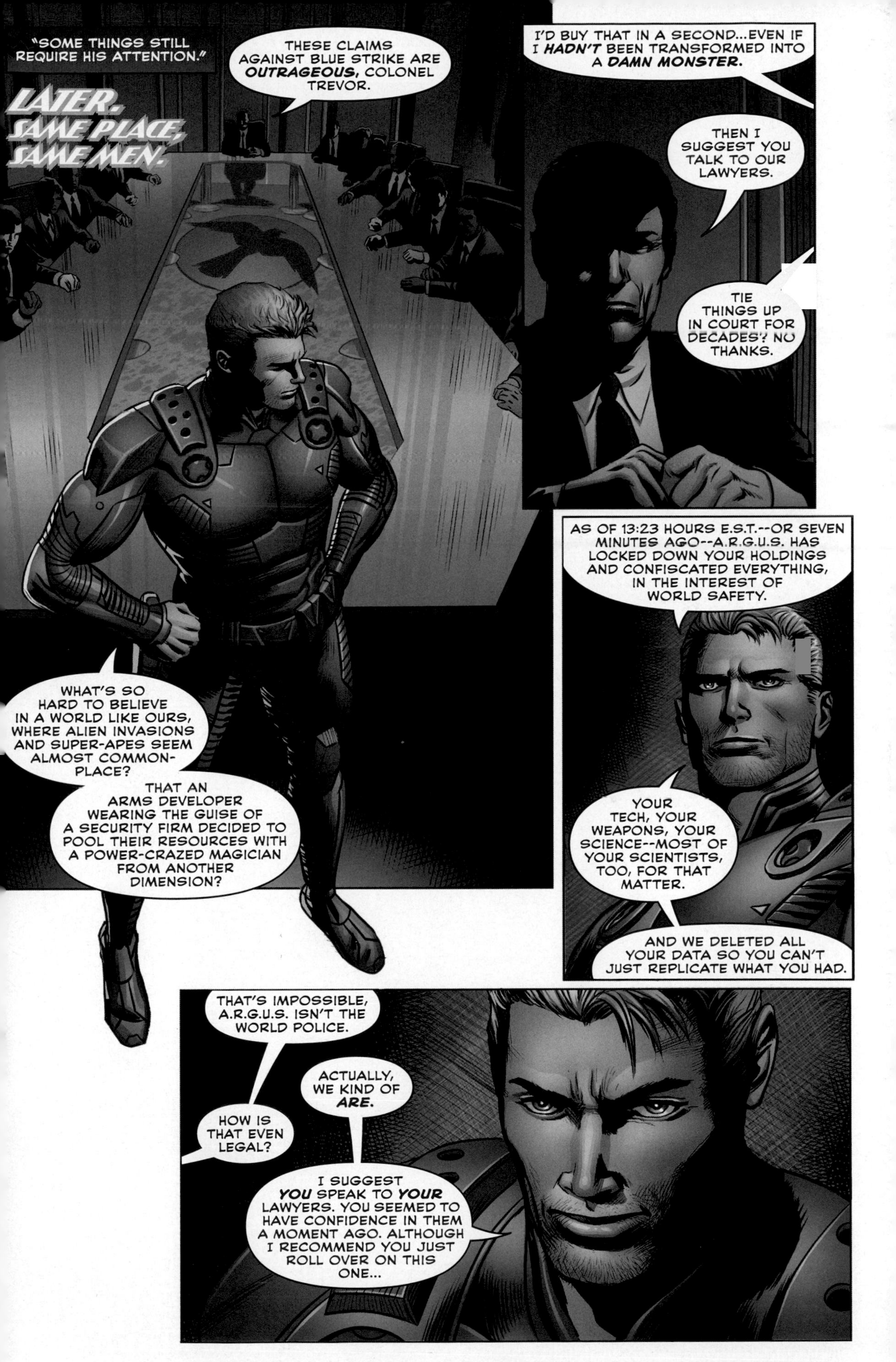
"SOME THINGS STILL REQUIRE HIS ATTENTION."
LATER. SAME PLACE, SAME MEN.
THESE CLAIMS AGAINST BLUE STRIKE ARE OUTRAGEOUS, COLONEL TREVOR.
WHAT'S SO HARD TO BELIEVE IN A WORLD LIKE OURS, WHERE ALIEN INVASIONS AND SUPER-APES SEEM ALMOST COMMONPLACE?
THAT AN ARMS DEVELOPER WEARING THE GUISE OF A SECURITY FIRM DECIDED TO POOL THEIR RESOURCES WITH A POWER-CRAZED MAGICIAN FROM ANOTHER DIMENSION?
I'D BUY THAT IN A SECOND...EVEN IF I HADN'T BEEN TRANSFORMED INTO A DAMN MONSTER.
THEN I SUGGEST YOU TALK TO OUR LAWYERS.
TIE THINGS UP IN COURT FOR DECADES? NO THANKS.
AS OF 13:23 HOURS E.S.T.--OR SEVEN MINUTES AGO--A.R.G.U.S. HAS LOCKED DOWN YOUR HOLDINGS AND CONFISCATED EVERYTHING, IN THE INTEREST OF WORLD SAFETY.
YOUR TECH, YOUR WEAPONS, YOUR SCIENCE--MOST OF YOUR SCIENTISTS, TOO, FOR THAT MATTER.
AND WE DELETED ALL YOUR DATA SO YOU CAN'T JUST REPLICATE WHAT YOU HAD.
THAT'S IMPOSSIBLE, A.R.G.U.S. ISN'T THE WORLD POLICE.
ACTUALLY, WE KIND OF ARE.
HOW IS THAT EVEN LEGAL?
I SUGGEST YOU SPEAK TO YOUR LAWYERS. YOU SEEMED TO HAVE CONFIDENCE IN THEM A MOMENT AGO. ALTHOUGH I RECOMMEND YOU JUST ROLL OVER ON THIS ONE...

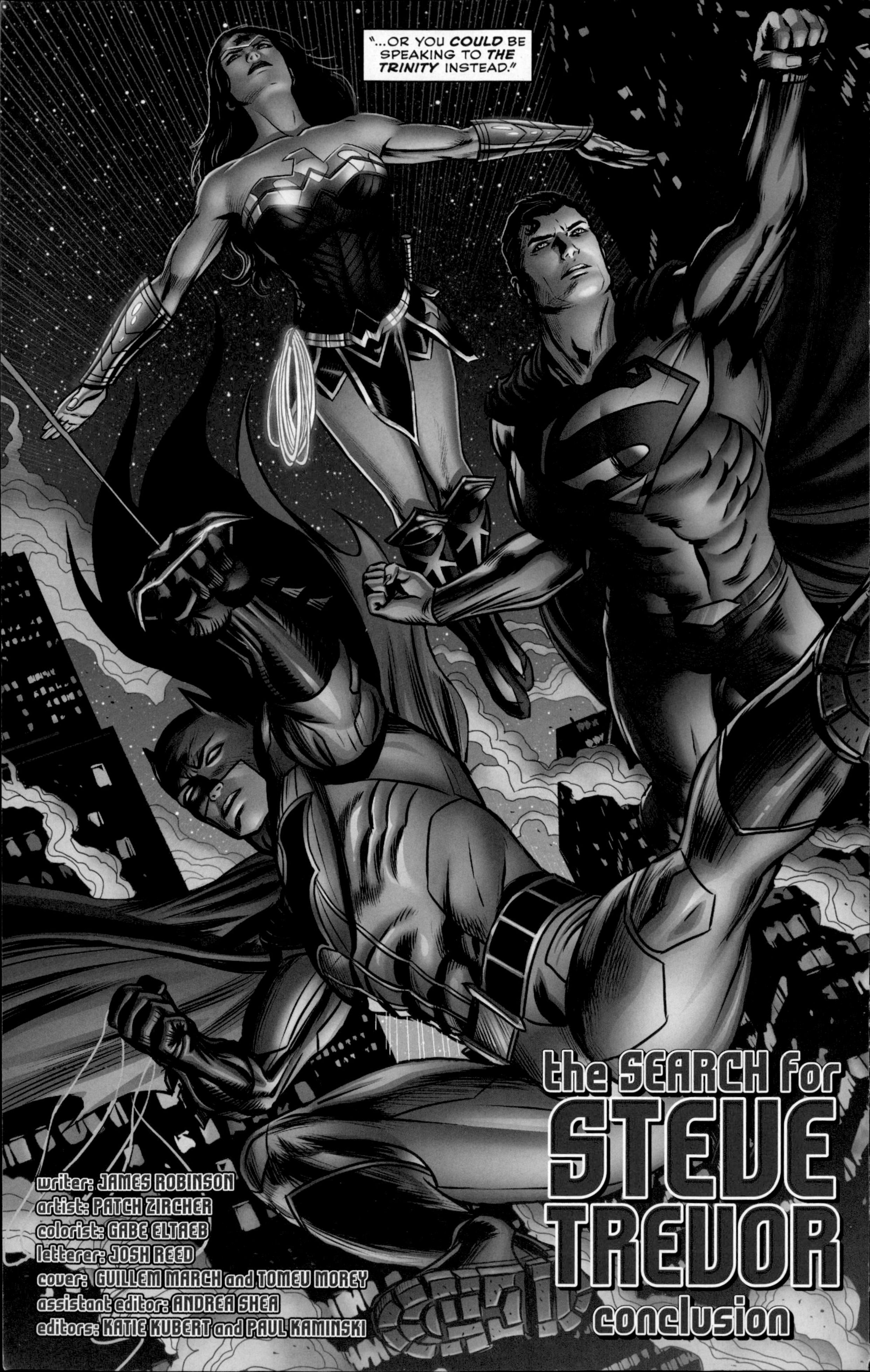
"...OR YOU COULD BE SPEAKING TO THE TRINITY INSTEAD."
the SEARCH for STEVE TREVOR conclusion
writer: JAMES ROBINSON
artist: PATCH ZIRCHER
colorist: GABE ELTAEB
letterer: JOSH REED
cover: GUILLEM MARCH and TOMEU MOREY
assistant editor: ANDREA SHEA
editors: KATIE KUBERT and PAUL KAMINSKI

TRINITY #17 variant cover by BILL SIENKIEWICZ

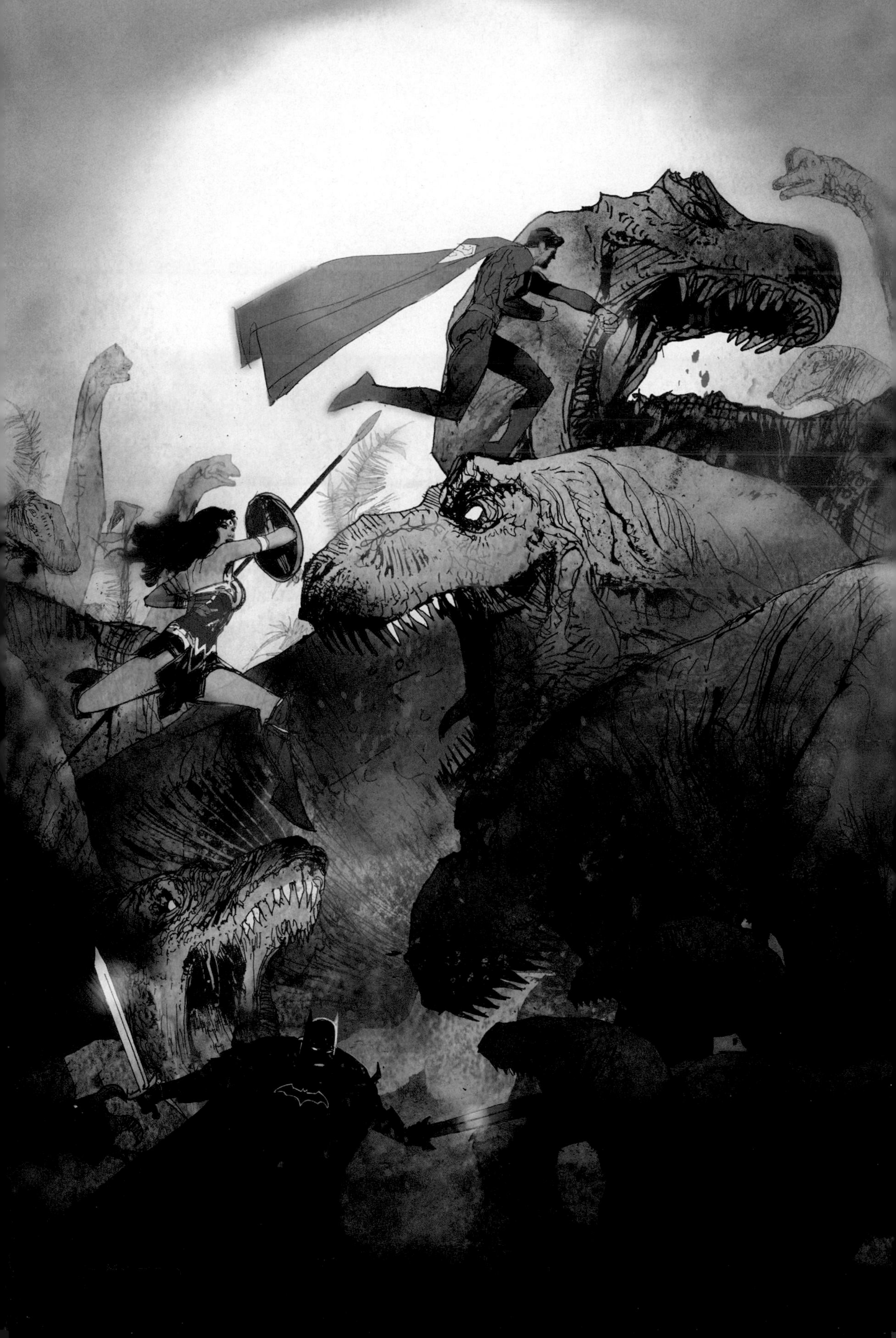

TRINITY #18 variant cover by BILL SIENKIEWICZ

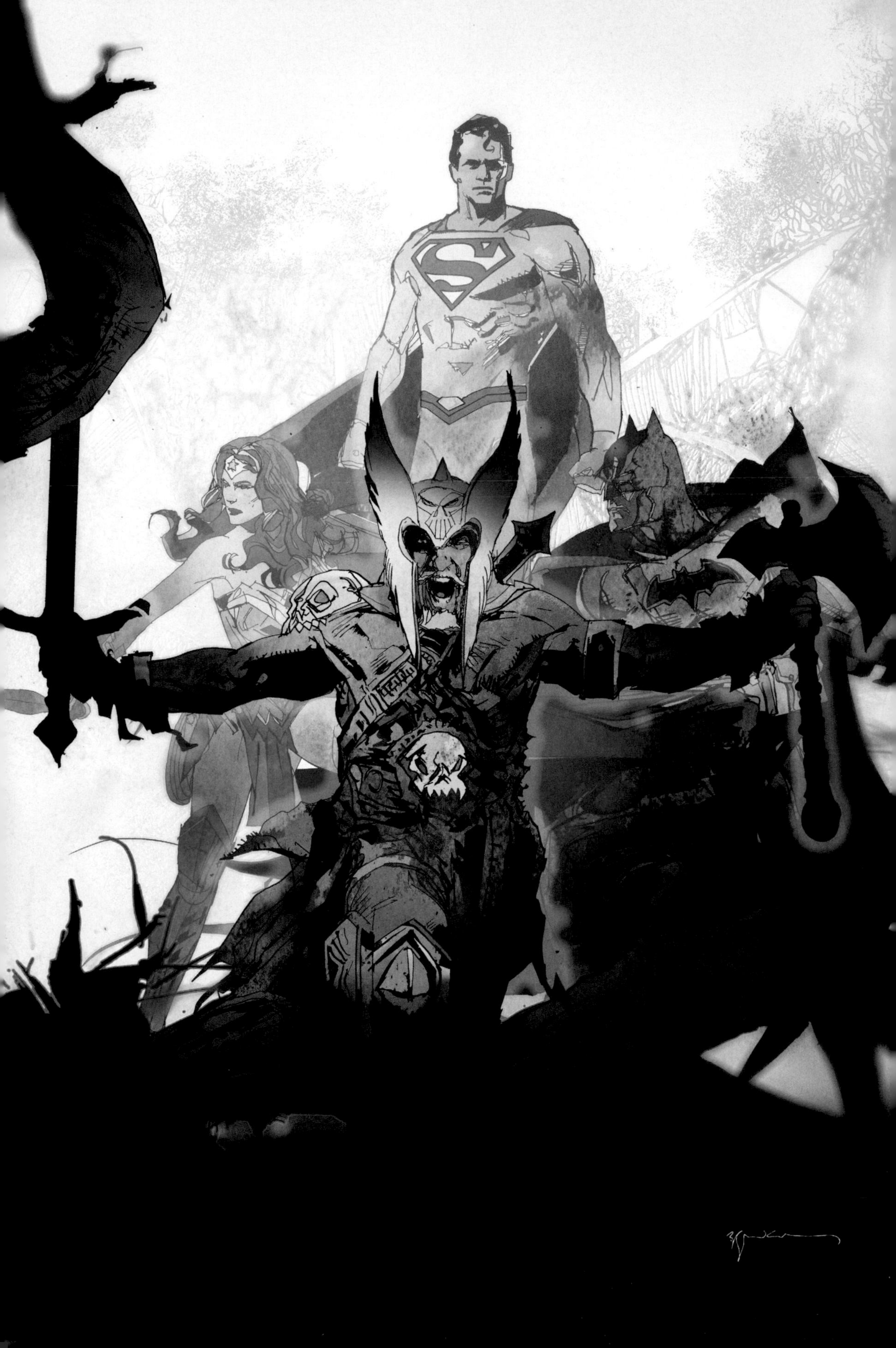

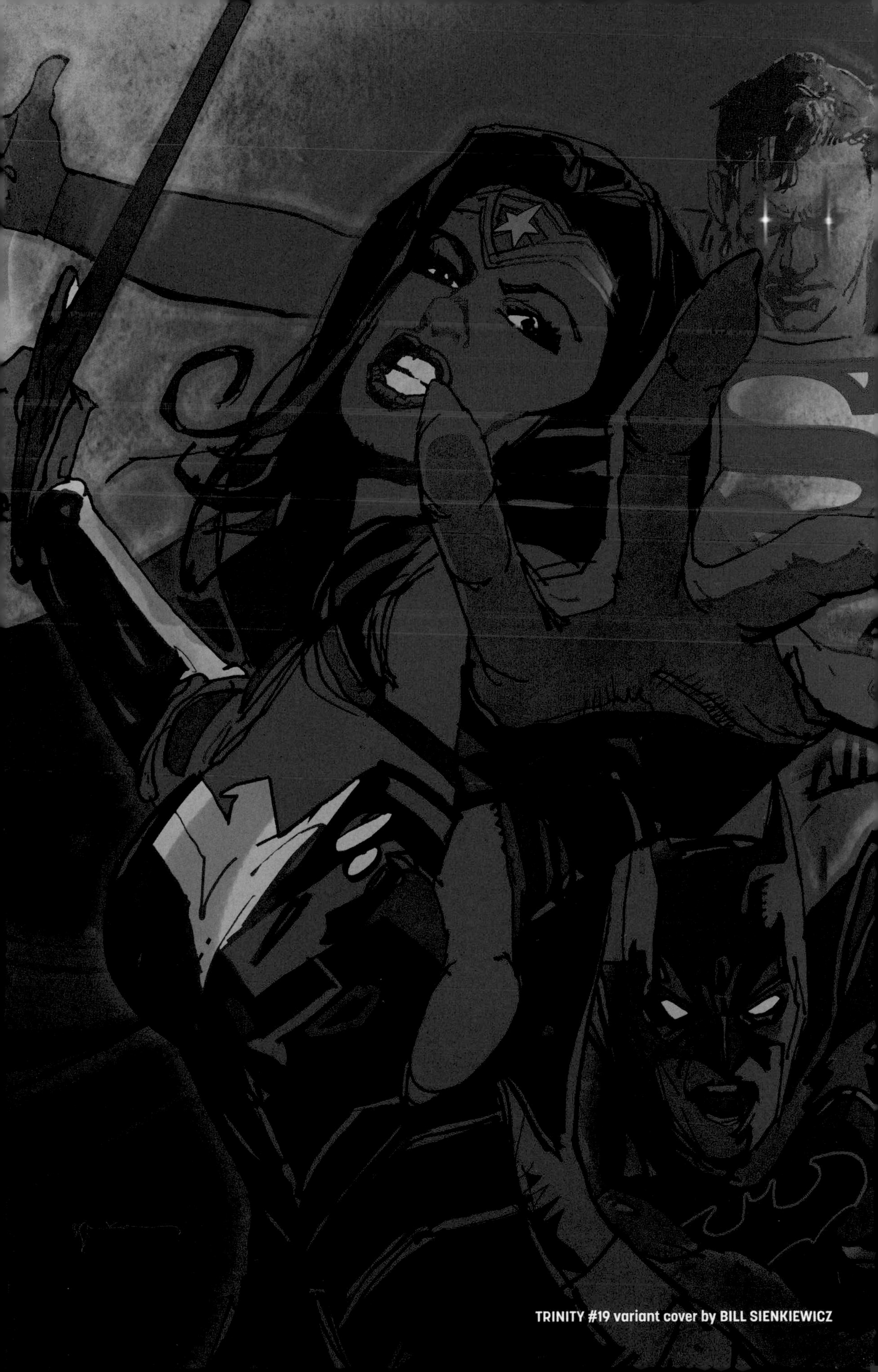

TRINITY #19 variant cover by BILL SIENKIEWICZ

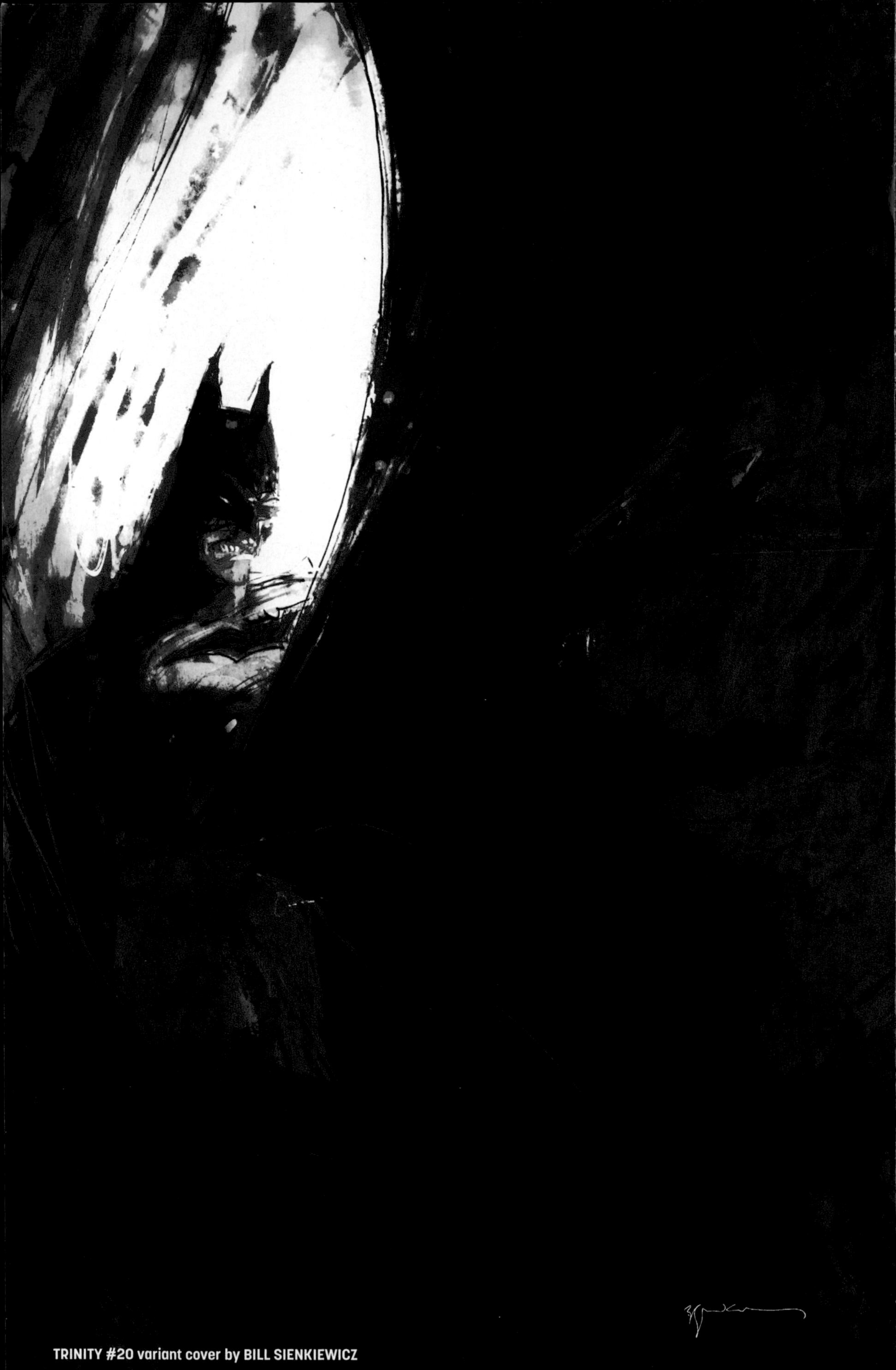

TRINITY #20 variant cover by BILL SIENKIEWICZ

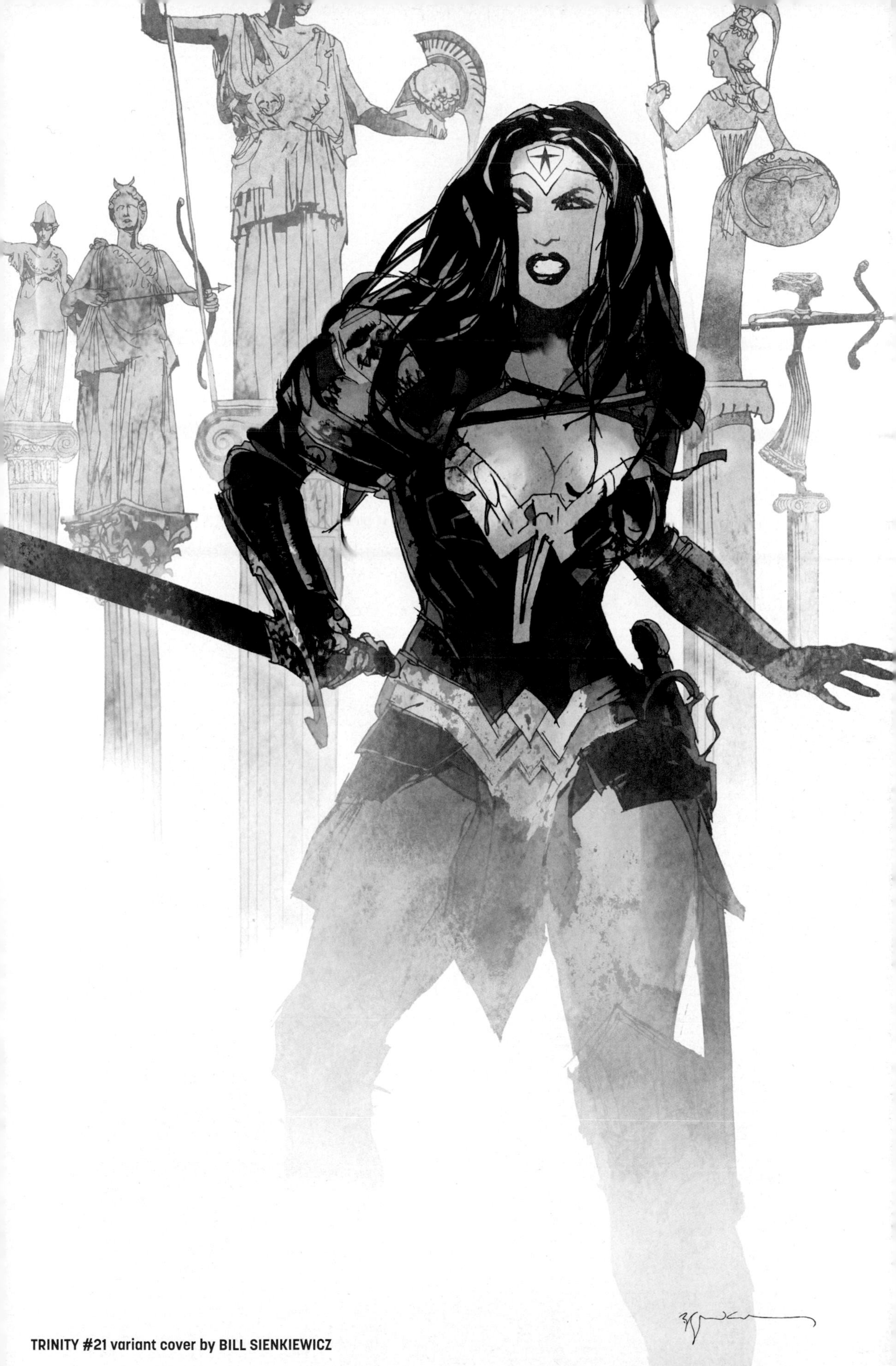

TRINITY #21 variant cover by BILL SIENKIEWICZ

TRINITY #22 variant cover by BILL SIENKIEWICZ

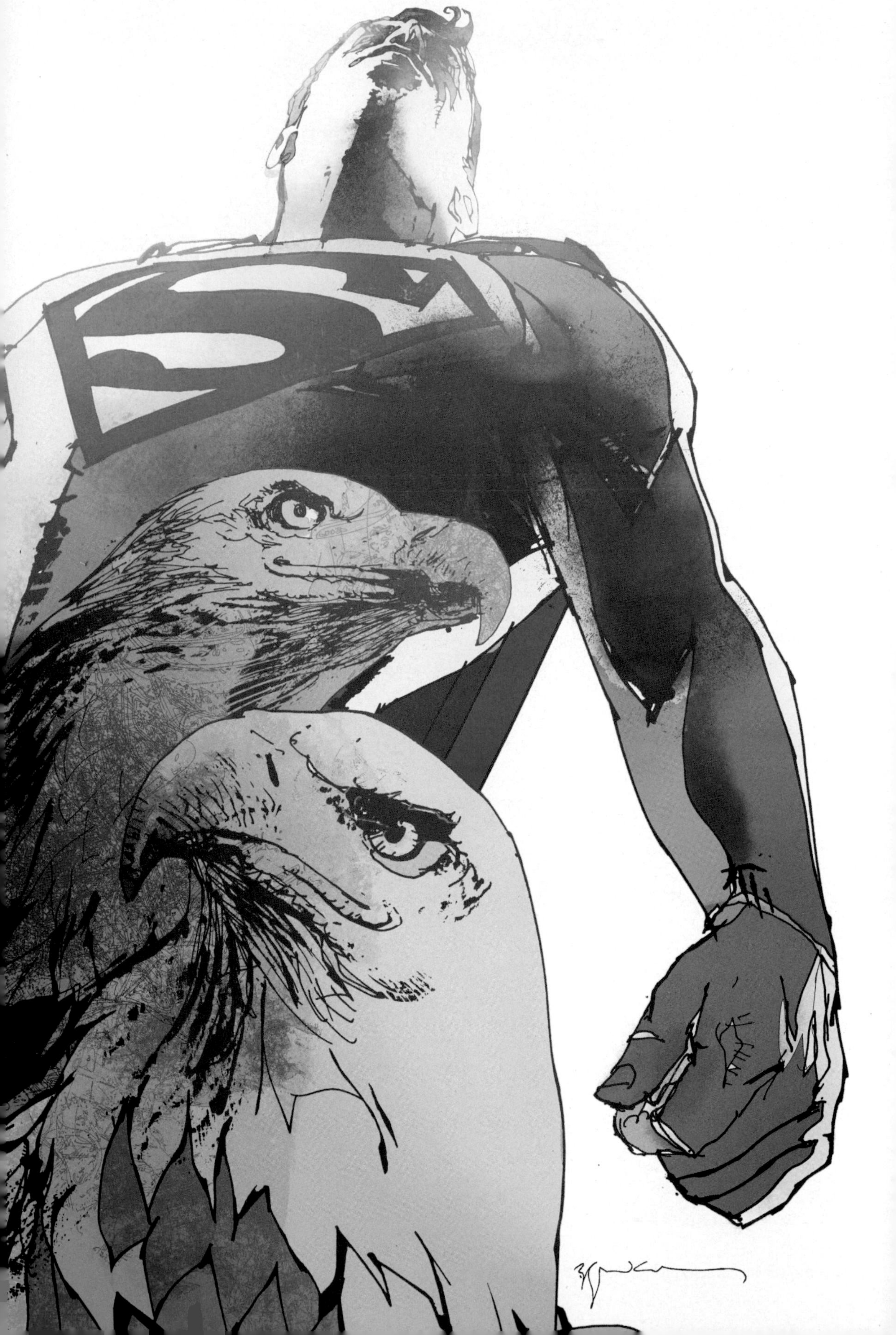

TRINITY #17 cover sketches by PATCH ZIRCHER

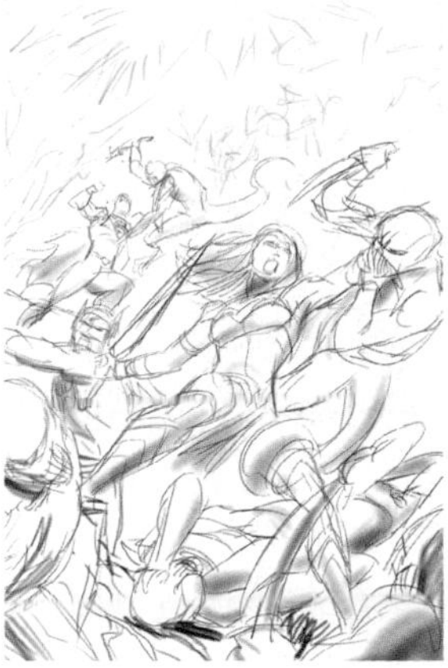

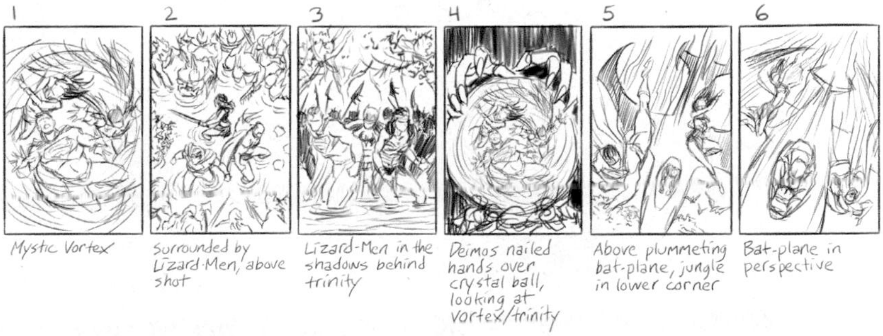
1
Mystic Vortex
2
Surrounded by Lizard-Men, above shot
3
Lizard-Men in the shadows behind trinity
4
Deimos nailed hands over crystal ball, looking at vortex/trinity
5
Above plummeting bat-plane, jungle in lower corner
6
Bat-plane in perspective

TRINITY #18 cover sketches by GUILLEM MARCH

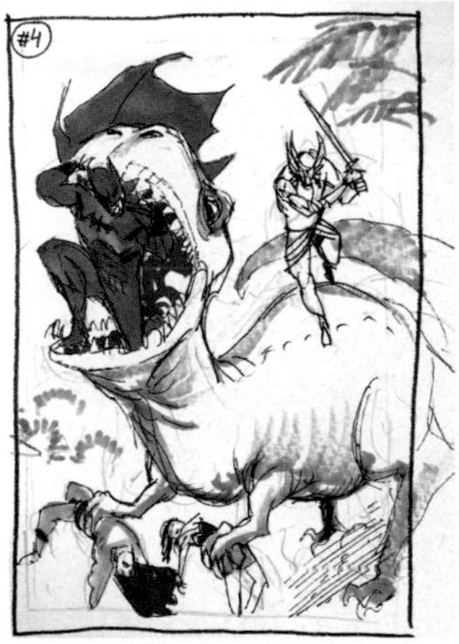
#4

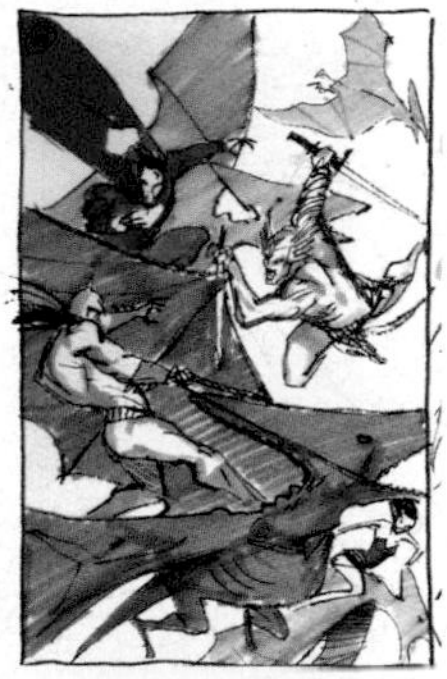

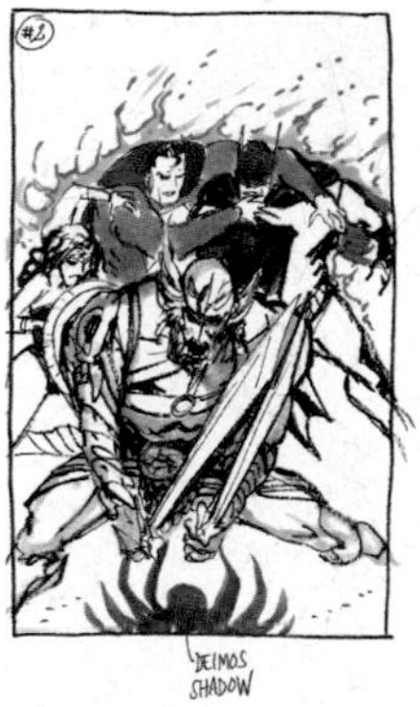
#2
DEIMOS SHADOW

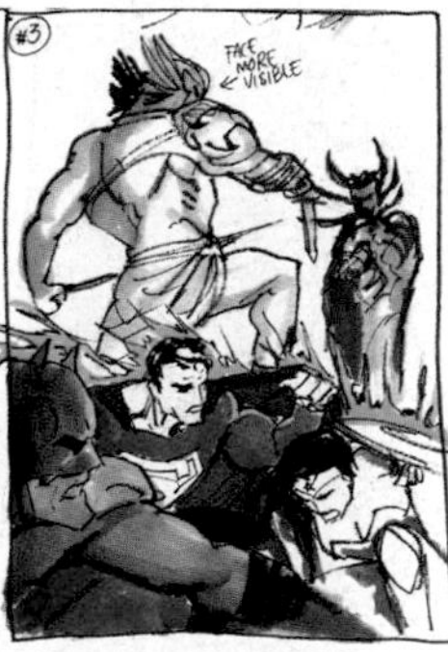
#3
FACE MORE VISIBLE

TRINITY #19 cover sketches by GUILLEM MARCH

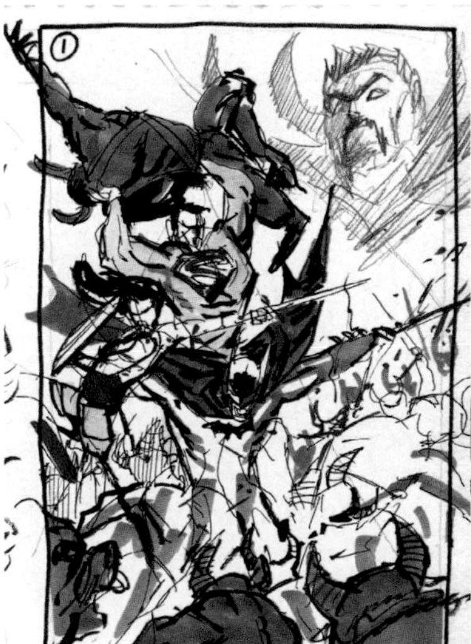
1

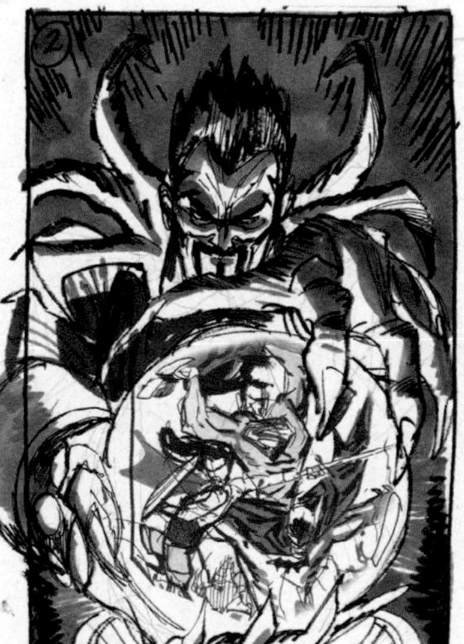
2

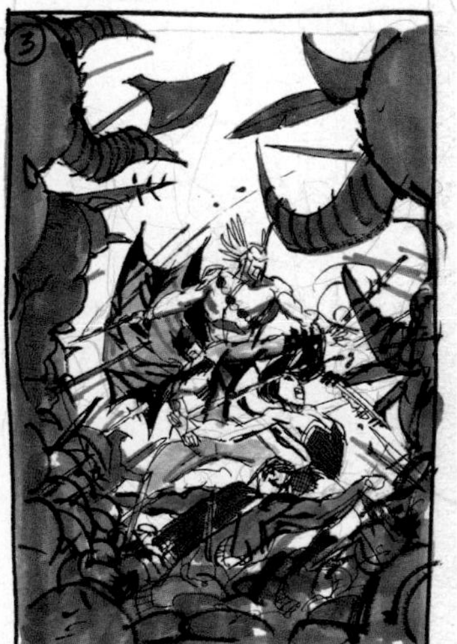
3

TRINITY #20 cover sketches by GUILLEM MARCH

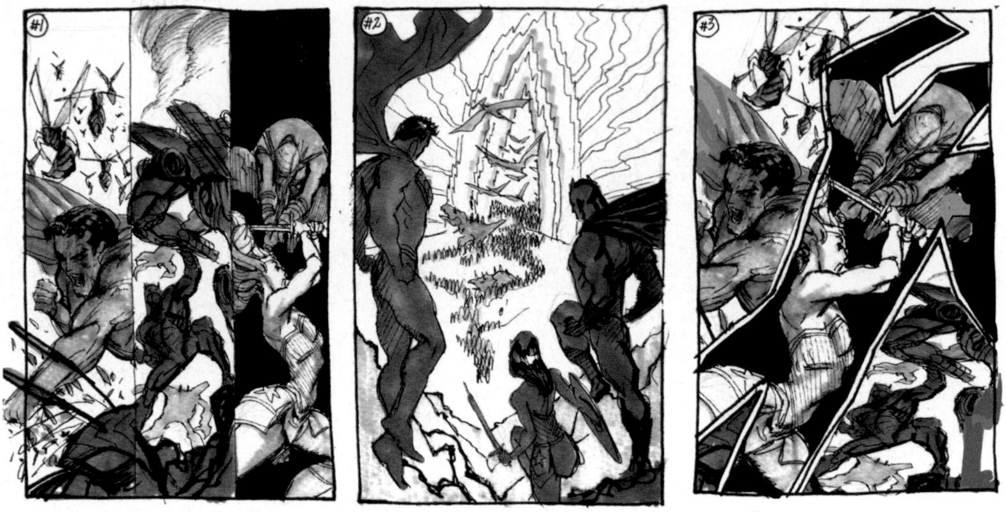

TRINITY #21 cover sketches by GUILLEM MARCH

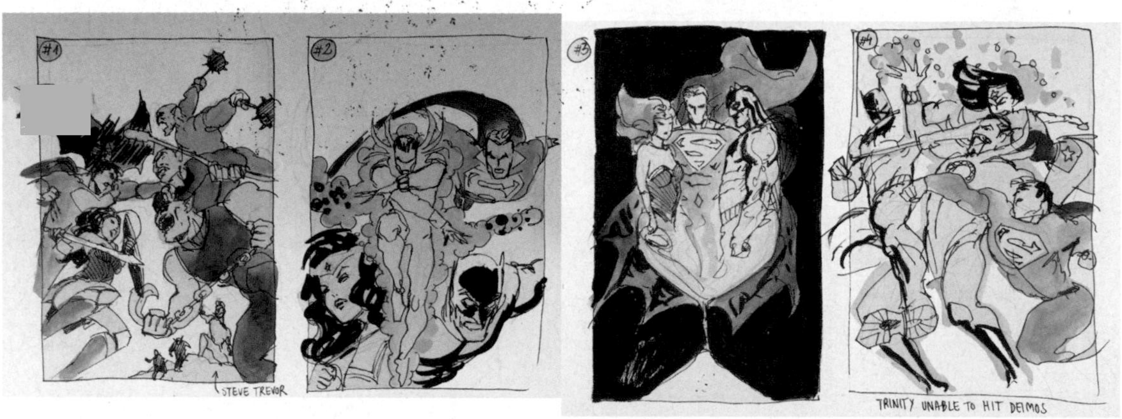
STEVE TREVOR
TRINITY UNABLE TO HIT DEIMOS

TRINITY #22 cover sketches by GUILLEM MARCH

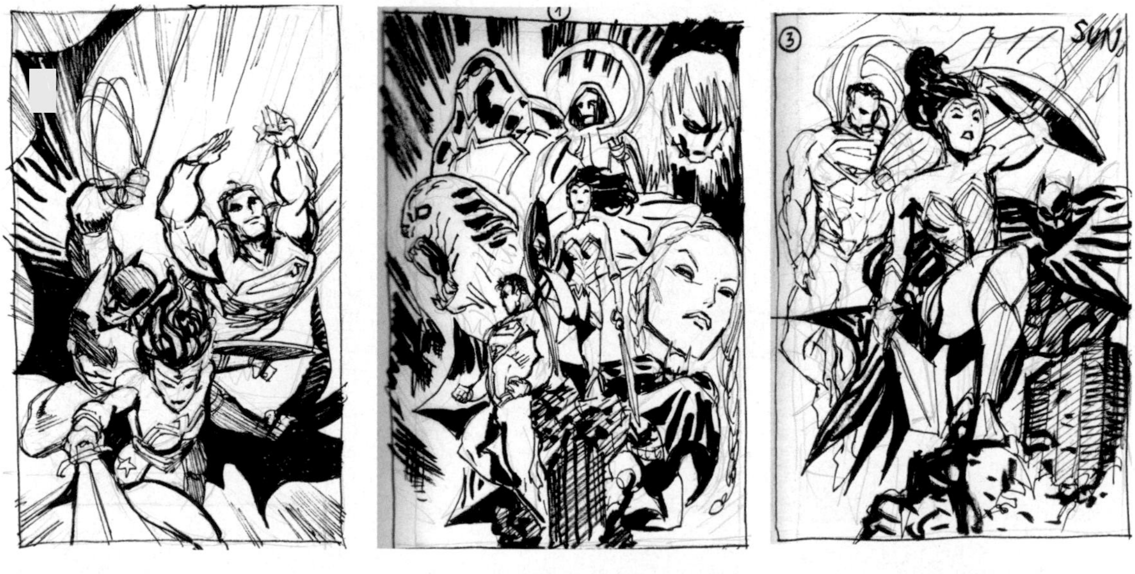